HEADING HOME WITH GOD

Jim McGuiggan

To
JIM, LINDA, and GEORGE
With love from
MOM & DAD

CONCLUSION

Now that you are connected and have bonded with your purpose, it's time to let it completely bless you! Do what you know you are called to do. If you need to revisit a purpose in this book to re-enforce its significance, please do so. It will only enhance your purpose experience.

I am excited for what is about to take place in your life! Your life will forever be changed. If you have not already done so; write down your purpose and begin working on it. Remember, "Your income is not your outcome, it is just funding what is to come (purpose)."

FOREWORD

This isn't a commentary but maybe there's a place for a book like this that takes the good work of others and makes some of it available for the rest of us who have neither the time or skill or patience to drill down deep for ourselves.

If it works at all you should come away from this volume with *something* of an improved sense of what the book of Exodus is about and a deeper realization that every generation of humans is on the same journey and is in need of rescue, challenge and guidance toward this planetary "land of promise".

I accept that there's too much in this work about "what should our response be?" rather than "What is it that God has done and means to do with the Exodus record of his mighty works?" We certainly need to think about our response in light of what God has done and meant to do in doing it but I'm certain that first and foremost it's the business of believers (Jews or Gentiles) to "learn the Story" and find out who and whose they are. If we do that then by God's grace we'll discover our identity in the new world we've become part of in the Lord Jesus. If we gain this we will know better how to live out our destiny and mission. Maybe Romans 12:2 speaks of that.

Contents

FOREWORD 3

Contents 5

Introductory Matters 9

I. RESCUE UNDER YAHWEH: 1:1—18:27 25

1 THE BLESSING CONTINUES 27

2 THE POWER OF THE POWERLESS 31

3 WHO'S IN CHARGE HERE? 35

4 NOBILITY IN STRANGE PLACES 37

5 EARTH'S GREATEST WONDER 41

6 THE IRISH WOLFHOUND 45

7 SO FAR FROM HOME 47

8 I SHOULD HAVE GONE BAREFOOT 51

9 AFRAID TO LOOK AT GOD 55

10 I AM COME DOWN TO DELIVER THEM 59

11 MYSELF! 63

12 THE RELUCTANT DELIVERER 67

13 SEE THAT JACKET? 71

14 THE HARDENED HEART 75

15 DRAMA AT THE INN 77

16 AND WHAT OF CIRCUMCISION? 81

17 ISRAEL WITHOUT PASSOVER OR CIRCUMCISION 85

18 DELIVERER OR TROUBLER? 87

19 LET MY PEOPLE GO 91

20 LET MY PEOPLE GO (2) 95

21 "LAZY, THAT'S WHAT YOU ARE—LAZY" 99

22 HURTING TOO MUCH TO BELIEVE 103

23 PAIN OR INCONVENIENCE? 105

24 ANOTHER FAMILY TREE? 109

25 STORIES IN CONFLICT 113

26 THE MESSAGE OF THE PLAGUE/SIGNS 117

27 THE REPENTANCE OF A SCARED MAN 119

28 A NIGHT TO KEEP VIGIL 121

29 DEATH OF A TYRANT..125
30 A SONG OF TRIUMPH 129
31 HE SHOULD HAVE SUNG 133
32 ISRAEL IN THE WILDERNESS 137
33 A SCHOOL IN THE WILDERNESS..........................141
34 THE NEW TESTAMENT CHURCH & WILDERNESS....145
35 THE SMITTEN ROCK AND AMALEK.......................149
36 REUNIONS IN THE WILDERNESS..........................153
37 LEADERSHIP AND WISDOM 155
38 LESSONS IN LEADERSHIP..................................159
39 POWER SHARING..163

II. COVENANT UNDER YAHWEH: 19:1—24:18....................165

40 THE NATURE AND FUNCTION OF THE TORAH 167
41 CHOSEN..179
42 TEMPTATIONS OF THE CHOSEN...........................183
43 A NATION OF PRIESTS.....................................187
44 THE DECALOGUE 191
45 YOU WILL HAVE ONE GOD— ME!.........................195
46. NO GOD BUT YHWH?......................................197
47. NO GOD BUT YHWH? (2) 201
48 NO GOD BUT YAHWEH? (3) 205
49 GOD OR THE WIZARD OF OZ?............................209
50 NO GRAVEN IMAGES 213
51 IN IT THOU SHALT DO NO "WORK" 215
52 THE LORD RESTED THE SEVENTH DAY....................219
53 THIS SHALL BE A SIGN 223
54 YOU WERE SLAVES IN EGYPT............................227
55 HONOR THY FATHER AND THY MOTHER................229
56 NOT MERELY OUR NEIGHBORS...........................233
57 HONOR THEM BECAUSE....................................237
58 THE IMAGE OF GOD IN PARENTS 241
59 DO NO MURDER..245
60 NOTHING TO DO WITH ME AND MY WIFE 251
61 YOU SHALL NOT COMMIT ADULTERY 255
62 YOU SHALL NOT STEAL 261
63 THOU SHALT NOT BEAR FALSE WITNESS................265

64 THOU SHALT NOT COVET..271
65 A FEW PRELIMINARY REMARKS 275
66 THE BOOK OF THE COVENANT.......................................277
67 I LOVE MY MASTER...279
68 THE REALIZABLE BEST 283
69 CRIME AND PUNISHMENT 287
70 THE KILLING OF WITCHES 291
71 WHO OWNS EVERYTHING ANYWAY? 295
72 DON'T SHARE A TABLE WITH FLIES................................299
73 HOW IT FEELS TO BE ALIENS..303
74 SO THAT YOUR DONKEY MAY REST................................307
75 THE HEART OF THE SABBATH 309
76 BOILED IN MOTHER'S MILK...313
77 HAVING DINNER WITH GOD 317

III.WORSHIP IN THE PRESENCE OF YAHWEH 25:1-40:38....321

78 GIVING AS WORSHIP 323
79 A HOUSE FOR GOD TO LIVE IN......................................327
80 WHAT DOES THE TABERNACLE MEAN?...........................331
81 SO WHAT'S WORSHIP FOR?...337
82 WORSHIP THE OXYGEN OF THE SOUL............................341
83 WORSHIP & THE SECOND GREAT COMMANDMENT.......345
84 HOLY FURNISHINGS 349
85 HOLY CLOTHING 355
86 THE BLESSING OF REPRESENTATION 361
87 ELECT OR ELITE? 365
88 SERVICE OR POWER?...367
89 MONEY THAT MAKES A CONFESSION.............................371
90 GOLDEN CALVES AND ELECTRON MICROSCOPES............375
91 THE ART OF BUILDING 381
92 A GRASS-EATING BULL...383
93 A HARD PILL TO SWALLOW 387
94 GOD IS IN EARNEST 389
95 I'LL TAKE MY CHANCES..393
96 LEAVE THIS PLACE 397
97 GO WITH US OR DON'T SEND US...................................401
98 AS A FRIEND TO HIS FRIEND 405

99 MY FACE SHALL NOT BE SEEN..407
100 THE DARK LINE...411
101 HE WAS NOT AWARE..415
102 A HOME BUILT OUT OF SUFFERING.....................................419
103 BEZALEL AND THE MESSIAH...421
104 THE KING IS IN RESIDENCE...423
SELECTED BIBLIOGRAPH...425

Introductory Matters

THE NAME OF THE BOOK
The Hebrews used the first few words of each book to name the first five books of their Bible. In the Hebrew Bible our book of Exodus is called 'shemoth" (names) since it begins with "and these are the names". Sometime around 250 B.C. the OT began to be translated into Greek (the LXX) and "ve'elleh shemoth" was given the name "Exodusos" ("the path or road or way out") because the major historical event was the leaving or exit out of Egypt. From there we got the Latinized form Exodus.

THE STORYLINE OF THE BOOK
A new Pharaoh is on the throne in Egypt. He doesn't know what Egypt and the throne owe to the former Hebrew prime-minister, Joseph, and he has become fearful of this foreign nation which is prospering within Egyptian borders. What if they sided with enemies who sought the throne of Egypt? A policy of ethnic cleansing and slave-labor was initiated. During this critical period Moses is born and is raised as the son of Pharaoh's daughter. When Moses kills an Egyptian official for harming an Israelite, events are set in motion that result in his fleeing to Midian where he marries Zipporah, a daughter in the family of Jethro.

For forty years the fugitive tends to his father-in-law's sheep and then God calls him to pastor his flock which is back in Egypt. The beginning of Moses' return to Egypt is the burning bush meeting with a God who reveals himself as YHWH. The man is enlisted by YHWH to help Him keep his promises to Abraham to rescue Israel from slavery and settle them in the land he promised would be their inheritance—Canaan. After initial objections, Moses obeys and appears in Egypt before Pharaoh, the 'son of Amon-Re'.

The stern demand, "free my people, says YHWH!" provokes the pharaoh's derisive response, "Who is YHWH that I should obey him? I won't let Israel go." A series of fierce blows (the ten plagues) from YHWH compels Egypt to hurry the slave-nation out of their borders and into the wilderness to worship this God of judgment. The army of Pharaoh pursues the Hebrews, catches up with them at the "Red" sea but the God of Israel puts himself between the two groups. The sea opens up to allow the Israelites to cross on dry land and returns to drown the forces of tyranny. The newly freed nation sings a song of praise and deliverance and turn to face the wilderness.

The people finally arrive at mount Sinai (Horeb) and there YHWH forms those who had simply been the seed of Abraham into a holy and priestly nation. The 'ten Words" (Decalogue) are followed by a series of laws which would govern their lives and a Tabernacle is built in which YHWH will dwell in the center of the people. The book concludes with the actual rearing of the sanctuary and the entrance of God into the Holy of Holies.

THE PURPOSE AND DIRECTION OF THE BOOK

The problem with incredible books like Exodus is that they are so rich that it's surely impossible to fully grasp their purpose. It isn't difficult to read the book and summarize the contents but that isn't the same as determining the purpose. Since it deals with ancient history you might say its purpose is to give us a history lesson. Hardly! While it offers historical information, its purpose goes beyond expanding our stock of historical knowledge.

The book of Exodus can't be understood independent of the other four books of the "Pentateuch" (five rolls). It is immediately and inextricably linked to Genesis, Leviticus, Numbers and Deuteronomy. It has its own peculiar thrusts, of course, but it has no themes that are completely independent of the other four books.

It tells its own part of the story of God's creative and redemptive work on behalf of the whole of mankind. In Exodus this work of God centers in the Hebrew nation. It is Act two of a drama in five Acts. Because this is so it takes from, adds to, shapes and enriches, is shaped and enriched by the other four books. To take our cue from John Bright, to see Acts 1, 3, 4 and 5 without Act 2 is to miss much of the meaning of all five Acts. So, whatever we say about the purpose of Exodus must be understood in that light.

And though what we think a writer's purpose is must be drawn from what the writer actually says it is possible for a writer to be revealing more than he knows. He may pass on words and laws that are richer than he understands or he may tell us of events that can only be appreciated fully at some later date and another perspective. (Haven't we all had experiences which, at the time of their happening, didn't appear to be significant, but which in later years we recognized as profoundly significant?) And if we have reason to believe that there is a divine hand at work, one who's superintending the record as well as the general course of events we'll be slow to think we have exhausted the purpose or purposes of the book.

Genesis deals with God's work with and for humanity through special individuals. Exodus deals with God's work with and for humanity through a nation, Israel. The worldwide scope of the earlier chapters of Genesis (1-11) is easily seen. With chapters 12-50 the universal scope of things remains but it's less obvious since special characters take the center stage (Abraham, Isaac, Jacob and Joseph). Exodus sees the God of Abraham as the central character and Moses as his special witness, but it's the creation of "a priestly nation" under God that has the lion's share of the Exodus material.

That creation of the nation begins with a mighty and gracious deliverance of the people from the power and oppression of one of the earth's powerful monarchs. It continues with the enactment of a covenant at Sinai, which constitutes the offspring of Abraham as that "nation under God". Exodus pays special attention to the covenant as the terms under which and the vehicle by which the nation lived in relation to itself, its neighbors and God. And Exodus pays special attention to the homage toward and worship of God as set out in the planning and construction of the tabernacle. This structuring of the nation's worship and governing of its life-style in terms of the covenant is not merely a response to the initial redemption it's part of the redeeming work of God. The Rescue is a gracious and liberating experience but so is the giving of the covenant and the structuring of worship. Exodus will have nothing to do with the notion that the "Exodus" is an event distinct from what follows. It is always a deliverance "in order to". The nationalizing of the Abrahamic offspring is no mere "extra" tacked on to the Exodus, it is one element in a grand purpose that embraces the deliverance itself but which is not exhausted by the deliverance. In accomplishing the "Exodus" (the "leading out"), God's purpose was to bring the people to himself (19:4). Their trek was not merely geographical (from Egypt to Sinai) it was spiritual/theological (from bondage to an oppressive master to freedom under God). It was a move from Pharaoh to God! This is especially clear in 6:5-9.

Israel's identity is unknowable unless it is sought and understood in relation to Yahweh. The truth is more radical than that. Israel's identity doesn't even exist outside of its relationship with Yahweh. "Israel" did not create herself, shape herself nor define herself. Israel did not even know herself. All this sprung from God as a source. The sound "Israel" might mean many things for modern people but in the Mosaic explanation of the sound, "Israel" takes its meaning from the purpose and actions of God! In one sense it's true that "Israel explains God". But it is more true to say "God explains Israel". To understand "Israel" we should begin with God rather than Israel. It's true of course that the God we begin with in Exodus is a God who is related to Israel rather than some "Eternal Being" who is the conclusion of an Aristotelian argument. Nevertheless, as with Man, so it is with Israel, we understand the creature when we understand the creator. It will probably be helpful, then, to break the book of Exodus into three grand segments:

1. **Yahweh, the redeemer of Israel**
    (The Exodus events)
2. **Yahweh, the covenant partner of Israel**
    (The covenant materials)
3. **Yahweh, the worshipful center of Israel**
    (The tabernacle materials)

The substance of the book is written from a post-Exodus standpoint and it is written from a pre-Canaanite perspective. It seems clear that the book of Exodus (along with the other books of the Pentateuch) was written for Israel to teach her whose she is, who she is and how (as a consequence) she should live before the nations.

In carrying out this purpose Moses:

Repeatedly links Israel with Abraham, Isaac & Jacob and with the God of these patriarchs;

Tells the story of their oppression by Egypt and their rescue by YHWH;

Tells of the giving of the Law at Sinai which shaped the people into a holy and priestly nation which was especially related to YHWH (though he was Lord of and cared for the entire earth);

Insists that Israel is a sign of the reign (kingdom) of God and that she is on her way to dwell with God in Canaan;

Tells of the Tabernacle, which was to be built by people of a willing heart, that YHWH might dwell in the center of them and be approached only as and when he prescribed;

And makes it very clear that this new nation was to be nothing like the people of Egypt from which they were delivered or Canaan to which they were going (compare Leviticus 18:1-4).

MAJOR THEMES OF THE BOOK

Later readings of a great book almost always end with our having seen so much more than we saw in earlier readings. There are numerous reasons for this, no doubt. See again paragraph 9 above. As we become wiser our eyes are opened to truths we hadn't seen before. As we become more familiar with the book, it often becomes more itself and rather less than we made it to be at first reading. As we become purer (and less selfish) we pick up on challenges and demands we subconsciously avoided in earlier days. As we become more acquainted with God's full counsel in Scripture we see more of what he was driving at in independent books. This should lead us to modesty and make us cautious in our judgments. Still, we'd have to suspend judgment altogether if we didn't think we could recognize some major themes in this incredibly rich book of Scripture.

The nature and character of YHWH.

There is for example, His centrality and supremacy. Believers would rightly insist that God is the center of the whole corpus of Scripture but it's clear that his centrality is more obvious in some books than in others. God is not thrust upon us as the leading character in, say, the Song of Solomon, as he is in Exodus.

The record of Exodus itself is saturated with YHWH and his activity. The "contest" between YHWH and the gods of Egypt proclaims his supremacy and the comments of psalmists and prophets on the material of Exodus herald his glory. No one is saved, enlightened, protected, judged, commissioned, fed, given water to drink, made victorious in battle, builds, serves, lives or dies without the directing and enabling hand of God! No one is to be praised, served, followed, feared, exalted, thanked, trusted, worshiped or obeyed but YHWH.

There is His faithfulness to his promises and purposes. The book opens with the Israelite connection with Jacob (and so, Abraham and Isaac) and the blessing aspect of the Abrahamic covenant. There is Joseph who spread blessing everywhere he went (see Genesis) and there is Exodus 1:7,12 where we have echoed the promise of blessing to Abraham. In 2:23-24; 3:6,13,15-17 God's redemptive purpose is linked with his promise to Abraham. This includes not simply the rescue from Egypt but the final rest in Canaan, the land of promise and gift.

And there is His creative power and purpose. It's true that Exodus doesn't have a doctrine of creation as it is developed in Genesis but it would be easy to overstate the difference. Since it's true that Exodus is part of a five-book story, it's interesting that Moses began the story in Genesis with "creation". Why with creation? It's not only that everything begins there historically; it all begins there theologically! Exodus is part of the story that God is faithful to his creation purposes. *Redemption serves creation.* God didn't wash his hands of humanity when they rebelled; his love of humanity, which was expressed in creative activity, then takes a redemptive aspect—God begins to work toward removing the curse, which resulted from sinful rebellion and to swallow up cursing in blessing. The book of Exodus contributes its part to that Story. (See the comments on the meaning of the Tabernacle.)

The words of Exodus 1:7,12 remind us of God's promise to Abraham but God's promise to Abraham reminds us of the words of Genesis 1. The whole notion of "blessing" and "cursing" has its roots in the creation and fall narratives. Words like multiply, teem, prosper, fill, grow, flourish or replenish are all in the semantic domain of blessing. What is happening to Israel (the seed of Abraham) is what God wants humanity to experience.

The same God who took formlessness, lifelessness and disharmony and brought about order and fullness of life in the beginning is able to do the same in Egypt. There, where they should not prosper and multiply, they do! By the power of YHWH! In the wilderness, which proclaims "curse" in the starkest fashion, God blesses and makes Israel to prosper. In the wilderness, with its chaos, disorder and stunted, lower life forms, we see a nation thriving. In Genesis 1, ten times we hear a creative "let" and in the wilderness we have ten creative "words" which form a nation out of a rabble of fugitives. The God who could create a wilderness out of Egypt (because they sought to curse those whom God sought to bless) could create a home within a wilderness. It's no surprise to hear that the God who divided the Red Sea is the creator who divided the waters from the land in Genesis 1.

There is His awful holiness, which sets him apart from humans. Throughout the book there are independent verses and events that stress this. There is the awful isolation of YHWH on the summit of Sinai, a mountain quaking, heaving and burning. There are the frightening blasts of a trumpet, increasing in volume with each sounding and the dread voice of God when he speaks like a man.

15

There are the boundaries set around the base of the mountain and guarded by fierce Leviticus with the threat that anyone, human or beast, that touched the mountain would be executed immediately. There were the special preparations, which the handful of leaders had to make in order to approach the Lord. There are rules and washings that must be obeyed by ministering priests and approaching worshipers. There are the spotless animals and scrubbed pots and pans involved in His worship and that silent, perpetually-shrouded-in-darkness sanctuary within Tent, where no one but the high priest could enter on only one day in the year and not without sacrificial blood. Then there are the many passages that teach us that even Moses came to God when he was called and not otherwise. And of course, there were the calamities, which he poured out on rebellious Egypt as well as the judgments at various points on a treacherous Israel. All of this and more was to stress the separateness of YHWH who nevertheless dwelled at the heart of a sinful people.

Then there is His never-ending lovingkindness. It's true that YHWH's fierce judgments call into question his lovingkindness but if one takes in the over-arching purpose of God toward all of humanity and the goals toward which he strives, the judgments on rebellious people take on a different complexion. In a world where sin has entered YHWH is more concerned about the character of humans than about their immediate happiness. What he offers is life but what he *is* often forced to execute is judgment. Any good government wants life and prosperity for its citizens but it often has to deal out punishment on criminals who oppress other citizens. Good governments reward those who approve of and contribute to justice and mutual prosperity but they also chastise those who oppose those ends. If we view a government only in the sternness of its judgments against criminals we might think it cruel and unjust or merciless. If we saw it, however, actively pursuing policies, which benefited all its citizens, our judgment about its sternness would be balanced. It isn't necessary for us to view people as vindictive and cruel because they punish offenders.

The Story as developed in the Scriptures tells of a "personal" God who seeks the blessing of all his creatures and who sometimes experiences a "conflict of interests" in the face of the oppressed and the oppressor. The book of Jonah assures us that YHWH cares deeply for the Assyrian nation, which is oppressing the other nations. The book of Nahum tells us that God cares for the nations that Assyria oppresses and so he is finally forced to bring judgment on Nineveh. The God who judges Egypt in Exodus is the God who blessed Egypt in Genesis. Difficult as it may be for moderns to swallow, God's judgments on people are severe mercies. Severity toward those who are cut off because they oppose God's purpose to bless and mercy toward all others who will benefit from the removal of that obstacle to blessing. YHWH's judgment on Egypt brought blessing to Israel and through Israel he would bless humanity. And we must remember that this purposes to bless and give life rise out of his lovingkindness (see Psalm 136:1-26).

The deliverance from Egyptian bondage.

Since this event takes up 14 chapters of the book and another is devoted to a song about the event, it's obviously of supreme importance. And we are told repeatedly that God is identified as the one who brought them out of the "iron furnace" or the "house of bondage". This strongly suggests that we are to view YHWH as a God of rescue or redemption. When the Tabernacle is completed we're told that the silver sockets into which the framework of the Tent is fitted are made of redemption money. In addition to this we have the perpetual ordinance of the redeeming of the firstborn established by God and linked to Israel's salvation on the night of the Passover. Books like David Daube's *The Exodus Pattern in the Bible* show just how crucial to Hebrew—Christian faith this event was and continues to be. Psalmists and prophets will, again and again, use the Exodus as the model for new national and individual deliverances from enemies whether spiritual or human, from sins or political/social oppression.

The covenant Law at Sinai.

The actual deliverance from Egypt was not an end in itself. The move from Goshen to Sinai was no more geographical than

Abraham's move from Ur to Canaan. Of course geography was involved but it was a movement of the spirit, a shift from the lower to the higher, from distance to intimacy. Israel wasn't brought to Sinai so much as they were brought to God (see on 20:3).

What the covenant Law did for Israel (and the world) can hardly be exaggerated. Jews since that day have exulted in the Law and what the Law means to them. This is not the place to say much about the NT's treatment of the Law (and Paul's treatment of it in particular) but a slow and thoughtful reading of Psalm 119 (and others) is an education in the effects of the Law on this nation. Whatever we should conclude about Paul's varied pronouncements on the Law we know that no enlightened Jew (and certainly not Paul!) would have viewed the covenant Law as given at Sinai to be a bringer of death. (This is especially clear from Deuteronomy, which repeatedly tells us that the covenant Law was given so that life might result!)

The Law was a gift of God to a nation in dire need of light! It was an expression of God's love for Israel and the patriarchs. It enabled them to live with this YHWH about whom they were so ignorant. It guaranteed justice to the defenseless and a way to redress wrongs committed by rebels against the Law (and so, against God and the people). It shaped worship and provided ordinances, which kept alive the Story of God's loving-kindness, which is the soil out of which Israel's ethical response grew and in which the noble life was nourished. Worship is part of what enables people to live nobly and gallantly because it keeps people aware of the living presence of the God who calls them up and strengthens their noble purposes. And the Law saw to it that the nation kept in close touch with its living Lord and never forgot her gracious roots. (See Exodus 22:21 and 23:9 which illustrate this.)

God always intended Israel to be a blessing to the world's peoples. One way in which the Jews have done that is their teaching of their covenant Law to the nations. To say that the Mosaic covenant has shaped the foundations of justice in (at least) the Western world is to say only what is common knowledge. It never failed to irritate T.H. Huxley, the Darwinian and agnostic, to hear

18

people glibly dismiss the Hebrew Law. He tirelessly insisted, and with great passion, that we should recognize its grandeur and the profound benefit it brought to the world.

The doctrine of Access through Sacrifice

There is an interesting tension in the book of Exodus between God's insistence on being removed from the people and his wanting them near him. He makes it clear their sinfulness is an obstacle to unbroken communion but makes it equally clear that he is working toward full and intimate fellowship. YHWH hides himself in a perpetually darkened sanctuary away from the people and yet will not dwell anywhere else but at the heart of those people. He stands aloof from them but invites them into a covenant relationship with him. He sets up numberless "hindrances" to communion with him but gives them a priesthood and a sacrificial system to enable them all to have communion with him (compare Leviticus 17:11). Their sins, he assures them, put up a wall between him and them, but he offers them a way to have those sins forgiven—sacrifice!

THE GOD GIVEN AUTHORITY OF MOSES

From Exodus 5 until his death, Moses functions as the clear leader of Israel but there is always a debate going on in that generation about his moral right to be leader. Exodus (and Numbers) stresses the divine commissioning of Moses in the face of opposition, which continues to rear its head. It is brought out and dealt with in the narrative.

While still in Egypt he rebukes an Israelite for wronging a brother and the offender snarls at him (2:14): "Who made you a ruler and judge over us?" Rejected as leader (Stephen in Acts 7:25 says Moses thought he would be recognized as a deliverer) and forced to flee, Moses may well have brooded over this and that would explain his reluctance to return as deliverer (see Exodus 3 & 4). Be that as it may, it's clear from chapters 3 and 4 that Moses didn't promote himself into the position of leadership and authority. He insisted he was not the man to the point where God became angry with him. All this being the case, later claims that it wasn't God but Moses who engineered the march into the wilderness (14:11; 16:3; 17:3; 32:1) are seen to be rubbish.

In Numbers14:2 we have Aaron and Miriam doubting the special commission of Moses and again in 16:3,12 we have the rebellion led by Korah, Dathan and Abiram during which Moses is accused of self-promotion and lording it over the people. This whole matter clearly bothers Moses and we find him constantly seeking assurance of God's presence with him as he leads the people. The narrative takes great pains to show that what Moses did and said came to him from the Lord. In the last two chapters of Exodus when we're told how the tabernacle was being set up, we're told seventeen times that they did it "as Yahweh commanded Moses".

WHO WROTE EXODUS?

Sometimes it doesn't matter who wrote the Bible book under consideration. Who wrote Hebrews doesn't matter much but if Jesus credits David with Psalm 110 and builds an argument on it (see Matt 22:41-46) that's an entirely different matter. Jesus, in keeping with the OT record, attributed "the Law" (the Pentateuch) to Moses (cf. John 5:45-47; Luke 24:27,44; Josh 1:7,13; 23:6; 1 Kings 2:3; Ezra—Nehemiah). R.D. Wilson reminds us that OT texts consistently tell us of new legislation ascribed to David, Hezekiah and others but they always distinguish between that and "the law of Moses".

I believe Moses "wrote" the Pentateuch so I believe he wrote Exodus. I don't believe he personally wrote every word in the Pentateuch (or Exodus). I think conservative scholars like E.J. Young and R.K. Harrison are correct when they say that the Pentateuch is "fundamentally" Mosaic. Harrison could be right when he says, "It may well be that the presence of third person pronouns in various sections of the Mosaic enactments indicate that these sections were dictated" (538). He goes on to say that many of the smaller sections of the Hebrew text may have been later "assembled into some sort of mosaic and joined together into a roll". If someone later, under God's superintendence, compiled Moses' materials that would suit us.

(We hardly need to believe that the prophecies of Jeremiah were written in the order we find them in the book of Jeremiah. Just check the dates of the various oracles. The same is true of Isaiah, Daniel and Ezekiel. But the dating of the oracles undermines the notion that men centuries after the named prophets wrote the oracles under the name of the named prophets. The same holds true for Mosaic materials. Many of them are dated.)

That Moses used earlier sources would be no more surprising than that Luke used them or the author/compiler of the Kings/Chronicles literature used them (see 1 Kings 8:8 and compare 2 Kings 25:27). Wilson characterizes the conservative position saying, "...the Pentateuch as it stands is historical and from the time of Moses; and (that) Moses was it real author though it may have been revised and edited by later redactors, the additions being just as much inspired and as true as the rest" (p.12).

That Moses wrote Deuteronomy without writing 34:5-12 is perfectly acceptable to me. I just know he didn't write 34:10, "Since then no prophet has risen in Israel like Moses..." And it looks like Exodus 40:38 is a later reflection on the whole wandering experience of Israel though it may have been written by Moses ("...in the sight of all the house of Israel, through out all their journeys" ASV). But vv. 36-38 would be separated from the events of 34-35 by something like forty years. I wouldn't think Moses would have written Numbers12:3 ("Now Moses was a very humble man, more humble than anyone else on the face of the earth"). In all this I'm saying, that holding to the Mosaic authorship of the entire Pentateuch (and Exodus in particular) doesn't necessarily exclude insertions and compiling under the superintendence of God.

What conservative evangelicals don't want, because they believe it dishonors the Scripture, is the claim that the Pentateuch made its appearance centuries after Moses, is clumsily put together, is said to be from Moses when it really isn't, is a compilation by unknowns from unknown periods for purposes that can only be guessed at. What they become irritated at is the often incredibly flimsy foundation on which all these claims are made. What is not, in and of itself flimsy, is sheer speculation and gratuitous to boot. To hold to the essentially Mosaic authorship of the Pentateuch is not something we need apologize for.

THE APPROACH TO EXODUS OFFERED HERE

There will be no verse-by-verse treatment but I'm hoping to say something useful about sections of scripture before "applying" them to 21st century believers. I want to keep in mind what Exodus meant to Israel as they were preparing to enter Canaan. If I do anything useful in that area you should learn something about what Israel was to make of the book in light of their peculiar needs and challenges.

But the "People of God" down the ages is one People—ancient or modern, Hebrew or otherwise, under this covenant or that covenant. That has to mean that while we must allow ancient texts to have their immediate message there are truths that transcend their immediate origin and immediate addressees. When Moses speaks to his peers, for example, in Deuteronomy, he speaks of their descendants as "you". He doesn't limit his words to the people he addresses. He sees the generations that follow his own, as the extension of his own generation. The Scriptures are for all the People of God in all generations. The Messiah himself placed himself under the authority of texts that addressed God's people more than a thousand years before he appeared (see Matthew 4:4, 7,10). And in the NT the apostles did what their Master did and called on fellow-disciples to do the same. Of course there are texts that can't be taken over and practiced just as they stand but all the texts bear truths that don't vanish with age! As Goldingay has reminded us, the form of the "People of God" has changed repeatedly. Once it was a wandering patriarch and his wife, then it became seventy people entering Egypt, later it was a host in captivity and later still the nationalized "seed of Abraham", the nation of Israel at Sinai. A little later it was a wandering host of rebels and later still a people settled in the land of their inheritance. Not long after they became a divided people in the land and then a nation in exile. By and by it was a Solitary One and then "the Body of Christ". In all these changed situations, there was still the "People of God" who needed the Word of God and who fed on or were smitten by the Law and the Prophets. The canon of the Church is the whole Bible. There are theological truths, which are just as binding on us today as they ever were on ancient Israel who stood under Mount Sinai for a year on their way to Canaan. I'm hoping we can feed on some of those truths.

In Exodus there are truths that will remain as long as God does and there are rules that should be reverently laid aside as belonging to an age that is past. There are rules in Exodus (about gathering manna, for example) that were not to survive Israel's entrance into Canaan. But even those rules have things to teach us as we bring our lives under submission to God.

But there's more than one way to teach people upright behavior and it isn't enough to "inform" people of what upright behavior is. People need rules and can't live without them but they also need an emotional attachment to rules to help them keep them. People need to be inspired and they need models. Birch argues that morality is not to be found solely in the legal, prophetic and wisdom texts, which seek to control conduct, but is observable also in the narratives that can disclose reality and transform the reader. Stories have power; power to motivate as they enlighten. Stories can woo us into loveliness as well as shock us out of moral ugliness so it shouldn't surprise us that much of God's word is narrative. One of the strengths of narrative is that it can convey and illustrate more than one truth and at more than one Level.

The book of Exodus records history but it doesn't record "brute facts". Like other biblical books it takes events and weaves them together for the purpose of making its points. The history Exodus records is *interpreted* history. The "gospel of John" unashamedly tells us of its theological and spiritual purpose (20:30-31). To understand the book of Exodus is to do more than rehearse its stories (which is a profoundly important thing to do), it is to understand the point of the stories and to be able to make use of its truths in our own culture and environment as part of God's continuing work. To know what it meant to and did for Israel is one part of understanding. To grasp it so that its truths bear fruit in our lives and attitudes, that's another dimension of understanding and to find our place in the theodrama is more again.

Missing the first produces "sermonettes" and pious platitudes where there was a revelation of the Lord God Almighty. Missing the second can leave us wishing God hadn't retired and pulled down the shades after Sinai. If we miss the first part, we're left with 'sermon thoughts" and "homiletical hints". If we miss the second part we're left with a book of antiquities about a generation of fellow-humans who long ago dried up and were blown away in the wind. Miss the first and our souls grow lean on 'dainties" while we long for something substantial to feed on. Miss the second and Bible study is like licking carpet. Thank God for those scholars and teachers everywhere who enable us to understand that it isn't just "Exodus" but "Exodus & Us".

But in addition to all the above and maybe more important to us who want to "hear" the message of Exodus—Exodus is part of a narrative, a drama, a Story in which God is the central character whose character and purpose generates and shapes the "script" of the Story. To look at Exodus as a compendium of rules handed down by God is to miss the essential character of the book. It is "a chapter" in his Story.

This means that it makes no sense to say we can dispense with it. Might as well say we can tear out a chapter of Dickens' *David Copperfield* because we don't need it, because it deals with Copperfield's boyhood rather than his manhood. To do that would be to violate the entire story.

When we read of rules and regulations, commands and instructions we're tempted to isolate them from the Story rather than to see them as contributing to the Story of God's relationship with and purpose in Israel. The rules and ordinances and such disclose the character of God and his dealings with Israel as well as defining what it means to be "Israel". The "rules" are more than rules! As surely as sadistic parents create sadistic rules and in this way reveal themselves and the situation in which the children exist so loving parents create life-furthering rules. In doing this they reveal their own hearts and shape the existence of their children.

I. RESCUE UNDER YAHWEH: 1:1—18:27

The creative Lord is still at work even in a world of sin and chaos, working blessing in the midst of cursing

1

THE BLESSING CONTINUES

*So God blessed them, and God said to them "Be fruitful and multiply, and fill the earth and subdue it "- **Genesis 1:26a***

Exodus takes up the story that ended with Jacob and his family going down to Egypt. He knew his inheritance was to be Canaan and appears to have been afraid to go to Egypt (see Genesis 46:3) but God assured him that it was there he would make of him a great nation.

Many years had passed since God had sworn to Abraham that he would multiply his seed and make of him a great nation and yet when Jacob entered Egypt there were only seventy-five of them (Acts 7:14), hardly a great nation. But it's there that they "were fruitful and multiplied greatly and became exceeding numerous, so that the land was filled with them" (Exodus 1:7).

The language echoes Genesis 1:26ff. The creative Lord is still at work even in a world of sin and chaos, working blessing in the midst of cursing. The language is also the language of Genesis 12:2; 13:14-15; 15:4-5; 17:2,6,15f; 22:17-18; 26:4,24; 28:3. God's creative purpose to bless as he redeems has never ceased despite the evil that has increased. No circumstances, however chaotic they

27

appeared, proved the point that God had changed his mind about what he intended for humanity and Abraham his instrument of blessing. This blessing language implies what we are expressly told again and again: *the Abraham file has not been closed.*

In Egypt the blessing work of God continues but sin arises to bring curse to those God intended to bless (1:8-22). Pharaoh makes it an "us" and 'them" matter and a policy of ethnic cleansing and exploitation is initiated. In this case the cursing work of Pharaoh is no match for the blessing work of God and the more he curses them the more they increase (1:12). This fear-inspired work of cursing those God intended to bless raises the Abraham connection again (Genesis 12:3) and ensures that the Pharaohs were spelling out their own future judgment.

The biblical Story insists that Israel is the blessed instrument of blessing by which God would bless the world. There is nothing elite about Israel but she is elect. Her election is not merely for personal gain, she is to be a blessing to all the nations of the earth. Those who opposed God's instrument of blessing opposed themselves and were an obstacle in the way of God's purpose to bless the world. That being the case, when he had to, God moved them out!

The political reason for this 'shrewd" (1:10) policy of Pharaoh is to make sure his own throne and his own people might be secure, free from future threat. The oppression, the ethnic cleansing he undertook wouldn't have been called "cruel" or "brutal," 'savage" or "unjust". Of course not! It was a question of "foreign policy" and "internal necessities". When has a group or nation of oppressors ever named their policy anything other than "good diplomacy" or "political necessity"? Ask Hitler or Stalin why they did what they. Ask Pol Pot, Papa Doc or the Shah of Iran why they tortured and exterminated. Ask Mao Tse Tung or Chiang Khai Shek why they did what they did. Ask the major powers why they've involved themselves in policies that everyone knows are monstrous. In most prisons they say there are no guilty prisoners. It seems there are no guilty nations either; none who have involved themselves in deceit, lies and injustice. Everyone is innocent.

We sometimes wonder why it takes God so long to get things done in this world. Because the corruption in the world is so widespread and the wickedness is so entrenched and governments are such liars and people are so self-serving. But in the midst of it all, is God, wading through the corruption and moving things to his purposed end.

The power of the powerless is the certain knowledge that no lie can live forever and no tyranny can reign forever.

2

THE POWER OF THE POWERLESS

Two things said Kant, fill me with awe The starry heavens
and the moral law,
But I know something, more mysterious and obscure,
The long, long patience of the plundered poor.

I think Edwin Markham wrote that. And haven't you felt that wonder? Sometime back my Ethel and I watched the news together. From Africa they showed an incredibly long line (surely it was a mile long) of people who needed medical attention. Most of them, or so it seemed, were skeletal women carrying dying babies. There was a single doctor sitting at a table and a solitary nurse assisting him. (Dear Lord, how this must hurt you!) Later that day Ethel had a fearful asthmatic attack. I bundled her into the car, drove her round the corner to the clinic, the sympathetic receptionist said she'd get one the doctors to look at her immediately one was free. I was grateful, Ethel was choking and I was anxious. Mere minutes passed and I began to feel my veneer of maturity peeling away. What was keeping them? What kind of medical service was this that my wife had to sit here choking for air?

In my head I was reading the riot act to the whole establishment and then the vision of these plundered poor crashed its way into my chaotic innards and for only another few minutes (when a doctor quickly came to our rescue) I felt their condition with special clarity. That evening, almost simultaneously, she and I brought up the two experiences of the day (the news report and the visit to the clinic) and we just had to speak to God about our situation and theirs. No one was to blame for any aspect of Ethel's hurt, the delay was very brief and a relief-bringing injection brought us both sanity. How different the situation was for this long, long line of waiting people. Quiet, patient, unprotesting sufferers, many of whom couldn't have made it to be two figures sitting at a single table away in the distance. Victims of warmongering, fratricidal governments and troops at home and predatory wealth abroad. The plundered poor! The powerless poor? No, not without power. Exodus 1:8-22 and 2:24 speak to all this.

• The power of the powerless lies in the truth that such a God exists as will not let wrongs go unrighted!

• The power of the powerless is the certain knowledge that no lie can live forever and no tyranny can reign forever.

• The power of the powerless is not in their capacity to absorb punishment or their intolerable meekness, it lies in the character of the God who now takes note of them and who assures them that the last word is not that of the earthly juggernauts that grind their bones to powder.

• The power of the powerless lies in the fact that their groans don't simply die in the still air that hangs above their squalid ghettos or sewer-pipe homes, that the God who hated pharaonic tyranny and oppression 2,000 years before Christ hates it still 2,000 years after him.

• Their power lies in the truth that the God who took grim note of the Jewish tragedy takes note of the black, yellow, white and brown groans rising from any street in any village, town, city or metropolis anywhere in the world. He hears the voiceless groans of the more than 36 million developing humans who are done away with each year. (Almost all of them are being hunted down because they get in the way of trouble-free life-style. And Westerners who have discriminated against the handicapped in the womb are aghast at Easterners who are discriminating against females in the womb. It doesn't matter that the Easterners are doing what they're doing for the same reason Westerners are doing what they're doing. Both handicapped and females are seen as obstacles to a self-fulfilled life for the adults.)

• The power of the powerless lies in the truth that God will not only punish the evildoers, he will right all wrongs. He will do what is right!

Well, that settles that. Since God is going to take care of it all in some future judgment, I needn't move my finger to lift a burden or redress a wrong. That response might do if God's righting of wrongs was confined to the future. It might do if we were not a vehicle of his justice and mercy, if Christians were not a sign and a manifestation of the reign of God. Since we are a sign and a manifestation of the reign of God, we'd best get on with it and embody a God-imitating justice and kindness. Anyone who is just going to "leave it all with God in the future" is asking to have Matthew 25:31-46 stamped on his forehead.

As amazing as it may seem in light of our excessive and growing interest in ourselves, part of the power of the powerless is the Church, the disciples of Christ (see Isaiah 42:1-4 as used by 2 Tim 2:24-25 which puts us in the "justice bringing" business). We are given the duty and privilege to (under Christ and as part of Christ) bring a glad-hearted justice to the world at large. It isn't an option— it's an obligation.

Harry E. Fosdick speaks of obedience when he tells of something his father said. As he left the house the father said to the mother: "Tell Harry he can mow the yard today if he feels like it." A few yards farther and he turned again and said: "And tell Harry he'd best feel like it." Fosdick said he mowed the yard utterly without rancor because he was being obedient to someone who was his friend as well as his father. I'm certain that's true, but he mowed it just the same. I was going to make an application of that to us but I've forgotten just how I would phrase it.

Sometimes the circumstances yell loud and it would appear that "Pharaoh" is running the show

3

WHO'S IN CHARGE HERE?

*The king of Egypt said, "If it is a boy kill him;
but if it is a girl let her live." **Exodus 1:15-16***

Goldberg reminds us that for all his power, Pharaoh couldn't even get his daughter to keep his rules. He wanted all the Hebrews boys killed and here's his daughter breaking the law (2:1-10).

Who would deny that the daughter made a choice? But, in light of the narrative, who would deny that God was at work in her choice? Had we asked the princess if she was a free agent she would rightly have said yes but how can a sensitive woman be utterly free when they see an abandoned baby at the mercy of the elements, destined to die if someone doesn't do something about it? And on top of that, when she opened the little casket, "he was crying" (2:6) so are we surprised when we read, "and she felt sorry for him"?

But the baby wasn't abandoned in the usual sense. This had been a protected baby—for three months a mother had defied the law of the land and when the baby's growth became a threat to himself, the mother acted wisely. She put the baby where one might least have looked for him—in the river where the law said he was to be

35

drowned. The divine irony is that the place designed to kill him becomes the location where he is preserved and the house (of Pharaoh) from which death is being handed out becomes his refuge. 2:10 speaks of some kind of public confirmation of Moses' adoption into the house of Pharaoh. While Egyptians kept a careful eye out for boys, for would-be deliverers, so that they might kill them, the adopted grandfather, Pharaoh, was bouncing on his knee the only boy in his whole kingdom he needed to kill! He was educating him, nourishing and advancing him (Acts 7:22). He would have been amazed at any Israelite who would think to warn him that his God was seeing all Pharaoh's evil and would work to bring him down. He would have found that hard to believe while he played with his grandson Moses.

Is it any wonder that David (Psalms 2), seeing the plots and schemes of his own people and foreigners as they opposed Yahweh and his anointed—is it any wonder, while looking at these judges and kings who thought they could successfully thwart God's purposes, he says, "The one enthroned in heaven laughs; the Lord scoffs at them"? To hear Pharaoh bellow about his power and what he would or would not do to Israel must have amused Yahweh. Pharaoh, who couldn't dress himself without the help of God was sovereign? Hardly!

The ancient picture is no more amusing than the modern ones. We listen to men and women who have achieved some acclaim speak as though they were gods, as though they were God. What the scientists will or will not do one of these days. (One prediction I read was that when our sun burns out in a million years or so, the scientists will put another, maybe two, in its place.) It's amazing what splicing a few genes and drawing out the implications of some phenomenon will do for some scientists. They begin to believe they are in charge and it isn't the first one I've heard snigger at a believer's claim that God was in charge. Sometimes the circumstances yell loud and it would appear that "Pharaoh" is running the show but one of these days someone will walk up to a modern pharaoh and offer him a ten-lesson correspondence course on who Yahweh is.

4

NOBILITY IN STRANGE PLACES

*He said to his daughters, "Where is he? Why did you leave the man? Invite him to break bread." **Exodus 2:20***

Presuming, as I do, that the midwives of ch.1 were Hebrew women, it isn't surprising that they favored the Hebrew mothers. I can see that it might be difficult for them when the Egyptian authorities were putting pressure on them to act against their own people. (We've read much about that during the Nazi regime and read of Jews turning against fellow-Jews to save their own skin. In view of their horrendous conditions I have no criticism to offer about that.) Nevertheless, Hebrew women stood by Hebrew women. And it isn't difficult to understand that Moses' mother, Jochebed and her daughter Miriam showed concern for Moses but it's nice to read that an Egyptian princess can show as much human decency and compassion as a Hebrew.

No group or people have a monopoly on nobility or honor. In 2:13 we have a Hebrew oppressing a fellow-Hebrew. When confronted with his wrong, rather than renounce it and turn from it, in a bitter sulk he insults and implicitly threatens one who sought to right a wrong the day before (2:12-13). We are all capable of oppressing our own. This Israelite snarls his bitterness at Moses and rejects him as an interfering and arrogant interloper.

In 2:17-20 we have an outsider taking an entirely different view altogether. Some shepherds bullied the daughters of a Midianite priest and Moses, who had been rebuffed the last time he interfered in a quarrel, couldn't stand by and see that happen. He stood up for the oppressed ones and the priest saw it as gallantry. When he was told the story of Moses helping the girls, he wanted to know, "Why did you leave him? Invite him to have something to eat" (2:20). Bear in mind, when he offered hospitality, the only thing he knew of him was that he was "an Egyptian" (2:19).

What might have made it even more difficult to offer hospitality to this stranger would be finding out that he was an Israelite. Jethro was a Midianite and that meant he was as much a descendant of Abraham as Moses but he was of the "rejected" line as were Ishmaelites and Edomites (Genesis 25:1-6 tells us the Midianites were deliberately separated from Isaac). Jethro treated Moses as Esau treated Jacob in Genesis 33. It's lovely to see healing!

Again and again in Genesis and Exodus we are shown that outsiders are capable of kindness, discernment and integrity. A stranger called Melchizedek blessed Abraham and a Philistine king called Abimelech rebuked Abraham for a callous rejection of Sarah as his wife (to save his own skin) leaving her at the mercy of anyone who came along. Jacob is completely forgiven by Esau the brother he conned and the Pharaoh who exalted Joseph welcomed him. Here in Exodus an Egyptian princess defies the law of Egypt and a Midianite priest praises Moses who was insulted by his own.

It's too easy to dismiss nobility in those who aren't of "our house". Wendy Kaminer in a *Theology Today* article some time ago took a severe look at the self-help books of evangelicals in which evangelicals praised themselves as people who loved their children, cared what happened to society, took marriage seriously and so forth. Looking at it through her eyes I began to feel my toes curl as quotation after quotation showed us up as smug and self-righteous, seeing ourselves as a cut above everybody else.

A godly Christian woman compared with a non-Christian decadent is a sight to behold but what about comparing a carnal, apathetic, whimpering and bigoted Christian with a patient, compassionate, socially-useful, un-embittered non-Christian? Jesus, it is said in the NT, marveled twice. Once he marveled at the unbelief of his own people (Mark 6:6) and on another occasion he was astonished at the faith of a foreigner (Matthew 8:10). And it isn't a rare thing to hear Christians confess one to another that sometimes "outsiders" show more love and compassion than the people we worship with.

We don't need to needlessly attack believers and praise the world to show the world we're really "honest" people or to curry favor with them. If we should show understanding and generosity to "outsiders" we should show it at least as much to struggling believers. But if the Bible shows us anything and if the Master's example counts for anything we should gladly recognize nobility, gallantry and compassion where we see it, no matter the immediate source, for in the end, it all has one source.

He who gives all humans food,

clothing, fruitful seasons and

glad hearts also helps them to

live lives of beauty and

strength.

5

EARTH'S GREATEST WONDER

"By faith when he was grown up, Moses refused to be called a son of Pharaoh's daughter, choosing rather to share ill-treatment with the people of God than to enjoy the fleeting pleasures of sin."
Hebrews 11:24-25

The sun shines down on nothing lovelier or grander than a boy, girl, woman or man of high moral integrity and cheerful endurance. Autumn forests are wonderful, snow-capped mountains or high and thunderous waterfalls are breathtaking, vast deserts and grand canyons are spellbinding but nothing's as awesome as a human who with cheerful stubbornness refuses to surrender her integrity! Nothing's as riveting or creates as many lovely, gallant dreams as a vulnerable little human who with a characteristic smile refuses to exchange his integrity for something less than the vision that has seized him.

And I know in a world of spiraling figures on divorce, crime, abuse; I know in a world where the bizarre and monstrous grab the headlines that it isn't always easy to look long at and appreciate the grandeur of such people. But they're there; the virgins, the un-embittered, the forgivers, the honest, the faithful, the straight, the kind, the clean, strong and compassionate people—they're all around us. They aren't Jesus but they're genuine!

If you think only Christians are like this—wake up! If you don't already know that there are people who profess no allegiance to Christ and still live lives of breathtaking loveliness I won't take the time to tell you about them. If you've never had an experience that led you to swear that "people outside the Church often treat you better than those in it" you've lived a sheltered life. God doesn't wait until people make a commitment to him before he makes a commitment to them! He who gives all humans food, clothing, fruitful seasons and glad hearts also helps them to live lives of beauty and strength. As Paul put it in Acts 17: 25, God gives all humans life "and everything else." I'm weary of a superficial use of Scripture that denies what is plain to be seen by anyone who is able to see—God's work of building character goes on with wonderful effectiveness even in the lives of non-Christians!

Where do people of moral integrity come from? How do they arise? What shapes them? The short and complete answer, of course, is God! That's enough. But let me isolate two things that God uses in creating and shaping such wonders:

1) Early experiences and environment, and,
2) An abiding sense of the invisible.

I don't know if any biblical character illustrates this better than Moses. Exodus 1—2, Acts 7:20-38 and Hebrews 11:23-28 would be helpful here.

When found by Pharaoh's daughter Moses was given back into his mother's arms for nursing. It wasn't unusual for a child to be four (in some cases, even five) when weaned from his mother. With a mother like Jochebed (Hebrews 11:23) you can be certain Moses was nursed while his mother sang and told him stories. And faithful Amram while leading Moses around by the hand would have told him stories of how God led Abraham here and there like a child. Day after day, knowing that he was to be taken from them soon and subjected to tremendous pressures and temptations, they would have filled his yielding mind with God, covenant, election and destiny. It doesn't surprise us, then, after he has been educated in all the wisdom of the Egyptians and showed himself to be a man, mighty in word and action (Acts 7) that he says "No!" to Egyptian glory, wealth and prestige. I'm not saying it was an easy decision or one quickly made. I've no way of knowing that; but we do know it was thoroughly decisive!

Is it pressing Heb 11:24 too far to see a public and formal rejection of the pharaonic family name? Was there a time when he was asked formally to accept the adoption into the family of the Pharaoh and in the sight of all Egypt's elite he turned it down? Formally or not, his "no" was one of the grandest in history (MacCartney). Illustrating this biblical truth Josephus tells us that even as a little boy Moses took the crown Pharaoh had playfully put on him and stepped on it. What we know for sure is this: he chose his revered past and painful future with his enslaved and oppressed people rather than the power and wealth of Egypt.

Who can estimate the power of childhood training? Or the power of a single noble deed in the life of an otherwise poorly trained child? We've all heard horror stories about the awful deeds which shaped a child for evil but we've also heard people tell us of some sublime single experience that never left them and kept a light on in their heart down the years. We can't overestimate the importance of catechizing our children with deep, rich, abiding and ennobling truths. And people we don't know but who are watching, can see us do something gallant, something stubbornly right and be redeemed by it without even knowing quite why.

Hebrews says Moses said "no" to Egypt's vast wealth and power because he knew what was ahead. Saw by faith what wasn't yet "seeable". He endured, it goes on to say, because he saw Him who is invisible. Faith is the substance of things hoped for, the evidence of things not seen. That's one of the key elements in these incredible people—they rise beyond the visible and grasp what is not yet subject to the eye or the senses.

The battle for full truth and faith, following George Roche, hinges on the meaning of a rainbow. Only a fool denies the physical. Only an ingrate uses the good things scientists and medical researchers bring and then dismisses the scientists with contempt. These professionals bring many of God's finest gifts to us but the worst kind of technology is the kind that kills rainbows, that takes the mystery out of everything and that substitutes equations, measurements and symbols for meaning. It's one of the glories of these remarkable people of faith and integrity that they will not allow rainbows to die; that they will not allow technology to dissolve mystery!

"What is a rainbow? Why it's an atmospheric optical phenomenon caused by water droplets refracting light." Of course it is! And who would want to deny that important truth? But that's not all. Beyond the physical, beyond the water droplets and refracted light there is Genesis 9 and a Story.

With sophisticated cameras, electronic microscopes and computers people can follow the path of a human from conception through cell division and replication to maturity and finally to death—from the womb to the grave. See? Pictures and physical explanations for everything, no mystery, no needless hypotheses (like "God" or "meaning" or "values")—all is naked to the eye and having sensed it—that's the end of it. But it's not the end of it, not for the "keepers of rainbows". And what do the defenders of rainbows have to offset the (partial but) powerful truth of the mere senses? A Story! These people know that beyond the bully now before us, beyond the seducer now before us, beyond the embittered, hand-wringing and cynical, beyond the statistics on crime, premarital, extramarital and perverted sex; beyond the rape of nations, unemployment, lords of porn, booze and injustice there is the Righter of all Wrongs! Not just the Punisher of the Wicked but the Righter of all Wrongs! Beyond the important temporal there is the eternal; beyond the important visible there is the Invisible. Beyond the microscope, the telescope and the theory— there are glorious humans and there is the Story!

6

THE IRISH WOLFHOUND

*"When he went out the next day, he saw two Hebrews fighting; and he said to the one who was in the wrong."Why do you strike your fellow Hebrew?" **Exodus 2:13-14***

The government was exterminating their little boys, they were enslaved to the point where they cried to God because the bondage was so severe and they were brothers and sisters. If that was the situation, how come they were oppressing each other? You'd think since they were enduring oppression from their enemies that that would be enough, how could they turn on each other and do the enemy's work for him? Wasn't there enough pain in the world for the People of God to face? Weren't there enough enemies who bullied and butchered? In 2:13 we have one brother wronging another (and by consequence, wounding the man's family—do we ever wrong only one person?). There, there, in the land of injustice, where Hebrews should have stood by each other, had good reason to stand by each other; there, we find brothers wronging brothers.

And in a world filled with tireless evil, vicious, brutal, evil; slimy, rotting evil; crushing, debasing, cruel evil—in a world filled with that we find churches grinding each others bones. We find journals, bulletins, taped-sermons and all kinds of church media devoted to the exposure of some preacher, church or other on matters of teaching. Ah, yes, but it must be on something foundational like the death, burial and resurrection of Jesus? Maybe his atoning death? The certainty of judgment? The one true God? The truth and trustworthiness of Scripture? Some central affirmations of Scripture—surely? No! Take one quick glance around at these papers and see for yourself. With the porn industry, the booze industry, the drug industry, the vice industry, the abortion industry; with the many open sewers pouring out filth, with countless open wounds around us, caused by gangsters, corrupt landlords, politicians and war-mongers—with all these in front of us as enemies, who do we pick a raging battle with? Some other little assemblies which, despite their limitations, with Bible in hand and God set in their hearts, have for years stood opposed to these monstrous tyrannies. That's who some of us devote our papers, sermons and letters against! These are the sort of little congregations that some huge assembly leaders dismiss as churches that should close shop. [It's amazing what a bit of "success" will do to some people.]

There's this story of the Irish Wolfhound that enjoyed a big juicy bone and then hobbled off on three legs. I don't believe I'll tell it.

7

SO FAR FROM HOME

*"She bore a son, and he named him Gershom; for he said, "I have been an alien residing in a foreign land." **Exodus 2:22***

On an old milestone, on the wild hills of western Ireland, miles from any house, some lonely soul scratched: "So far from home". I think there was more than geography included in that pathetic line.

Genesis 1—11 tells us again and again of people who were made homeless as a result of their wickedness. Adam and Eve lost the garden, Cain lost the place where he communed with God, the antediluvians experienced loss of home when their world was desolated by the waters coming back up over the earth in an act of "uncreation" (contrast Genesis 1) and the Shinar people lost the center and city they were creating for themselves and became wanderers again over the face of the earth.

Exodus 2:21-22 suggests to us that Moses felt this sense of homelessness when he called one of his sons, "Gershom" that sounds like a word that means "an alien" or someone living in a strange land. Maybe "homeless" would be best in our context. I'm of the opinion that Moses was embittered, felt let down by God and that that is shown in the name he gave the child and the fact that he didn't circumcise him (see *Drama at the Inn*). Just the same, if he felt like that he could only be missing his people. Chapter three tells us that in response to Israel's sadness and cries God is going to take them out of Egypt and bring them to the home he had promised (3:7-8). Living away from home beats dying but there may come a time when even that isn't true. Food in a pigpen is still away from home and a good-paying job in a distant city won't always make up for the absence of the family and all that that means.

To have no one to answer to, no schedules to meet, no place you have to be has its pleasures but for most of us there is the longing to belong and to be. An Irish poet describes an old woman of the roads, who is tired of her vagrant life, heartsick of the tramping through wind and rain, and who prays to God for a little house of her own, where she could find peace in homey duties during the day, and then, she says:

I could be quiet there at night
Beside the fire and by mysef
Sure of a bed and loth to leave
The ticking clock and the shining delf.
Och! but I'm weary of mist and dark
And roads where there's never a house or
bush And tired I am of bog and road
And the crying wind and the lonesome hush.

Christians look for their home too. Sometimes they look for heaven just as passionately as Israel looked for Canaan and finally they look for their post-resurrection life with its unbroken peace in righteousness and holiness. There were those among Israel who quite enjoyed the leeks and onions and garlic of Egypt (as they should have) but for most of them, home after a painful journey was better than leeks and fleshpots in a temporary station. There were times when the hope of a future in Canaan wasn't popular and there are times when heaven and a new creation isn't especially sought.

But I suppose it depends on how you view the future under God. If you see it as an eternal prayer meeting, or an eternal hymn-singing service where all we do is tell God how wonderful he is, that might not appeal to us. If it's seen, as I believe the Bible implicitly teaches us it will be, then how could we not look forward to a state free from ignorance and racism, free from radical nationalism, free from ill health and oppression, free from disease and warmongering, free from predatory wealth and unbridled individualism? Home is about life. More life, not less.

A burning bush is a good symbol of individual people who go through some horrendous experiences or prolonged suffering without being destroyed.

8

I SHOULD HAVE GONE BAREFOOT

*"Moses, Moses!" And he said,, "Here I am." Then he said, "Come no closer! Remove the sandals from your feet for the place on which you are standing is holy ground." **Exodus 3:4b-5***

The Hebrew text of Exodus 3:1 indicates the shepherd was doing what he usually did—taking care of the flock for Jethro. It's possible that the shepherd, though an embittered man, was thinking about his people back in Egypt. He named one of his children "Gershom" because he couldn't forget that he was exiled, separated from his own. Be that as it may, it was in the middle of another ordinary day, or at least, in the middle of one that began that way, that the man met God in an extraordinary way. There, with sand in his clothes, hair and between his teeth; there, with the parched land, the whispering wind, the throbbing heat and the smell of sheep he was confronted with an old and awesome Ally.

Was it some natural event? Like St Elmo's Fire, which sailors often see out at sea? Perhaps, but after forty years of shepherding wouldn't you think the shepherd had seen more than a few instances of all those natural things? Wouldn't you think he had

51

become at least accustomed to such sights? And doesn't the text suggest that the man finds this experience unusual? He came near and someone (who knew the shepherd's name!) told him to go barefoot, the ground had been made holy, not by the bush, but by the presence of an indwelling God. Among other things, this text suggests we find God at times in surprising places.

A burning bush is a good symbol of God who burns without needing any external help. If the shepherd had ever lit a fire he would have seen a bush burning until it was consumed and known full well that the fire died with the bush. That was because the fire was taking its strength from and depending for its existence on the materials surrounding it. When they were gone, the fire was gone. It had no independent life.

On this occasion, the fire continued to burn without having to draw on its surroundings. We're told that God appeared to Moses in a "flame of fire" which is self-sustaining. Here is a God who depends on nothing and no one for his existence, one who isn't kept alive by the power/strength/life of his worshipers or servants. This truth mustn't be lost on us. We need a God who is close to us, a God who is like us (since we're "in his image") but we're in dire need of a God who is unlike us, who is altogether other than us, who is in that ultimate sense independent of us. God forbid that we should depend on a God who depends utterly on us!

A burning bush is a good symbol of Israel which was even at that moment in the heat of trouble and trials but would not be consumed. Given Israel's situation in Egypt—still they flourished. How was that possible? What was it that was frustrating the purpose of Pharaoh to consume and curse Israel? It was the blessing of God who dwelled in them and was always with them. The God who spoke from the bush had assured both Abraham and Jacob that the people would go down into Egypt and although (he tells Abraham) they would be oppressed while there, he would preserve them and bring them out of bondage (Genesis 15:12ff; 46:3-4). The secret behind the blessing in the midst of oppression and the deliverance from the rapist was the presence of the indwelling God. The Church of God needs to experience and enjoy this truth.

A burning bush is a good symbol of individual people who go through some horrendous experiences or prolonged suffering without being destroyed. Haven't you seen people who left you speechless with their bravery; by their refusal to be embittered, by their refusal to be put off as they seek God in righteousness and sincerity? Aren't we persuaded that whatever else is true about situations like that God is showing himself in it, that we should go barefoot because we're on holy ground, we're in the presence of the holy One?

I know a woman who had thirteen children, whose life was way too hard (the details only her family really know), never got her head above water, suffered numberless disappointments, wrestled with illness and debt. It's now when I look back on my mother's life and remembering her cheerfulness, her compassion toward needy neighbors and the sick in our district (only God knows how many came to our door to see if *Cassie McGuiggan* could advise or help). It's now when I think of the nights with very little sleep or none at all because one or more of the children were sick, of too little food for herself, too few clothes, too little help, too little encouragement and then dying before her time—it's now, looking back on all this and remembering her faith that I realize I was in the presence of God— I should have gone barefoot.

When I think of the women I saw in my boyhood around our district who quietly but bravely opposed (often at awful cost) the whining or bullying of their husbands and insisted that they act like men; who bore the indignity of their poverty with the dignity of princesses—I realize now, I should have gone barefoot.

When I look at some of the TV documentaries and watch people who live with brave eyes and unbowed hearts through an endless stream of abuse and injustice, who ask for nothing, who aren't part of the protesting crowds when the TV pictures are taken because they are out there somewhere scratching in the ground trying to feed their families—when I look at them, I know I'm in the presence of God. I should go barefoot.

When I see the masses of people being worn down, lowering their standards, joining the crowds of those who insist that society owes them "a living"; when I see the bulk of us settling for the pathetic, lapsing into bitterness, endlessly finding fault with everyone else, acting as though we were one of the people in the Third World or Eastern Europe when in fact, things could hardly be better, just needing a bit of fine tuning; when I see people whose days are frittered away in doing nothing but what their impulses suggest, in passing what's left of their lives planning and doing only what is pleasant to them—when I see all this, I realize that while burning bushes aren't completely absent, they are few and far between. And it's because our societies are so filled with those of us who throw in the towel so easily that "burning bushes" are so special. You see a different indwelling spirit there, you hear God speaking to you out of a common burning bush, the place becomes holy and you have to go barefoot. Now and then, as I go through another ordinary day I see visions. Like the gentle and cheerful woman who lived two hundred yards from me and whose crippling illness made her walk bent almost double and she had to look up just to say hello. Or the bright-eyed, giggling woman with her daughter and grandson I saw some time ago in a distant city. She was the most disfigured lady I've ever seen. In coming into contact with such people I suddenly see something that makes me wonder and I feel the impulse to go barefoot.

9

AFRAID TO LOOK AT GOD

*And he said further, "I am the God of your father, the God of Abraham, the God of Isaac, and the God of Jacob" and Moses hid his face, for he was afraid to look at God." **Exodus 3:6***

Exodus 3:6 offers this, "...At this, Moses hid his face, because he was afraid to look at God." I think we need to note that it was when God said he was the God of Abraham, Isaac and Jacob that we're told Moses was afraid. The God who made promises to Israel, the God who watched Moses run from Egypt and live for forty years in a sulk—that's who spoke to Moses that day. The conversation that follows makes it clear that Moses doesn't want the job God calls him to so maybe when we're told Moses was afraid that we're to suspect that there was more than one face to his fear.

However that may be, he was afraid! Does this surprise us? When asked if he was afraid of God, C.S Lewis said, "Of course not! And yet..."

I must confess I wonder about those who can speak so familiarly about God, as though he was their "pal" or their "chum". Maybe it's just jealousy on my part because I don't feel that much at home with him and maybe there's more truth in that than I care to admit even while I tell myself it isn't the whole story. To enter too easily into His presence might suggest we don't have a balanced view of him. To saunter into his presence, hands in pockets, so to speak, is surely a sign that we haven't grasped it at all; that we haven't seen ourselves with sufficient clarity.

We hear Peter gasp in amazement and then beg the Master to depart from him because he himself was a sinful man. It wasn't only that the Christ was holy, different; it was that Peter suddenly realized he was in the presence of someone far above him even though that one was pleased to be near him.

And we hear Isaiah, confessing that his sin was the sin of the nation (6:1ff) and that in the King's presence he was "undone" and "unclean". I hear of Moses being afraid and averting his eyes.

Ah, yes, but that is our fault. God would not have it so. So some say but it was God who told Moses not to come any closer! It was God who shut himself off up the trembling Sinai and dwelled in fire up there. It was God who shut himself off behind curtains and hid himself in a constant cloud of incense in the Holy of Holies. "Even the angels are not pure in his sight" one of Job's friends rightly said. This is God who lives, said the apostle of grace in 1 Tim 6:16, in unapproachable light. Pursue holiness, said the NT book of Hebrews, or you won't see God (12:14). And it was the same writer who urged Christians who are the ones receiving the kingdom of God, "let us be thankful, and so worship God acceptably with reverence and awe, for our God is a consuming fire".

Should we then come groveling into the presence of God? Should we come crawling and quaking as into the gloomy presence of someone who is always on the verge of destroying us with a holy blow from his huge fist? Hardly, for the same man who is afraid to look at God in Exodus 3:6 wants to see God's glory in 33:18 because God has assured him that there is a friendship established between them. But even in that moment of warmth and intimacy, even in that moment when Friend met friend, there is this word, "But you cannot see my face, for no one may see me and live" (33:20). But even that

56

was an act of friendship, an act of compassion on the part of a Friend that protected his friend (33:21-23).

Should we be afraid to look at God, now that Jesus has come? Of course not! And yet...

But since the Fall of humanity God's gracious work is always characterized as a rescue mission—there's always someone in need of saving from some tyranny...

10

I AM COME DOWN TO DELIVER THEM

So come, I will send you to Pharaoh to bring my people, the Israelites out of Egypt. **Exodus 3:10**

George A.F. Knight reminds us that ancient gods came down to glorify themselves but the God of Abraham, Isaac and Jacob comes down to rescue the suffering from the oppressors. This is no surprise to those who know the Story—we expect God to be a liberator. Isn't that what the philosopher said of God's forgiveness, "Of course God will forgive us—that's his business"?

But since the Fall of humanity God's gracious work is always characterized as a *rescue* mission—there's always someone in need of saving from some tyranny of some kind whether it's an individual or a nation from some desperate situation or the human family from the powers that alienate it from the Holy Father. This is *not* a passing theme in the Bible—we find it everywhere. Most notably we see it in a young man hanging on a stake, spit, sweat and blood streaked. A young man who, even as he rescues us, exposes what it is above all that we need rescued from—our sinful and oppressive selves!

In the Exodus part of the Story the reason God "comes down" is because he has seen and heard the pain of the plundered [2:23-25; 3:7-9] and he remembered the covenant he made with Abraham [2:24]. The God who was coming down was a God who made covenants with actual people, like Abraham; he is a God who was faithful to his word and [as Brueggemann likes to remind us] he is a God who is provoked into action by the cries and the misery of the tyrannized. Then there's this: we need to keep in mind that the people he came to rescue were not paragons of virtue as God himself knew full well; they will break his heart in the Wilderness once they are delivered and they will forget him before Joshua's corpse is cold in the ground—as the book of Judges tells us. This is the nation he has come down to liberate because though they would prove themselves faithless to their word he could not be faithless to his.

But the deliverance was not to be by magic though miracles would be involved and while it is God who will do the liberating he will not do it alone. Note what he says in 3:8,10: "So I have come down to deliver them...Therefore, come now, and I will send you to Pharaoh, so that you may bring my people, the sons of Israel, out of Egypt."

Moses had understood more than forty years earlier that God had commissioned him to deliver Israel and he thought Israel might have understood that [see Acts 7:20-25]—but they hadn't. Back then he was a prince in Egypt, learned, courageous and revered as the son of Pharaoh's daughter [Acts 7:22]. Now he was an eighty-year old shepherd making a precarious living looking after someone else's sheep. The strange name this God would soon give himself hardly seems stranger than the way he works—rejecting the royal power Moses once had and now sending him to Pharaoh in social and political weakness with a shepherd's staff in his hand. There are plenty of stories in the Bible that tell us God makes his power perfectly present through weakness. There was Gideon's three hundred, David's sling and a smooth stone, there was the boy Jeremiah who would tear down kingdoms with words and there was the Galilean prophet who would ransom a world by serving until death.

The God who willed not be God without us has also willed that he will deliver his children through the devotion of their brothers and sisters; delivering them by mothers who will defy a tyrant's decree and save a child and a rejected brother who will carry a nation on his back until they are safely home though he himself doesn't make it!

He can't be summed up in a

sound even if it is a truthful

sound like

El Shaddai. While he is

almighty, he is more than that.

11

MYSELF!

For from him and through him and to him are all things. To him be the glory forever. Amen. **Romans 11:36**

The God with a strange way of working adopts a strange way of naming himself. Let's see what the scholars tell us about God's response to the request for "a name". They tell us he took a verb as a name. "Tell Israel 'I am' sent you." Scholars tell us that "ehyeh" is the first person singular in the imperfect tense of the verb "to be," hayah, and the imperfect tense speaks of action not completed.

This being the case, they tell us, God defines himself in terms of continuing existence. God is not "I was" but "I continue to be". If Israel asks for his name, Moses is to tell them, "*Always Is* has sent me".

But the imperfect tense often functions as a future this is how some scholars render the word: "I will be" (as it is, in fact, in 3:12). So, "I will be what I will be" is given by all the versions as an alternative to "I am what I am". This will make no difference if we

63

take etymology and grammar as defining God. If he "always is" then he "will be". But if there's a play on words (see below) it might make a significant difference.

There are scholars who insist that we should ignore the verbal element. They tell us that "ehyeh" in this context is not a verb. It lost its verbal nature long ago and is a personal name, the precise meaning of which is long lost and is not recoverable.

Other scholars tell us it doesn't matter whether it is a verb or not, that God is simply making a play on words and that what "ehyeh" means is determined by what God does and is in relation to Israel.

There are scholars who tell us that "ehyeh asher ehyeh" (I am what I am) is a refusal to be named. In that case, Moses asks "who are you?" and God says, "I am who I am". If you asked someone who he was and he said, "I am who I am" you would probably understand it as evasion rather than revelation. His tone would suggest if he meant to be rude or that the question was irrelevant or some such thing.

But it need not be an outright refusal. If God is making a play on words ("I will be what I will be"), he may be saying, "You'll know who and what I am by what you see me doing." While this is indeterminate in one respect, it is a positive affirmation in another—I am who I will show myself to be.

The end result is that some scholars are sure they have the situation understood and others who are sure they don't. They all read the arguments the other makes but remain unconvinced on the main issue.

Everyone agrees that Yahweh (or something like that) is related etymologically or phonologically to the verb "to be" (hayah). It is YHWH (with some vowels supplied) that God takes as his covenant name.

To the hopeful patriarchs he had revealed himself as El Shaddai but now to the bewildered, alien and suffering descendants of these patriarchs he adopts the name Yahweh. That he is God almighty (El Shaddai) is plain enough but what does he do with his almightiness? What does his almightiness mean when they remain bewildered and

64

suffering aliens? Wouldn't you think that the Almighty God of the fathers would have fulfilled his promises and protected their children from all this alienation and suffering?

Linking the relationship, "the God of your fathers..." with "Yahweh" stresses both predictability and unpredictability. The same God who sends Moses calls himself "I will be what I will be". He can't be summed up in a sound even if it is a truthful sound like El Shaddai. While he is almighty, he is more than that. While he is the God of your fathers, Abraham, Isaac and Jacob he is more than that. All these names and phrases, if people aren't careful, will only serve to box God in and he won't allow that. His purposes are too grand, his wisdom in carrying them out is too vast and his Person is beyond complete human comprehension so he calls himself, Yahweh; he will be what he will be.

In C.S.Lewis" *The Horse and his Boy*, the human hero, Shasta, has been stolen in infancy by the evil Calormen. The Narnian horse, Bree, and Shasta are on their way to freedom in Narnia but they suffer much on the way. One of the central trials was the constant threat from lions which seemed to Shasta (and, at one critical point, to Bree) to be the worst trial of all. In discussion with a great lion who professes to be his helper, Shasta is whimpering about how tough things have been for him and went on especially about meeting up with all those lions. The great lion tells him there was only one lion. Obviously he didn't understand, so Shasta tells him there were many lions. Again he is told, there was only one lion, swift of foot. It turns out that the great lion was everywhere where needed, he drove off the jackals in the night and he gave Bree the strength of fear just when he needed it. Finally Shasta is sobered and asks, "Who are you?"

Three times the lion answers him. First in a deep resonant tone which shook the earth he said, "Myself!" A second time, in a tone of gaiety, as though he was completely satisfied with who he was, he said, "Myself!" And a third time, in a whisper so low you had to strain to hear it and yet it seemed to come from everywhere, "Myself!"

There's something of this in Yahweh. He's the incomparable one, who can only be compared with himself. Who tells us who he is and yet because of what we are in relation to what he is, he can't tell us at all. He speaks to keep from saying nothing. He isn't the utterly unknown but he is the unknown and in this he glories because it can be no other way—he is what he is and he is beyond finding out. It is Romans 11:33-36. The evasive and yet revealing, Yahweh, is what God chooses as his covenant name with Israel.

12

THE RELUCTANT DELIVERER

"Who am I, that I should go to Pharaoh and bring the Israelites out of Egypt?" **Exodus 3:11**

The whole of chapters 3 & 4 are a "call narrative" that isn't completed until Moses reaches the border of Egypt when a patient God again (4:14,24) shows his anger against an overly reluctant and not wholly committed Moses. God was going to deliver Israel from Egypt and Moses was the agent he chose to use. "Who am I, that I should go to Pharaoh and bring the Israelites out of Egypt?" (3:11) In saying that Moses wasn't asking for information, he was declining the job.

Stephen in Acts 7:25 said Moses thought Israel would understand that God was using him to deliver them, but they didn't. When he acted on their behalf they rejected him as deliverer (Exodus 2:14) and the God who (Moses thought) tried to deliver them forty years earlier had failed (compare 5:22-23). Was the failure because of Moses? If so, the "Who am I?" in 3:11 makes sense.

Was God unable or had he changed his mind (see 5:22-23 and note 4:18 which seems to be sarcastic)? Or was it both?

One of the underlying themes in Exodus is this: Moses was truly commissioned by God and that he was faithful in exercising that authority. This phrase, "God said unto Moses" occurs something like 90 times in Exodus, Of the building of the Tabernacle and the arrangement of the sacrificial system, in the last two chapters, we hear again and again and again [sixteen times] that whatever was done was done "as the Lord had commanded Moses." Whatever else is true in chapters 3 & 4, we know Moses wasn't seizing any authority; he was having it pressed on him by God. This reluctance pattern is seen in later cases like Gideon, David, Jeremiah and numerous others.

The thrust of Exodus 3:11-20 is not to convince Israel and verify Moses commission but to convince *Moses* and deliver the "subpoena" to someone who didn't want it. The record of the events shows that Moses didn't seize a place of authority and it does it by showing that Moses was reluctant to take the job on.

The shepherd has a numbers of excuses to hide behind. He doesn't want the commission, he tried it and was rebuffed, so sulking and hesitant he complains, "Who am I to do this job?" And how could he persuade Israel he was their longed for deliverer? They would ask precisely what God was going to be to them that he hadn't been in centuries of alienation and generations of suffering— what "name" could he give them, what guarantees? If God had ignored them for so long what would make Israel think he was interested now? This skeptical people wouldn't believe his word— 4:1. Even miraculous signs had their limits; he would still have to talk and that wasn't a strong point of his he said (4:10-12). When all his excuses are taken away the real problem is laid bare, "O Lord, please send someone else to do it" (4:13).

Later, when Moses" commission and authority is called into question (see Numbers 12:1-9; 16:3, 13 as typical), the events recorded in these two chapters will be recalled. In a dispute with his opponents it's easy to hear Moses say, "I didn't want the job! He made me take it."

But for all the debate Moses became their shepherd. The Mishnah tells us God saw Moses tenderly shepherd a little thirsty goat and said, "Thou hast compassion with a flock belonging to a man of flesh and blood! As thou livest, thou shalt pasture Israel, My flock".

But the dialogue between God and Moses isn't really strange though it wasn't all to Moses' honor. No leader worth the name ever grasped at authority. It has happened in the world of politics and to our shame it has happened in religious circles and churches but it ought not to be (Matthew 20:25-26). To seize leadership is to "lord it over" but to be seized by God to lead is to serve.

The People of God is not a democracy! There is freedom but when men and women who are chosen as God's appointed instrument to accomplish a purpose, the Bible makes no bones about it—to oppose that person is to oppose God himself.

The rich biblical notion of faith is more than mere belief, more than simply "the acceptance as true any given proposition"; it involves trust. And trust can't be compelled!

13

SEE THAT JACKET?

"Believe me that I am in the Father and the Father is in me; but if you do not, then believe me because of the works themselves."
John 14:11

"What if they do not believe me or listen to me and say, 'the Lord did not appear to you'?" he wants to know (Exodus 4:1). Though the problem, at this point, is more in Moses than in the people, it isn't an irrational request. The "God of their fathers" had been around a long time and yet they were murdered and enslaved. If one comes with promises of a new future, it would hardly surprise us that they would have their doubts (6:9).

So God offers him credentials (4:2-9). Turning the staff into a snake and back again was "so that they may believe that the Lord...has appeared to you" (4:5). If that wasn't enough, there were two more signs (vv.6-9). Someone met and was with Moses. Whoever he was, he had power over the Nile (the Egyptian god Osiris), serpents and disease—to create and cure.

I know philosophers and philosophical theologians debate the credential power of miracles but you only do that in your study or lecture hall. You only do that when you calmly abstract the events from reality and reason on logical relations. We've heard plenty about Lessing's ugly ditch and how that miraculous power doesn't "prove" this or that. Yes, yes, but when you meet the real thing in a real setting where the event is contextualized and invested with meaning, all those arguments vanish like vapor.

G.K. Chesterton's poem on Lazarus [*The Convert*] sums it up well. Lazarus dies and is called back to life by Jesus the Christ. He wanders down the road, stops by a group of wise men who are matching words, laying out syllogisms, rattling out reason through a sieve which holds the chaff and lets the wheat go free. And what are they proving; that men cannot be raised from the dead! Lazarus listens to their arguments for a while then walks off saying of their wisdom, "But all of this is less than dust to me—for I am Lazarus, and I live!"

But the truth is I'm not very impressed with the whole school of thinkers who are so good with words that they can't assure us that what the Nazis or Stalin or ten thousand other tyrants have done is evil! The man or woman who stands to say there is no way to prove the right or wrong, the morality or immorality of what such people did to tens of millions—should I be surprised that they see no proof in the biblical miracles or what they are said to support? The word "proof" is not the problem any more.

For those who wish to believe, said God, these signs are proof enough. Ah, but a real miracle would compel faith. No sir! The rich biblical notion of faith is more than mere belief, more than simply "the acceptance as true any given proposition"; it involves trust. And trust can't be compelled! They'd seen miracles all over the place but wouldn't believe and so the Messiah would work no signs for them but he did believe in their credential power (John 15:24). To the strugglers who were not hard of heart but needed help at a critical time Jesus offered his works as proof (John 14:11; 20:24-31).

In a house in Troy, Ohio many years ago I was in the company of a boy called Tad Powers. I had spoken at the nearby building and he and I came on home ahead of the rest. He followed me around as boys are apt to do with a visiting speaker. I don't know what got into me but I turned to him and taking off my glasses I said to him, "Do you know who I am?" "Yes," he said, not especially impressed, "You're a preacher!" I looked at him solemnly and said, "I'm superman!" Quick as a flash he said, "Prove it!" Here's this, what? nine year old boy and he knew the difference between an ordinary claim and an extraordinary one. Had I said, "I'm Jim McGuiggan" he might have said, "You're secret's safe with me". Since I made an extraordinary claim, one that the circumstances made it hard to believe, he made an understandable response.

I had made a "power" claim and he asked for "power" evidence. So I gave it to him. I must have been out of my head but I looked around and there on the stair-post a jacket was hanging. I think it was mine but I can't remember. "See that jacket?" I asked. He grunted assent. I said, "Watch it!" He watched it for a few seconds and saw it fall. It nearly floored him (nearly floored me too). He turned with eyes like organ-stops and whispered, "Do some more!" At that point others were coming in and I whispered I didn't want everyone to know who I was. He watched me even more closely for the rest of the evening. (I even made a quick visit to the bedroom to check under my shirt for the big red **S**.)

The biblical credentials are not just raw acts of power. They have a moral and contextual fitness to them though there are a few which must be taken up into the larger context of the entire biblical corpus if we are to see them at their best.

The miracles of Jesus were more than raw acts of power, they expressed character, compassion, continuity with the OT concerns and directions and they were creative promises of a future and complete redemption. In any case, Moses didn't go unaided to Egypt.

Pharaoh and God were
involved in the hardening
process.

14

THE HARDENED HEART

*"But when Pharaoh saw there was relief, he hardened his heart and would not listen..." **Exodus 8:15***

"But I will harden his heart so that he will not let the people go" (4:21; 7:3; 9:12; 10:1,20,27; 11:10; 14:4,8). Nine times we're told in Exodus that God hardened the heart of Pharaoh.

We're also told that Pharaoh hardened his own heart. "But when Pharaoh saw there was relief, he hardened his heart and would not listen..." (8:15; 9:34—see also 7:13,14,22; 8:15,19,32; 9:7,35).

A surface reaction to the first group of texts suggests arbitrariness on God's part. They would seem to say the Pharaoh had no choice; as if God's hardening his heart left him without power to do other than God decreed and, in those cases, God has decreed rebellion and sin.

The second group of texts, on the surface, would seem to suggest that God had nothing whatever to do with the hardening of the king's heart.

Neither of these surface reactions is the right response. Pharaoh and God were involved in the hardening process. God was no spiteful and arbitrary tyrant and Pharaoh wasn't hypnotized or turned into a mere puppet.

Hardening is a judicial act of punishment. God is never said to harden the heart of a righteous person. The person whose heart is hardened is one who has already committed himself to rebellion against the will of God and as such, God uses his commitment to rebellion against him and to further His own agenda.

Hardening is the action of God in such texts. God's approach to one committed to wickedness, calling him to do what is right, is done with the full knowledge that that person will refuse. God's decision to force the wicked one to choose even when God knows he will choose evil is God's hardening work; it has the effect of driving the wicked one deeper into rebellion.

Hardening is God's act of demanding that the sinner choose good. What God demands is not that the wicked choose wickedness but that he choose good. God tempts no one by calling him to choose evil (James 1:13-15). God changelessly calls people to do what is right and good. That he knows they will choose evil does not alter the fact that he calls them to choose the contrary. Just the same, it is God's deliberate act of demanding obedience of such a person that is the occasion of his further and deeper rebellion.

Hardening is the act of the sinner on himself. It is perfectly proper that God should ask of anyone that they obey him. One who is committed to rebellion should not *be* committed to rebellion and is responsible for his rebellious state. When God comes to him demanding that he obey, he should obey and when he chooses further rebellion he is hardening his heart against God.

What God foreknows is *the sinner's* choice of evil. He does not foreknow that he (God) has chosen evil for the man. He foreknows that the sinner will choose evil. His foreknowing the sinner's choice doesn't alter the fact that it is the sinner's choice. When God exercises his right to make the sinner's choice of evil serve his purposes, it is God hardening the sinner by providing the occasion by deliberately making the demand and the sinner hardening himself by providing the choice

15

DRAMA AT THE INN

*On the way at a place where they spent the night, the Lord met him and tried to kill him. **Exodus 4:24***

"And it came to pass on the way at the lodging-place, that Jehovah met him and sought to kill him. Then Zipporah took a flint, and cut off the foreskin of her son, and made it touch his feet; and she said, Surely a bridegroom of blood art thou to me. So he let him alone. Then she said, A bridegroom of blood in regard of circumcision" (Exodus 4:24-26, ASV with footnotes).

Goldberg says, "These three verses constitute one of the Torah's great enigmas". God met "him" and tried to kill "him". Is the "him" Moses? Perhaps. Is the first him Moses and the second him the son? Perhaps. Why was any life threatened? And why threatened by God? Whose feet did the foreskin touch? Moses' or the son's? Why were the feet (or legs) touched? Why did that lead to "so he let him alone"? What does a "bridegroom of blood" mean? What made Zipporah think that circumcising the boy had anything to do with the death-threat or its removal? If the uncircumcised condition of the boy had been a real problem with God, why only now after all these years did it become a threat to life? Were both boys uncircumcised? I've read no one who has certain answers to these questions. That's why Goldberg and many other baffled commentators say what they say.

God assured Moses that Egypt held no danger for him since everyone who wanted to kill him was dead (4:19) and now he or his son is in danger from God himself on the way to Egypt.

Whichever son of Moses and Zipporah this is that's now circumcised, he probably isn't an infant and may be as old as late thirties since Moses had lived there with Jethro forty years. In any case, this son of Moses, the deliverer of the people of God, has not been circumcised. That in itself is strange since Moses would have been well aware of the ordinance and would be expected to have circumcised him. Furthermore, the Midianites were descendants of Abraham through Ishmael and they were well acquainted with circumcision. Zipporah would have known all this and would have learned about Israel's faith down the years from Moses. In dealing with the text all kinds of guesses must be made unless we decide to read it, say what it says and pass on without comment.

Here's my sense of it right now. Moses was rejected by his own people and it was something of an embittered man who went to Midian and married Zipporah. Later he had a baby he named Gershom which reminded him that he was away from home, from his people and all that that meant. The boy wasn't circumcised perhaps because Moses was embittered and disappointed and the token of the covenant (see Genesis 17:10-14) was ignored. The boy wasn't brought into the covenant with God as he should have been—he was God's child and Moses withheld him [by withholding circumcision]. Later still he mellowed some and called the next boy, Eliezer, realizing that God had been his help through these years. Later still he met the God who had claimed the seed of Abraham in covenant (Ex 3:1ff) and on hearing him identified as the God of Abraham was afraid (3:6). His fear was almost certainly multifaceted.

God commissioned him to go to Egypt to deliver Israel, who was God's firstborn and belonged to him, but was being withheld from him by Pharaoh. God would vindicate his claim that Israel was his firstborn even if it meant killing Pharaoh's firstborn (4:22-23). All this God told the reluctant Moses (4:13-14) about the reluctant and stubborn Pharaoh (4:21).

Still Moses seems reluctant (4:18, where his "to see if any of them are still alive" sounds truculent or trustless) and even after he sets out toward Egypt he still has not delivered his firstborn over to God in covenant by circumcision. In Midian there had been a disgruntled and stubborn Moses withholding his firstborn from God while in Egypt there was a stubborn king who was withholding God's firstborn from him.

How serious is God about claiming his firstborn in Egypt? Will he allow stubbornness to deprive him of his boy? He will not. Not from a Moses or a Pharaoh! If this boy Gershom is not given to God in covenant by circumcision, if he is not covered by the blood (in circumcision) God will kill him. God will not have a stubborn Moses withholding His son standing before a stubborn Pharaoh who is withholding God's son. He will settle this before Moses enters Egypt.

So he threatens to kill the child (had he wanted to do more than threaten the boy with death, nothing anyone could have done would have made a difference). Zipporah circumcises the boy, takes the foreskin with the blood and smears the child's legs (check the lexicons) and averts death. Moses by his negligence had forced her to hastily shed the blood of her sick boy. Moses arrives on the scene and she says to him in connection with the circumcision and blood-letting, "Surely a bridegroom of blood art thou to me". The result of Zipporah's act is that God "left him alone". (Did the child's fever drop, his seizure depart, or what?)

As many places in the narrative of Exodus connect with other places, my guess is that this section connects with the Passover and the redemption of the firstborn by the placing of blood on the door posts. Moses' firstborn was redeemed from death by the application of blood so Israel (in the firstborn) was redeemed by the application of blood. Without the blood (in this case at circumcision) Moses would have lost his firstborn so without the blood, Pharaoh (and Egypt) and Israel will lose theirs.

But why is this section here? I think it's part of a large section beginning with 3:1 which stresses the truth that Moses had not seized authority over the nation. He was a reluctant deliverer, even to the point of passive rebellion. God had laid hold on him and dragged and threatened him into the job (cf. Amos 7:14-15; Jeremiah 1:4-7). I'll come back to the authenticity of Moses' commission when we get to the last nine chapters of Exodus.

16

AND WHAT OF CIRCUMCISION?

Any uncircumcised male who is not circumcised in the flesh of his foreskin shall be cut off from his people he has broken my covenant.
Exodus 17:14

This section, though it has its own peculiar context, introduces us to circumcision in the book of Exodus. Perhaps it won't hurt us to make some remarks on that rite at this point.

What are we to make of circumcision?

1. It speaks of God's grace since it is initiated by God as a sign that he has received Abraham and his descendants as objects of his covenant love and purposes.

This is made clear in Genesis 17:1-13. In the NT, Paul will make the point that circumcision followed Abraham's gracious election rather than being a condition of his election (Rom 4:10-12).

2. *It also marks those out who have it as a people who live in covenant allegiance to and in service of God.* A circumcised person was a person given over to and recognized as belonging to a Holy Father.

We learn from Genesis 17:14 that it is a covenant that could be broken by the human "junior partners" to the covenant. Of course, to reject the will of the "senior partner" was to reject the ethical implications of the sign so in embracing the mark as a sign of election and grace, they were also receiving it as a token of their commitment to God. (The ethical implications of the mark would rise out of the character of God and would be developed and spelled out in Israel's experience and covenant Law.)

Deuteronomy 10:12-16 develops this point. What God requires of them, says Moses, is for them to love him and let the consequences of that ripple out into their life with each other. He elected them (15) and the token of that election should be in their hearts as well as in their flesh (16). Jeremiah calls on his peers to circumcise themselves "to" the Lord by circumcising their "hearts" (4:4). Stephen in Acts 7:51 speaks of his Jewish critics as having uncircumcised hearts and ears. In all this we hear Stephen talk about hearts and ears that are not devoted to God, not inclined to lovingly understand or listen to him. An uncircumcised heart doesn't understand or appreciate well, such an ear doesn't listen well and uncircumcised lips don't speak well for God (Ex 6:12). The underlying suggestion is that uncircumcised hearts and ears are not acknowledged to belong to the Holy Father.

In the NT, Paul will argue that the physical mark of circumcision binds the one wearing the mark to the life-style laid out by the Torah. Since there were Gentiles living a life characteristic of the Torah and there were Jews living a life unlike the Torah, the presence or absence of the mark becomes irrelevant (Romans 2:25-29). It only truly means something, he claims, if a godly life accompanies it. In this text the real Jew, Paul teaches them and us, is a Jew who is circumcised in heart as well as flesh.

3. Circumcision is immediately connected by scripture to the production of descendants.

Genesis 17:2 confirms to Abraham a covenant made by God with him. 17:4-6 explains a central aspect of the covenant. "As for me, this is my covenant with you: You will be the father of many nations. No longer will you be called Abram; your name will be Abraham, for

I have made you a father of many nations. I will make you very fruitful; I will make nations of you, and kings will come from you..." In light of this, it isn't surprising that the physical sign of the covenant is placed on the organ of reproduction. "You are to undergo circumcision, and it will be the sign of the covenant between me and you..." (17:11). Compare Genesis 24:2 where an oath related to the family is undertaken by placing a hand under the thigh and making contact with the genitals and swearing.

4. Its association with the "eighth day" suggests it has to do with "a new beginning," a radical departure from the past, new life.

Genesis 17 has Abram getting a new name in connection with his circumcision. The name speaks of a new status, a new and enriched set of circumstances with and under God. The male child born into the family belonged to God before the eighth day, but on the eighth day something new happened (17:12) and he entered a covenanted relationship with Yahweh.

So many things in the OT covenant Law were associated with the number eight. The leper is cleansed on the eighth day after seven days of purification, the year of Jubilee follows seven sevens of years and everyone gets a new start; sacrificial animals only become worthy of that status on the eighth day, after seven days with the mother.

Building on OT background Rev 17 sees the "resurrected" beast as appearing in an eighth head. In the Sibylline Oracles, the resurrected Lord is described as 888. In Colossians 2 there seems to be a close association with uncircumcision/death and circumcision/resurrection. Before the "old man" was cut away they were dead in their trespasses and uncircumcision (2:13). Their union with Christ is related to their being circumcised "with the circumcision of Christ" (2:11) and so made alive. Whatever else is not clear, it's clear that Paul uses circumcision as a metaphor that results in a radically different state, a new life or beginning. The past is gone (Colossians 2:10-13 and 3:1ff).

The Passover marked Israel

out as a redeemed nation...

17

ISRAEL WITHOUT PASSOVER OR CIRCUMCISION

And the Lord said to Moses, "How long will this people despise me? And how long will they refuse to believe me in spite of all the signs that I have done among them?" **Exodus 14:11**

In Joshua 5:2 God instructs Joshua to, "make flint knives and circumcise the Israelites again" ("a second time"—NRSV). This again, since it can't refer to individuals, must refer to Israel as a nation. We're seeing here the renewal of the covenant (cf. Genesis 17:9-14) with Abraham's seed. And since they were soon to eat the Passover (Joshua 5:10) they needed to be circumcised (Exodus 12:47-49). The biblical record suggests that the nation observed the Passover only once in the wilderness before a period of judgment fell on them. See Numbers 9. If, as seems to be the case, they did not eat it repeatedly it would be another mark of the judgment laid on them by the God who "passed over" them in bringing them out of Egypt. All the males in a family had to be circumcised or the family couldn't eat (Exodus 12:48) and The Passover marked Israel out as a redeemed nation that was in Abrahamic covenant with God (circumcision being the sign) so that both Passover and circumcision went together. To deny them one, was to deny them the other. *With both signs denied them, they were a wandering group of nobodies, having been covenanted to no one and having been redeemed from nowhere and destined to die in the wilderness.*

This was the reproach Egypt would heap on Israel if God did not spare them, said Moses (Numbers14:13-16), "Then the Egyptians will hear about it!...And they will tell the inhabitants of this land...The Lord was not able to bring these people into the land he promised them on oath; so he slaughtered them in the desert."

Now in the land, dedicated again to God by taking on themselves (in the heart of hostile territory and made vulnerable through pain) the sign of their identity and their allegiance and reenacting the night of their deliverance from Egypt, the reproach of Egypt has been fully dealt with—they didn't die in the wilderness!

Instead of wiping out the whole nation for their utter faithlessness, God consigned a generation of them to death in the wilderness (Numbers 14:1-23). Their children would bear the weight of the fathers' sin and wander for forty years (14:33). It might be because the whole nation was under God's judgment that the younger generation was not circumcised during the wanderings in the wilderness. God, as Calvin has suggested, would not allow them to place on their children the mark of the covenant they had so scurrilously and repeatedly violated (Numbers 14:22). The fathers would see their sons as uncovenanted, like all the nations around. In Joshua 5 the circumcising of the Israelites at the command and permission of God signals their acceptance back into the covenant, the past is gone, there was a new beginning.

86

18

DELIVERER OR TROUBLER?

"May the Lord look upon you and judge you! You have made us a stench to Pharaoh and his officials and have put a sword in their hands to kill us" Exodus 5:21

Here he comes striding in from the desert with a staff in his hand and a message in his mouth—"Let my people go!" He came to the leaders of the wounded people and told them he had come, in the name of God, to set them free. He even gave them signs that seemed to confirm his commission (4:29-31). And were they glad to see him? "And they believed. And when they heard that the Lord was concerned about them and had seen their misery, they bowed down and worshiped." At long last deliverance had come!

But when the hero went before Pharaoh, he didn't believe! "Look," he said (5:5), "you are stopping them from working" and that same day the king gave orders to make their work harder. The people in the brickyards had to make as many bricks but they now had to go and find some of the materials for themselves (5:6-18).

The king is now in a screaming fit. Things were bad before but now they were worse. Some deliverer. Some deliverance!

"May the Lord look upon you," they said, "and judge you! You have made us a stench to Pharaoh and his officials and have put a sword in their hands to kill us" (5:21). Before he came they could keep up with difficulty, ensuring that Pharaoh wouldn't turn on them and kill them but now he has an excuse to decimate the ever-growing people of Israel (5:5). Should it surprise us to hear the reluctant messenger of Yahweh complain to him in 5:22-23? "And you have not rescued your people at all." At all. This has all the marks of a bitter accusation laced with disappointment but God seems to take it in his stride, as if he fully understood this reaction (6:1ff).

Because we know how it turned out, it's harder for us to feel what they felt or what Moses felt. Since we know the script we can smile through their tears. It's a horse of a different color when the pain is our own and someone, in the name of God, quotes us the promises of God and speaks to us of rescue and a rose-garden. We suspect they're a bit too glib about our pain, we suspect they don't fully appreciate the depth of our suffering. The texts we read when we weren't hurting so bad are simply not as inspiring now that we're hanging by our thumbs.

The Israelite experience surely teaches us that God might work miracles but he doesn't work magic. He works his miracles within the human system and his activity allows for human response, creative or rebellious. He waves no wands to make all pain vanish; he works no cheap miracles and if we're looking for a pain-free existence we're wasting our time. He doesn't (and won't) pick us up and drop us in paradise. There's no rubbing of lamps, billowing smoke and a magic-working genie. There is Yahweh, up to his elbows in pain with his people, feeling their hurt (2:25; 3:7).

I notice that Christ proclaimed both deliverance and suffering. He called his people "blessed" but said they were also "blessed" when they suffered in his name (Matthew 5). There's no doubt about it that Jesus often brings trouble to a life that has known ease because he often leads us into conflict with the powers that be (within and without). To confront wickedness, our own or others' will sometimes bring hurt we never had. Who knows the power of a chain or a chain of wretched habits until they try to break them? And it's only God who leads us to tear at those links that bind us so powerfully. Only God leads us to enrage the Destroyer by engaging him in conflict. Who but God will lead us to speak against injustice at our own cost?

"Let not your heart be troubled..." is a faithful saying and worthy of all acceptance but it is only one scripture, only one precious truth. This is another, "Think not that I am come to send peace on the earth. I am not come to send peace, but a sword..."

On one occasion when he called for a child to be brought to him for healing the unclean spirit had his last spiteful throw. "Even while the boy was coming, the demon threw him to the ground in a convulsion. But Jesus rebuked the evil spirit, healed the boy and gave him back to his father. And they were all amazed at the greatness of God" (Luke 9:42-43).

Pharaoh's spiteful last throw lasted for an extended period but they were rescued for all that. Our own pain, heartache may last much longer. Some of it coming because we're part of the human race and some of it coming because we have said "yes" to God in Christ but rescue is ours just the same.

An intelligent, cheerful, life-loving woman became a Christian and found her life to be tougher than when she was out of Christ. She told me she thought it would be easier when she would enter into a life-giving union with the Lord but she hadn't found it so. She turned from him. That was more than twenty-five years ago and she's still away.

If you enter into covenant with me, said God, you will be mine in a way that others aren't.

19

LET MY PEOPLE GO

Now therefore if you obey my voice and keep my covenant you shall be my treasured possession out of all the peoples. Indeed the whole earth is mine. ***Exodus 19:5***

You can't read the Bible very long before you realize that Israel was a special people. If you enter into covenant with me, said God (19:5), you will be mine in a way that others aren't. "My people!" There must have been moments despite their obvious weaknesses and their fickleness when Israel felt good about that! There must have been moments when it sank into the heart of each one of them that there was a new wonder in the world and that they were part of it. It wouldn't have happened to them all at the same time or under the same circumstances. For some it would have been a moment of solitude while working in the field alone. For others it would have been as they looked in on their children while they slept, before they themselves settled down to a refreshing night's rest. For some it would have come in the middle of a noisy and joyful "riot" with special friends when everyone was silly with laughter.

For others it would have a moment of national praise or mourning; when in their desperation or in their worshipful mood the nation came together as one person. To be a part of all this; to have been "lucky" enough to be invited into such a nation and heritage; at that moment all of these wonderful occasions would become sacraments, bringing the individual into the very presence of the Lord who had graciously chosen him. Only now and then, perhaps, would the astonishing quality of their privilege and honor come home to Israel but that flash of insight could be enough to create a brilliant view of life and the world. The moment would pass but the impression left would last a lifetime and beyond. "My people!"

The nation is bigger than the individual. The People are grander than the sum total of all the citizens. God's astonishing claim is that Israel is "my people". Leaders they had, elders they had, kings they had, prophets and priests and judges they had but it was the "People" that God calls "my". The elders, priests, prophets, kings and judges are servants to the "People". It's true that the individual mustn't be completely swallowed up in the corporate whole and become a statistic but it seems to me that people today in the Western world need to learn the major truth about solidarity, about "corporate personality". It's true that the OT, even in its earlier periods, stressed the importance of "one man" but it had (or so it seems to me) a healthier view of "solidarity" than the Christian Community.

For good or ill we're linked together. Organized crime knows what organized good only pays lip service to— there's more power in organization. Independent thieves and gangsters can make "a living" but criminals who band together can make "a killing". When the People of God fully acknowledge God's intention to create a "People" and not just to save "individuals" and when that truth becomes a guiding principle, the world will see, more clearly and with more effect, the sign of God's presence in the world. In society there will be a People who move together, give and forgive together, praise and protest together, sing and suffer together, debate and worship together, work and weep together. When that time comes, the redeeming and creative acts of God, which formed such a People, will become matters of inquiry and wonder and God will be glorified in his people.

The People are stronger than the individual. One cannot do without the other but something happens to an individual when he becomes part of a great heritage. It gives him added significance, added strength since he shares in the grand mission and purpose of countless men and women. It gives a woman additional reasons to remain true because others are depending on her. Alone she is more vulnerable to doubts and despair and discouragement. As part of a People in whom God has invested strengths of many kinds she finds people to bolster her where she is weak and keep her from straying.

One army of the living God,
Before one throne we bow,
Some of the host have crossed the flood,
And some are crossing now.

What happened in Egypt was more than Moses against Pharaoh—it was God against a world!

20

LET MY PEOPLE GO (2)

The cry of the Israelites has now come to me: I have also seen how the Egyptians oppress them. ***Exodus 3:9***

What God meant to do is to create a new thing in the earth—a people who will rejoice in righteousness and will prosper in loving God and one another. Because the old and coercive power of Egypt opposed that God would dismantle the Egyptian world. The Egyptian "world"—what was that? It was human existence structured by those who had the upper hand. It was a world of "us" and "them" [Exodus 1:9-10], it was a world where enslaving others was "wise" and where national groaning—the groaning of men, women and children—was a sound the power-brokers easily got used to [2:23-24]; it was a world where the killing of children was no bad thing when it was to secure the peace and prosperity of the powerful. It was a world in which certain kinds of speech were forbidden and protest was savagely dismissed and threats were issued.

There's no reason to believe that every Egyptian man, woman, boy and girl approved of the wretched treatment of Israel. But empires have the big-hitters, the power-brokers, the law-makers, the story-tellers and they are the ones who shape the thinking of the empire. Lower Egypt was often at odds with Upper Egypt [Ethiopian kings and dynasties] and see how the king of Lower Egypt uses this as an excuse to begin sanctions and oppression against Israel [1:9-10]. Was there ever a powerful empire that didn't give "good reasons" for its savagery and oppression and shape the thinking and feelings of the home-born?

Egypt was only one expression of what has been since the beginning and what is going on even now in the year 2011. Such kingdoms are energized by the world-spirit, the satanic and demonic. Pharaoh was an actual person and perpetrated actual crimes against an actual people but the OT writers used his when they wanted to describe what is wrong with any generation that has taken leave of God [see Isaiah 31:7 and 51:9-10

What happened in Egypt was more than Moses against Pharaoh—it was God against a world! And what God fully intended to do was more than to deliver a mass of oppressed individuals; he purposed to create something new—he purposed to create a kingdom [note Exodus 19:5-6] and a kingdom entirely different from Egypt. It would be a kingdom opposed to oppression; it would be a kingdom with laws that would reflect the character of Yahweh **and** his purpose to bless the entire human family [note Isaiah 49:6].

God did not intend to free Israel from Egyptian cruelty and bondage that they might serve themselves—"Let them go that they might serve *me*" he said. He did not intend to dismantle one Egypt and establish another one in the land of Canaan.

What God began in Egypt was brought to an initial conclusion at Sinai when he called Israel to give itself freely to his service under the terms of a covenant that he revealed to them [24:1-8]. In Egypt and *as slaves* they built treasure cities for the powerful and at Sinai *as a liberated people* they built a Tabernacle for God to dwell in and they did it out of willing hearts [Exodus 25:2; 35:5, 20-29, illustrates]. The God they invited to dwell at the center of them had

96

shown himself to be a God that hated oppression and cruelty so when he calls them to serve him they knew what was expected of them and God spelled it out for them to some degree.

God didn't call Israel to be yokeless though he broke the yoke that Egypt had hung around their necks and enabled them to walk upright—he cured the stoop of the nation [Leviticus 26:13]. But he called them to take his yoke on them and serve him—and he was no Pharaoh who enjoyed the groans of people who were enslaved [compare Matthew 11:28-30].

to engage in healthy worship
is not to withdraw from the
real world, it is to withdraw
into the real world

21

"LAZY, THAT'S WHAT YOU ARE—LAZY"

"Go now and work; for no straw will be given to you, but you shall still deliver the same number of bricks." Exodus 5:18

That's what Pharaoh said to those who wanted to take time off from work to worship God (5:17). They wanted to down tools, to shirk their responsibilities, to avoid the real world and wander off to some place of worship while obligations stared them in the face.

It's an old accusation leveled against worshipers, and not only by outsiders. Karl Marx insisted that religion was the opiate of the people—which no doubt it is for some. It took away their will to do anything about the injustice that was all around them. The early Malcolm X talked of Christianity as a white man's religion given to Afro Americans to keep them content with injustice with promises of a better life in the hereafter. Friedrich Nietzsche was incensed with religion in general and Christianity in particular because though he respected Jesus highly (he said he was the only Christian and they murdered him) be believed that Christianity produced

99

weaklings and sniveling cowards. The Christians made no attempt to be strong so they made virtue out of weakness and vice out of strength. Numerous Christian writers have scalded evangelical believers for being out of touch with the life that now is and for ducking passages like Matthew 25:34-46.

Fosdick never seemed to tire of warning people against the dangers of worshiping God since it's too easy to substitute worship that costs nothing for costly service; too easy to flee from the real world into the world of pious hymns and prayers. We need that sort of proclamation but as Willimon and others have reminded us, to engage in healthy worship is not to withdraw from the real world, it is to withdraw into the real world. The world outside, for all its reality, is passing, it isn't permanent and it certainly isn't how things should be.

It's the balance, isn't it? It's finding it difficult to recognize when we're out of whack, unbalanced. It isn't easy for us to know ourselves and to be certain that we aren't just ducking and dodging, so it must be more difficult to know about others. I can't think there was a lot of sincerity in Pharaoh's remark. He'd been working them to an early grave and increased the pressure on them at the least excuse so his "You're lazy" was only his way of denying them their legitimate request.

I take more seriously the accusations of church leaders when they speak to their flocks. Since we're guilty of every other kind of wrongdoing we must be guilty too of avoiding costly service by hiding behind worship but I'm becoming more and more convinced that that kind of assessment and consequent judgment is beyond our powers. Who knows what I'm living with? Who knows me well enough to know I'm an "arm-chair general" or one who sings talks and prays about service but is involved in none? Before God, I'm not always sure about me so how could you be? It is enough for me to judge what deeds have been done or words spoken and assess them in light of God's teaching. I should leave the invisible realm of motives and other intangibles to the one who died and rose again that he might be the judge (Romans 14:9-11).

God forgive me, but years ago I used to see a brother at a mid-week Bible study fall asleep in the pew. Every time, without fail. I recall distinctly that I inwardly read him the riot act. Some time later I got a job in the factory where he worked and saw the nature of the job he did. It was enough to kill an iron horse. No wonder he fell asleep at Bible study. The wonder is that he ever dragged himself out to the meeting place at all! I wonder if the "Great Controller in the Sky" is keeping an eye on all the whip-cracking preachers, noting how they're using their time and energy. And I wonder if he spoke out of the heavens to them if he might not say to a lot of them, "Lazy, that's what you are—lazy".

But we need to keep in mind that what God was calling for was not Pharaoh's approval that Israel might "attend a church service" and then go back to work for Pharaoh. He knows full well that his sovereignty is being challenged. Some God or other was claiming this vast crowd of slaves as his "people"—they don't belong to Pharaoh. This Yahweh was calling him to admit Israel was his son and that they were to cease serving Pharaoh and become his servants.

The Scriptures acknowledge
that sometimes faith is harder
to sustain under real injustice
or deprivation

22

HURTING TOO MUCH TO BELIEVE

"Never shall I forget those flames which consumed my faith forever."
Elie Wiesel in 'Night'

It's easy for people who are healthy and adequately supplied to claim that they would have deep trust even if they were deprived, oppressed and exploited, plagued with ill health or some such chronic condition. Only the tolerably well off can be glib in this way but there are millions now and in the past who have lived under suffering so stark that people comfortably placed should first look at it in awed silence and then do something about it where they can.

Elie Wiesel, a Jew, born in a Hungarian ghetto, went to Birkenbau, a reception center for Auschwitz, when he was nearly fifteen. The inexpressible horror of it all led him to say: "Never shall I forget that night, the first night in the camp, which has turned my life into one long night, seven times cursed and seven times sealed. Never shall I forget that smoke. Never shall I forget the little faces of the children, whose bodies I saw turned into wreaths of smoke

103

beneath a silent blue sky. Never shall I forget those flames which consumed my faith forever...Never shall I forget those moments which murdered my God and my soul and turned my dreams to dust. Never shall I forget these things, even if I am condemned to live as long as God himself. Never."

The Scriptures acknowledge that sometimes faith is harder to sustain under real injustice or deprivation. Christ marveled that Capernaum, with all its synagogues found it difficult to believe and marveled too that a centurion who lived in that town could believe so greatly. In a town filled with hypocrisy this foreigner amazed Christ with his deep faith. We too admire those who live under terrible conditions but who remain cheerful and trusting but we'll also keep in mind that there are those who collapse under the pressure.

And we'll leave God to render judgment on them because we aren't capable of judging under such circumstances.

23

PAIN OR INCONVENIENCE?

*"Have fought against all odds, and not despaired
Have fallen and died exulting. So may I Keep an undaunted spirit all
my days..."*

L ook at these few texts from Exodus 1:10-14; 2:11,23; 3:7,17; 4:31; chapter 5 and 6:9. These texts are talking about people in real trouble.; those who wrestle with more than inconvenience. We're too quick to turn difficulties and challenges into calamities and tragedies, to exaggerate our loss into a catastrophe, our struggle into a drama. In a world of real and crushing pain it gets a bit wearing to hear healthy, well-fed people on low incomes but not utterly impoverished tirelessly whine about how hard life is for them. (One critic noted that it is the living who whine about life not being worth living.)

But people who can eat three times a day, buy knick-knacks, fill their houses with the bits and pieces we all enjoy, who are able to go shopping anytime they're good and ready, these can hardly be the kind we should pity. We will hardly class them as people living under great injustice.

Moses had come on God's errand of mercy and deliverance but the people were deaf. We might have thought his message would have gotten a better reception. To slaves it promised liberty, to homeless people it promised a home, to humiliated people it offered dignity and glory but the heart had been beaten out of them. Most of us can't even imagine such a situation since our lives, while they may be hard, are well within the bearable. It isn't so with everyone. Looking at some lives we're amazed at their resilience and when others fold under awful pain, we can't find it in us to fault them.

Governments have a great responsibility here; a responsibility for which they'll be held accountable before God. We can't legislate people into moral greatness or spiritual nobility but we can enact laws that make it easier to choose what is honorable. Laws can be enacted which promote and encourage honest citizens. Laws can be enacted which make it more difficult for the oppressor to oppress. We can so govern as to reward honesty, fairness and social usefulness. We can make it harder for the criminal element and we can defend the law-abiding and raise their opinion and support of the courts.

"There is a worse waste of life than killing a man in battle," says Ruskin, "the whistling bullets have brought pleasant messages to many a man—orders of sweet release, and leave to go where he will be most welcome and most happy...But if you put him to base labor, if you bind his thoughts, and blind his eyes, and blunt his hopes, and steal his joys...you have done all that in you lies to make the walls of his grave everlasting."

At the personal level we can brutalize our families and friends, until we crush the heart right out of them, until hope, values and honor are near dead and then we ask them to behave as if we had filled their lives with kindness, encouragement and challenge.

So let university professors and philosophers brutalize us, let school-heads dehumanize us but let them not look shocked when we act like animals without values.

So let's brutalize our friends, let's gossip and spread the shame of our neighbors but we mustn't act wounded or surprised when we find ourselves friendless.

Let's walk all over our families, humiliate and scourge them, drive them to tears and fear but we mustn't act amazed when they tell us our fine words mean nothing. How would Israel have reacted if Pharaoh had come speaking sweet words to them? What if we had watched what he did to them and then heard him speak words of affection to the weeping families and communities?

Yet God still makes his claim on people in pain. The hard conditions that make it difficult for people to hear provoke God to speak to their healing and bring about justice.

Pain, treachery, insult and the like can make people dead to higher things but it isn't true that they will do so. Millions live in pain and are sustained by God. They aren't dead to higher things. Yes, they struggle with real pain, they do their weeping but they still hear God speaking to them: "Come worship and serve me". Edith Banfield offers this fine word:

This do I glory in beneath the sun
That men have lived brave lives in evil times
Have kept glad-hearted under stress of pain
Have fought against all odds, and not despaired
Have fallen and died exulting. So may I
Keep an undaunted spirit all my days
Lose not the larger view, hold fast the joy
And with high courage come unto my grave.

And R. Louis Stevenson had this to challenge us with: "Our business in this world is not to succeed, but to continue to fail in good spirits." He tells the story of a friend and says, "The tale of this great failure is, to those who remained true to him, the tale of a success. In his youth he took thought for no one but himself; when he came ashore again, his whole Armada lost, he seemed to think of none but others...He had gone to ruin with a kind of kingly abandon, like one who condescended; but once ruined, with the lights all out, he fought as for a kingdom."

And so did the believers in Israel. So will the believers everywhere. And they will do it by the enabling power of God who will not allow them to be wimps.

This is a witness against radical nationalism, racism or any other form of elitism or discrimination

24

ANOTHER FAMILY TREE?

And Aaron took him Elisheba, daughter of Amminadab, sister of Naashon, to wife; and she bare him Nadab, and Abihu, Eleazar, and Ithamar. **Exodus 6:23**

Most people find the genealogies in the Bible difficult to read. That's hardly surprising but there is much to learn from the lists. Sometimes they are of interest because they have prominent names in them but much of their value lies in why they were inserted.

They serve different purposes and what follows suggests some of the ways they are meant to help us. It isn't simply that we can "draw lessons" from them, sometimes they are written for specific purposes. They may serve more than one purpose.

1. They show that God's "blessing" works. In Genesis 5:3ff the list is immediately connected with God's word of blessing on Adam and Eve. The blessing to be enjoyed (not a command to be obeyed) "be fruitful, multiply and fill the earth" is seen to work. What follows is a list of descendants. When God blesses he enables and empowers his creation to flourish and prosper. Compare Genesis 9:1,2 and chapter 10.

Additionally and connected with that, the genealogy of Genesis 5:2ff shows humans as co-creators with and under God in bearing children in their own image and after their likeness (see Genesis 1:26ff and 5:3).

2. They show that sin reigned through death. In the same text which is set in the larger context of human transgression and punishment, we not only hear that humans flourish we hear the repeated words, like a slow somber drumbeat, "and he died". In the midst of blessing there is death resulting from rebellion but in the midst of rebellion resulting in death there is a compassionate and pursuing God who continues to bless.

In addition to the connection with curse, the genealogies make the more general point that humans are creaturely and limited since they all die.

3. They show God's purposes are being forwarded. In Genesis 11 we are given the line of descent through major figures to Abraham who is central to the unfolding of God's purposes to redeem and bless the whole world and central to the record of that unfolding.

4. They show how life is organized under God (priestly line) and verify commission. The priesthood itself is central to the life of humans before God and in Israel it is of the utmost importance since it is a "kingdom of priests". The lists of priests stresses the organization of that priesthood and therefore of Israel's life before God.

In addition and connected with that, being able to find one's name in the list of priests verified one's place of authority and service. See Ezra 2:36,61-63; 1 Chronicles 24, Nehemiah 12 and elsewhere. See this also connected with the kingly lists in the Kings and Chronicles literature.

5. They show the solidarity of all humans—one common origin. No Israelite reading the Genesis lists would be left with any doubt that ethnically speaking we're all one. That in itself has vast theological ramifications. If we all come from a common root and that root was created by God, then God cares for all of us since we are all his creation. This is a witness against radical nationalism, racism or any other form of elitism or discrimination.

In addition to that and connected with it, they show us that the great are borne and nurtured by the unknown and unheralded so they aren't self-made people. The reverse is also true, in our family lines there are those we wouldn't want to brag about so snobbery is baseless.

6. They show us the purpose of God as developed down to the Messiah. The NT takes up the line of the Messiah in Matthew 1 and Luke 3 (see also Ruth 4:17-22).

In Exodus 6:14-27 we have a genealogical list that clearly has the purpose of legitimating Aaron and Moses. If there were times when Moses was called into question there would certainly be times when Aaron would be doubted. In some passages Aaron is given a very prominent place indeed but in others he appears as something of an assistant to Moses.

It is by Moses he is enlisted to bring Israel out of Egypt and it is by Moses he is called to the priesthood. If Moses' place is in doubt, why wouldn't Aaron's be in doubt? Add to that Aaron's part in the golden calf incident. In Numbers16-17 we have a record of at least one rebellion against Aaron as priest. Exodus 6 clearly means to legitimate them by placing Moses and Aaron squarely in the Levitical line and at the center of God's self-revelation and commissioning activity. Aaron is named first which might suggest that he is the central figure in this section.

God was angry at the stories;

the lies, the rubbish which kept

people from the truth and

therefore kept them from him;

25

STORIES IN CONFLICT

*And that you may tell your children and grandchildren
how I have made fools of the Egyptians and what signs I have done
among them—so that you may know that I am the Lord.* **Exodus 10:2**

When a child in ancient Egypt asked questions like: "Why doesn't the sea come in and overwhelm us? Why is there night and day? How can seeds become crops? Why is there desert and fertile land? How do things live? Where do people go when they die?"—when they asked questions about reality and the world around them the priests and teachers told them stories. It's true the stories were a "complex of tangled myth" or a "chaos of contradictions" but people aren't logic machines or breathing computers so they are able to live with unsolved tensions in the stories that shape them.

There were stories of gods that were born and died; gods that began and ended; gods that married and had children and gods that fought with each other and joined forces to defeat a common enemy. Gods, at the same time were forces, elements, animals and humans.

There was Anubis who attended to the dead or Apophis, the dread god of darkness. The earth was Geb and the chaotic seas were the god Nu in which Re, the sun, the supreme cosmic god of Egypt, was born and Re, who warmed the world and made everything fruitful. There was Ptah who (some said) gave life to everything and was in everything and there was Thoth, the moon god and lord of letters. There were gods and goddesses of love and joy (like Hathor) or gods which brought the menace of pestilence (like Sekhmet) or those who blasted harvests and created deserts (like Seth) or gods of truth and justice (like Maat). Different generations and different nomes saw different gods gain the preeminence but the most popular of all the gods, perhaps because he was more human than all the others, was Osiris. Osiris, god of vegetation; the one who conquered death and became the hope of all who died and who gave life to all of Egypt and was worshiped as the Nile river (which was also associated with Hapi). There was Horus, the loyal son of Osiris, who defeated Seth, the murderous brother of Osiris, and gained the rule of all Egypt (except, perhaps, the wilderness). The kings were the embodiment of this Horus who, when they died, reigned in the underworld as Osiris but were succeeded on earth by their sons as Horus. The stories about these were important to the continued stability and order in the land. There was the cobra goddess, Wadjet, which represented lower (northern) Egypt, who indwelt and empowered the king.

Was God angry at the Egyptians for what they were doing to Israel? Of course! But behind them, God was angry at the stories; the lies, the rubbish which kept people from the truth and therefore kept them from him; stories that shaped the life and thoughts of the nation, generation after generation. That's when he sent this dust-covered, staff-carrying shepherd into Egypt, right up to the palace of Pharaoh with another story: The story about meeting a God in the wilderness. It would be story against story—snake against snake.

In a series of plagues the true Story exposed as lies the story which justified idolatry, murder and slavery. The plagues (with a couple of exceptions) would follow the course of natural disasters. For those with eyes to see, the plagues were the hand of God but early on Egyptian magicians thought they were the tricks of a marvelous magician—tricks they could duplicate to some degree.

But Yahweh had paralleled the natural sequence of disasters sufficiently to allow a stubborn and cruel king to think that that was all they were, natural disasters (9:15-16). On this side of the Story we wonder how he could have continued in his evil purposes but our own vested interests often drive us down roads we should know, with startling clarity, are the ways of death. (Dishonorable relationships, crooked dealings, self-serving ventures—all rationalized as we recklessly plunge on, bringing suffering not only to ourselves but our families, friends and communities.)

Pharaoh and the Egyptians had seen the Nile go red before, they'd seen dead fish and they watched frogs leave the river, they'd seen flies and gnats, disease of cattle, hail, electric storms and darkness which covered the land as a result of the awful khamsin wind. All these things the slave-leader "brought" were familiar. True, they were more severe than what they'd experienced, true they seemed to come and go at the word of this troubler from the desert, but Egypt mustn't panic and they mustn't give in to lies. The stories of the gods of Egypt remain true and Egypt will come out of these troubled days even stronger in faith in the gods. Psalm 78 makes it clear that Israel would later be every bit as stubborn in their rebellion against God as Pharaoh was and with less reason.

God struck the Nile (Osiris) the life-bringer and made it a death-dealer. Here is uncreation. In the waters he made teem with life in Genesis 1 he multiplies death. Frogs (perhaps associated with Hekt or Ptah) forsook their own place and invaded the houses and palaces. The earth, vegetation, air, sun and moon, the god of storms, the animal embodiments or symbols of the gods—all these were attacked or used against Egypt by this Yahweh.

But God wasn't angry at the water, earth, sky or heavenly bodies—these were his creation and therefore his servants. They weren't foes to be subdued and they certainly weren't gods to be worshiped. They were made to bring blessing to Man and glory to God. He was mad at the stories! The stories, which denied him as the creator and kept humans estranged from him. So he who created, who multiplied life and gave everything its place, producing harmony and peace—he who did all this became the uncreator. Undoing what he had done; uncreating at a local level what he had created universally. Bringing curse in the face of cursing he becomes the great Uncreator.

26

THE MESSAGE OF THE PLAGUE/SIGNS

*On that same night I will pass through Egypt and strike down every firstborn—both man and animals—and I will bring judgment on all the gods of Egypt. I am the Lord. **Exodus 12:12***

*I*n Relation to Creation: Creation is the work of the Creator to bring into existence, to bless by making to flourish and exist in harmony. Uncreation is the act of judicial cursing in the presence of rebellion. See this beginning with Genesis 1 and 3—11.

What happened in Egypt was a local manifestation of uncreation. Waters teemed with death instead of life, heavenly lights were blotted out instead of governing the day and night; creatures left their own place (like frogs, for example) instead of maintaining harmony and life diminished rather than flourishing.

In Relation to the Abrahamic covenant: Genesis 12:1-3 speaks of God blessing Abraham and his seed (with a view to blessing the world). We see this promise at work especially clearly in the case of Joseph who was both blessed and became a blessing the house of Potiphar and in the prison (Genesis 39:2-6,23; 40—41).

Genesis 12:3 speaks of cursing for those who would curse Abraham and his seed. Egypt, which sought to curse Israel, was cursed by God. Note the verbal connections between the "toil" as a result of the curse in Genesis 3 and Pharaoh's imposition of toil on Israel.

In Relation to the gods of Egypt: "Beneath and above everything in Egypt was religion," said Will Durant. Different gods at different times and in different locations became the primary deities but some of the chief gods and goddesses that remained prominent included Re (the chief cosmic deity—the sun); Osiris (most popular of all the gods, god of vegetation and life, immortality—the river Nile); Horus, son of Osiris (embodied in the kings—the falcon); Isis, wife and sister of Osiris (the black soil of the Delta and the "mother goddess"). Other prominent gods were Geb (the earth), Set (wilderness), Sekhmet (pestilence), Thoth (the moon), Nun (the ocean and seas); Nut (heaven); Apophis (the serpent-demon of darkness). Important sacred animals which were regarded as embodiments as well as symbols of the gods were—the goat (Amon); the cow (Hathor); the cobra (Wadjet); the bull (Ptah); the crocodile (Sobek); the frog (Hekt?).

All these were attacked and/or used by Yahweh against Egypt on behalf of Israel to show that Yahweh alone is God (7:5; 8:22; 9:29; 18:11; Numbers 33:4).

"On that same night I will pass through Egypt and strike down every firstborn—both man and animals—and I will bring judgment on all the gods of Egypt. I am the Lord" (Exodus 12:12).

118

27

THE REPENTANCE OF A SCARED MAN

But Pharaoh hardened his heart this time also and would not let the people go. **Exodus 8:32**

Paul Scherer said, "The repentance of a scared man isn't worth much". He had a point though it could easily be overstated. If fear is the occasion of our turning from darkness to light, from wickedness to uprightness, from death to life, from Satan to God, fear has been a good friend.

Who puts traffic lights at junctions or intersections? Fear does! Who puts lifeboats on ocean-going liners? Parachutes on test pilots" backs? Who puts guard rails around parapets, builds hospitals, insurance companies, make some garments of non-combustible materials? Fear does! Fear isn't all bad though F. D. Roosevelt had good reason on one occasion to say, "The only thing we have to fear is fear". It's the timing and the depth of it. Does it paralyze and possess us? Or is it our servant.

Still, Scherer had a point. Said Pharaoh, (8:9 and elsewhere), "Stop the plagues and I'll be good". And haven't I said, haven't we all said or been tempted to say to God, "Don't let judgment fall on me and I'll never do it or say it again"? No one is impressed with himself when "I'm definitely going on a strict diet" is said only and always after a large meal. After each cigarette and the consequent choking, "I'm definitely going to give these up". New Year's resolutions are easier to make than live with, emotional commitments, which don't sound quite the same days or weeks or months later. Rabelais said, "When the Devil was sick—the Devil a monk would be."

But maybe it isn't all bad news. Maybe it's something to be thankful for that we feel the need and the want to express regret, remorse and even repentance. If he sins against you seven times in the one day and comes saying "I repent," forgive him. Isn't that what Jesus said (Luke 17:3-4)?

But that's just it, if he repeatedly sins against me he cannot be repentant, he cannot mean he's sorry or purposes to turn from his offending. I must say I feel the power of that protest, especially when I'm the one taking the beating but what are we to make of Jesus' teaching?

Putting together Luke 17 and Matthew 18, the Messiah made it clear he wasn't talking about a glib dismissal of wrongs. ("There, there, you didn't mean it, and anyway, it's no big deal.") The transgressor is to be rebuked and pursued; he is to be regarded as of value, as worth bothering with and certainly as one to be forgiven even though the transgression occurs more than once! For as sure as you live everyone goes to God again and again for forgiveness and often for forgiveness for the same wrongs. Is the repentance genuine then?

It sets my teeth on edge to read or hear that so-and-so isn't repentant, she's only sorry because she was caught. I don't doubt that's the case sometimes and with some people but how would we ever know such a thing in specific? I know God knows and I know, because we have the script in front of us, that this was so with Pharaoh, but the repentance of a scared man may well be worth a lot. When a sinner comes weeping, confessing wrong, offering apologies and promising reformation, by the grace of God, who are we to sit in judgment on such people if they re-offend? Whatever else is to be done for and with them (and there's a lot that should and could be done for and with compulsive offenders) there must be the offer of free forgiveness.

28

A NIGHT TO KEEP VIGIL

"When I see the blood, I will pass over you. No destructive plague will touch you when I strike Egypt" Exodus 12:13

Exodus 12 presents the original Passover as a special meal eaten with speed and anxiety. There was nothing gay or light-hearted about it, no one reclined, leisurely nibbling at this or that as if he had all the time in the world. As darkness fell, moving toward midnight, there was the soundless approach of One who had held his wrath in control long enough, had tolerated rebellion long enough and who would now grimly punish captors and set prisoners free.

The trembling, maybe whispering, slaves hid behind closed doors under the protection of the blood of the spotless lamb on which the family fed. Their door-posts and lintels liberally smattered with blood shed in death that certainly saved the dwellers from dying. 'the Destroyer" was about this night and while his intentions had been made perfectly clear—he would deliver a final stroke that would break the fetters of Israel's long slavery—there was danger even for Israelites.

It was to be eaten by a nation that survived by grace. The plagues had been falling on Egypt—Israel's enemies and Israel knew what it was like to be exempted from the scourge of flies and ulcerated cattle. This kind of "favoritism" would tempt the Israelites to despise the Egyptians, to feel smug, self-righteous and superior but the solemn words about a flock-animal (sheep or goat) and about its redemptive death would go a long way to balance things.

His words to Moses were, "When I see the blood, I will pass over you. No destructive plague will touch you when I strike Egypt" (12:13). There was no word about seeing their good works, their faithfulness, their loyalty, their fleshly connection with Abraham—only, "When I see the blood". There was no word either about seeing their crimes, their injustices, bitterness and insolence—only, "When I see the blood" because between them and death stood the sacrifice that kept them from dying. In the final analysis, what made the difference between the dying and the living was not character or ethnic pedigree but the blood of an innocent sacrifice.

It was to be eaten in unity as a nation—as one people. They were sanctified in families and neighbors (12:4) but their families were brought together under the clear word (12:3), "Tell the whole community of Israel" they are to do this or that. Here is a unity meal in which the whole community of Israel is brought under the protection of the blood and marked out as a having-been-ransomed people. There are no individuals or individual families here except as they were part of the Community.

This oneness, this cohesiveness was underlined by the way the meal was to be eaten. The lamb was to be roasted whole (not boiled or sodden which produces the breaking down of tissue, dissipation) and the smoke of it would be like the smoke of a burnt offering, whole and entire. It was to be completely eaten or at least totally disposed of (12:8-10). The sacrifice was not to be dismembered but left whole (12:46) and by morning, the meal was to be completed, finished, done with. Everyone acted in concert—a nation acted as one in doing what was done in one continuous act.

It was to be eaten by a nation in haste (12:11) for it was a nation ready to move so that for all its somberness this was a meal which had implicit in it the word of promise. "I will bring one more plague on Pharaoh and on Egypt. After that he will let you go from here, and when he does, he will drive you out completely" (11:1). Bread made without yeast (12:8) would later remind Israel of what God had promised as a result of the final and decisive plague (12:39; Deuteronomy 16:3). Egypt would be glad to be rid of them and so hurry them out of the land.

It was to be eaten by a nation who remembered their afflictions as they toiled under taskmasters. But it would come to remind them also of their hurried lives while in Egypt, the endless labor, no time to relax and bake their bread with yeast, allowing it to rise. So it would be the "bread of affliction" (Deuteronomy 16:3), driving home the point of slavery and adding to the restless nature of their lives—"bitter herbs" (12:8).

It was to be eaten by a covenanted nation that renounced evil and devoted itself to Yahweh. The absence of yeast from all their dwellings also served the purpose of reminding them who and whose they were. The word *chemotz* means "bitter" or "sour" and easily lent itself to the notion of what spreads corruption. The NT has numerous references that undergird that idea. Israel purged their homes of ferment prior to the Passover and only those who were circumcised could eat; those who were covenanted to God within the Abrahamic community.

the years of bondage were
forgotten in the joy of liberty
as they gaped on the corpses of
their oppressors on the shores
of the Sea

29

DEATH OF A TYRANT

"...see the deliverance that the Lord will accomplish for you today; for the Egyptians whom you see today you shall never see again, The Lord will fight for you and you have only to keep still."
Exodus 14:13b-14

The ancient Greeks told stories of Sisyphus, the cunning founder of Corinth. For making fools of the gods of the underworld he was punished to labor at a hopeless task. He was to roll a huge block of granite up a high, very steep hill and roll it down the other side. Each time he got the huge stone to the pinnacle his strength was gone and it rolled back down to the bottom. It wasn't just the effort that bathed him in sweat and exhausted him completely that made the punishment intolerable; it was the "almost but never" aspect of it coupled with the unceasing conviction that the next time he could manage it.

Exodus 14 tells of Israel trapped between the Red Sea and the most powerful army in the world, between an insurmountable obstacle to freedom and pitiless tyranny. In response to their despairing protests Moses assures them God will deliver them. "You see these Egyptians?" said God (14:13), "you will see them again no more, for ever!" The waters opened up for Israel and closed to bury forever the army of their bitter oppressor. The text tells us that Israel looked at the dead bodies of their once feared tormentors and believed in God and Moses. Finally! Those who picked their bones clean, those who bled them white were dead! "You will never see them again" said God. Whatever they had to face in years ahead—this battle was won and it would remain as a prophecy, a promise that nothing was beyond their hope!

Years of torture, generations of humiliation—ended. How many rebellions had been planned and come to nothing? How often had they turned their eyes heavenward in despair? The hope born in youth would often die in old age. Optimism and cheerfulness would have been replaced in a nation's heart by grim submission and a sullen endurance. Then with such speed and finality the tyranny was obliterated and the years of bondage were forgotten in the joy of liberty as they gaped on the corpses of their oppressors on the shores of the Sea (14:30).

And has "the Exodus" no message for the world at large? Is there any aspect of biblical teaching more eagerly sought than the message that the God of all the earth hates oppression, punishes oppressors, takes note of the weeping of the poor and exploited and that the Lord of all the earth will right all wrongs? Israel wasn't just lucky that their God happened to hate cruelty and felt the pain of the defenseless. No, Israel's God is the God of all humans and they all need to hear that he is as opposed to their tormentors as he was to Israel's! This is the one true God we must take to the nations of the world who have turned their eyes to lifeless idols or dark and savage deities. Well-bred and well-fed secularists sneer at a message which has become too familiar to them but which has laid the foundations of their freedom and prosperity. Clark Pinnock protests that we in the West allow the bored and argumentative secularists to set the agenda for our proclamation while multiplied millions of religious people are eager and need to hear about the true God who delivers the oppressed from the clutches of their enemies (see

126

Psalm 10). Since secularists thrust the message from them perhaps we should turn to the rest of the world and (maybe) they will hear.

But the message of "the Exodus" is not only for brutalized nations and communities; it has a word of assurance and hope for all who suffer under tyranny of any sort. Too many of us have lived under a tyranny of a personal nature such as uncleanness, bitterness, drunkenness, greed, gossip, arrogance, immorality and self-righteousness. To be endlessly assured that we we're forgiven is grand but not nearly enough. Years ago we became captives; so long ago, perhaps, that we can't remember when we knew what freedom was. There was never a doubt in our minds that it was slavery and there never was a time when we didn't long to be free but endless rebellions, countless uprisings against the dictator came to nothing, hope died and we were left with gloomy a view of the future; a future in which we saw ourselves as old men and old women still in the clutches of a cruel parasite and when that became our vision life became grim submission and a joyless patience. Better than nothing, of course, but so far beneath the life in which the soul dares to believe that the tyrant can and will be destroyed.

Then one day it happened. For some of us the calendar could be marked because on that day our Redeemer arrived, not silently and in secret but as though with a mighty rush of water and we saw the enemy dead and lying all around us. For many of us the passage from death to life, from slavery to liberty, from shame and humiliation to honor, happened without our noticing it and the tyrants we saw in former days passed away. We saw them again no more. Whatever the future was to hold, whatever tyrant we were to face—we'd see that slave-lord never again—not ever.

(I don't believe every person is enslaved to a particular besetting sin that is of life-destroying proportions. I believe that every person—no exceptions—is in dire need of saving and keeping grace. I believe that every person—no exceptions—can be humbled by a tyrant and I believe that there are those who haven't yet seen their bondage. Comparing themselves with themselves they're blinded by their own glory. I believe that God is anxious to deliver hosts of us not from particular and grievous wickedness but from pathetic lives, shallow views and trivial pursuits. But it's mainly for those who struggle with evils that single them out, evils that make others doubt the genuineness of their discipleship, evils that cause even themselves to doubt their longing for a holy freedom—it's to those that these words are especially aimed.)

The healing of others must not be viewed as one more nail in your coffin but as another prophecy, another assurance that tyranny will die. That God will not allow his child to vanish without rescue. Your day is coming. Your name is not Sisyphus. Those who have never known a deep, enduring and awful struggle can still sympathize and are praying you on. Those who have finally found God's redeemer in a friend, a husband, a wife, a child, a parent, a doctor and now know the joy of liberation, they are urging you on. One day God looking out of heaven will hear you, out of the darkness of your own crucifixion, taking on your lips the words his own Son had on his: "It is finished!" Finished the power and lure of the evil; finished the shame and humiliation of it; the bird has escaped the snare and the tyrant is dead!

30

A SONG OF TRIUMPH

"I will sing to the Lord for he has triumphed gloriously; horse and rider he has thrown into the sea..." **Exodus 15:1**

I admit I have heard songs of triumph sung with vindictiveness. I was born and raised in a country where people sing their rebellion, their triumphs, their hate, scorn as well as their laments. Such singing can perpetuate division and bitterness but that depends a great deal on the spirit in which they are sung and what precisely it is that is being proclaimed.

Now and then I feel a little irritation rise in me when I read that songs like Exodus 15 are bloodthirsty, vindictive, sub-Christian or some such thing. There's no doubt in my mind that the previous paragraph is true, but I must protest against our "Christian sophistication" which chooses to interpret almost everything biblical, especially if ancient, in the worst possible light.

The hymn is praise to God! The hymn is praise to God for the defeat of a bitter oppressor. The hymn is praise to God for the defeat of a malignant and bitter oppressor. Was anyone displeased to see the defeat of the Nazi regime? Or the downfall of Pol Pot or Papa Doc or Stalin? Is it only vindictiveness and mean-spiritedness that muttered thanksgiving when the defeat of ruthless armies was announced? It is only scholars who sit in comfortable chairs surrounded by books who can indict Exodus 15 as simple vindictiveness. Change the names from "Israel" and "Egypt" to "Nazis" and "Allies" and put these scholars in the thick of it, their families included, children and grandchildren, parents and grandparents. Place them there for decades and accuse them of vindictiveness when they pray for God to bring an end to the torment by the downfall of the tormentors.

Once across the Red sea, the path to Canaan was by way of Philistia and the word of what Yahweh had done to Egypt had spread, causing fear everywhere (vv.14 and15 and Joshua 2:9-11). Exodus 15:16 pictures the awe-smitten nations Israel would pass through standing as still as the walls of water (15:8). In any case, the Red Sea incident makes it clear that the future is secure, Israel would indeed inherit the land of Canaan because the Lord would cause the people he bought to pass over into it (15:16). It's interesting to hear that God "bought" the nation and Isaiah will later say that God gave Egypt as a ransom for Israel (Isaiah 43:3). We're not supposed to take these metaphors literally and base some convoluted theory of atonement on them and carry it over into the NT and the atoning sacrifice of Jesus. He brought Israel out from under oppression, freed them and identified them as his the way people buy things and the way they bought slaves in those ancient times. But there was no actual purchase and there was no "seller" or previous owner to whom a purchase price was given. See 1 Peter 1:18-19 where people were redeemed from a vain way of living.

In keeping with his promises to the fathers (3:8) he "will bring them in and plant them" (two imperfect verbs with future reference—v.17) "on the mountain of your inheritance".

The "mountain of your inheritance" may here refer to what turns out to be Mount Zion, which David chose as a sanctuary for God and where Solomon built the temple. On the other hand, which is much more likely, the phrase might simply be another way of describing Canaan, as distinct from, say, 'mount Seir" (see Deuteronomy 2:1 and Mal 1:3 where the mountains of Esau are explained as "his inheritance". In Deuteronomy 3:25 Moses pleads with God to allow him to go over into the promised land. "Let me go over I pray thee, and see the good land that is beyond Jordan, that goodly mountain (a singular, with the definite article), and Lebanon" (ASV).

If "the mountain of your inheritance" has reference to (as it turns out to be) Zion, it would be in view of the fact that God had manifested himself on a mountain, Sinai, as mythical deities were often said to do and that he had promised he would later dwell in Canaan with Israel. I much prefer the other view, that "the mount of your inheritance" is the land of Canaan, taking one of its prominent topographical features as descriptive.

Whatever later theological reflection is embodied in the song it is presented as the song Moses, Miriam (15:20-21) and Israelite men and women sang at the time.

The People of God have always

taken singing seriously...

31

HE SHOULD HAVE SUNG

Sing to him, sing praises to him, tell of all his wonderful works.
1 Chronicles 16:9

Who sang the first song only God knows. Why they decided to sing is another mystery. Why don't we simply talk everything?

We feel the need to be musical. It's been this way since ancient times. God has gifted those who enjoy music. I suppose there is one here and there who has no pleasure whatever in music but it's clear that those who enjoy it have been given a gift and those who have no pleasure in music we would regard as suffering loss. It's clear, of course, that the human capacity for music doesn't only show itself in a religious context but if "the sons of God" in Job, who sung for joy when the foundations of the earth were being laid, were angels, maybe we have the first song and the first singing in connection with the work of God.

One of the deadening things about Buddhism was that it was toneless. In Japan a Buddhist confessed to me that Christians had something great in music and song so the Buddhist splinter group he was connected with [30 million of them] adopted it into their practice.

The People of God have always taken singing seriously. Long before David there was Moses and in the days of the Judges we have the famous victory song of Deborah and Barak. David and Asaph are two very famous song-writers. Those who were concerned about keeping the message about God alive were anxious that the people sing! What we call the "book of Psalms" is a collection of smaller books of numerous psalms. These psalms were not meant just to be read—they were meant to be sung. You can see this in some of the instruction that is placed at the head of the Psalms by ancient editors and song-service people (Psalms 22, 57-59, 69, 75, 80). Sometimes they were to be sung to an already existing and favored tune. In Hebrew the collection is simply called "tehillim" (Praises)

When returning to Canaan after the exile Zerubbabel saw to it that there were lots of singers. There were villages where the singers lived and like Levites and priests they were given tithes. There were professional singers and even song-leaders. Take a look at these texts: 2 Chronicles 29:27-28; 35:25; Ezra 2:65; Nehemiah 12:28,42,45-47. Was there ever a man more practical than Nehemiah? And yet he thought singing and singing leaders to be of central importance in the newly restored Israel.

Jesus himself, we're told, sang a hymn after the Supper [and note Hebrews 2:12] and throughout the NT we hear of singing. Hebrews 13:15 calls singing a sacrifice of praise, the fruit of lips that make confession of his name.

The songs they sang from ancient times rehearsed the wonderful victories of God on behalf of his people (and therefore on behalf of all nations). They sang of hope for the future, they sang of God's good guidance in days when they especially needed it, they sang of the friend they had in Christ, they sang confessional songs in which they admitted their weaknesses and entreated God for help and forgiveness. They sang of their pain and disappointment, their joy in deliverance and in all the other times when humans feel the need to do more than *talk*.

134

There is power in music and song that seems to show itself in no other way. Charlotte Elliot's brother, H.V. was a minister for many years. In reference to his sister's hymn, *Just As I Am*, he said, "In the course of a long ministry I hope I have been permitted to see some fruit of my labor, but I feel that far more has been done by a single hymn of my sister's."

The Welsh people have always understood the power of song and once, on hearing an eloquent preacher speak, a Welsh lady said, "Ah, yes, but he ought to have sung the last part of the sermon".

It's tragic ignorance that leads people to feel they, "do nothing but sing" in an assembly of Christians as if they were doing something insignificant and were virtual spectators. Leadership ought to thoroughly expose the ignorance of that view not only in what they teach about singing but in how the assembly singing is structured.

Curse was "uncreation". The water returned over the land and covered it; life died rather than burst forth, disruption spread, sweat, thorns, thistles, back-breaking toil...

32

ISRAEL IN THE WILDERNESS

"Remember the long way the Lord your God has led you these forty years in the wilderness..." **Deuteronomy 8:2a**

Exodus 16:1 would suggest "let down" to Israel. A month and a half after leaving Egypt and they were still in the desert. To appreciate what Wilderness meant to Israel we need to have some idea what land meant to them. Walter Brueggemann's *"The Land"* is an eye-opening study on that major OT theme. "Land" is the place of blessing, it's where God is present and where fellowship with him is assured; it's home, security and true peace with God. It stands over against "wilderness" as "blessing" stands over against "curse".

In Genesis 1 God gives form to formless, life to lifeless, harmony to chaos (at least from a human habitation point of view). Everything had its place and "cooperated" with the other elements. The sun and moon were where they should be doing what they were supposed to do, the birds were in the air, the fish in the sea, there was life, swarming, teeming, abundant life and it was all pronounced "good", even "very good".

With Sin came "curse" and with curse, death, disharmony, conflict, distrust and the violation of appointed places. Curse was "uncreation". The water returned over the land and covered it; life died rather than burst forth, disruption spread, sweat, thorns, thistles, back-breaking toil—all this entered.

Nothing showed "curse" so vividly as Wilderness. Homelessness was never so clearly brought home. The absence of blessing was glaring and with the absence of blessing, the absence of God was deduced. Blessing was only possible in land that could be tilled or sowed (see Jeremiah 2:2) so wilderness, wasteland, was a visible reminder of curse, a visible reminder of the gulf between God and Man. To be driven from land (think of Adam, Eve, Cain, or Israel in exile) was a horrific experience for those who had this conception of land.

Suppose we're on a high place overlooking the wildernesses in the Sinai peninsula and we're panning it with our binoculars. As far as the eyes can see there is barrenness, stunted growth, waterless land, lower life-forms, pitiless heat, erratic boulders, a struggle for survival, scorpions and serpents, dust and the weary wind. Then down below us, suddenly, we're met by a profusion of color and life. Tents pitched in thousands, all in order and placed with precision around a central Tent. We see herds of goats, flocks of sheep, we strain our ears and the wind carries the sound of laughter up to us, a joyous shout now and then rises to us or the sound of music meets our ear. How's this possible? Is it a mirage? Here! In the middle of all this absence of promise there is life, real life, flourishing and abundant life. How did they get here? How do they sustain themselves? In the midst of curse there is this blessing? In this chaos could we expect this order and harmony?

Israel's experience in the wilderness was to be remembered for all their generations. Yahweh established the Feast of Booths (Tabernacles) so that they would never forget the time when God guided them through the trackless desert (Deuteronomy 8:15), and spread a table for them in that inhospitable land (Psalms 68:8-10; 78:18-30). It was a test for them, of course (Deuteronomy 8:2ff), and

God wanted them to grow in their trust of him through and by means of the testing.

What he wanted was for them to respond nobly, gallantly, but the Wilderness almost always became a token of their unbelief, their bitter complaining because freedom involved pain and very often they preferred slavery if it was dished up with onions and leeks to freedom if it involved a tough pilgrimage (but see Jeremiah 2:2).

Israel's Messiah, Jesus of Nazareth, came to represent Israel (and consequently, humanity at large) and endured a Wilderness experience (Matthew 4 and parallels). In the Wilderness he did all that Israel was supposed to do and didn't. He rejected the temptation to bitterly demand bread since he was God's Son and was entitled to it, he rejected Satan as the god who would go before him and bring him into the kingdom and he humbly submitted to the wilderness experience rather than tempt God for proof that he was there with him in it. Centuries earlier the Tempter had met Israel in the wilderness and brought it to its knees but by the grace of God, the elect survived and in the person of the Messiah the Evil One met "Israel" again and lost. What the Messiah did in the Wilderness was what Yahweh wanted from the nation.

For Israel the Wilderness became, though it did not have to be, a time of punishment and judgment. Numbers14:34 speaks the judgment on distrust and Israel was divided into two groups. "Wanderers" who were going nowhere and "pilgrims" who were going somewhere even if took a while to get where God was leading them. The NT bears witness to this punishment element in Israel's Wilderness experience (Hebrews 3—4).

And although many Israelites didn't believe it, the wilderness spoke of freedom. It isn't possible to understand the Wilderness experience of Israel without the Exodus as prologue and settlement in Canaan as epilogue. How did they get there (and where were they going)? However harsh and without promise the Wilderness was, it was "out of Egypt". It may have been away from cucumbers, leeks, garlic and flesh-pots but it was also away from slavers, murderous overlords, seven-day-schedules which ran from morn till night.

It may have been a brutal environment for the body but for the heart and soul, for Israel's heart and soul, it was another realm. The sun rose on free men, women and children (who were going home).

For some who say yes to God in Christ, life becomes harder, there are more pressures, there's more pain but it's still a different world. They've been freed from the Evil Prince who enslaved them. The very pressures now on them as disciples of Christ are a token of their freedom, their salvation (Philippians 1:28-29).

33

A SCHOOL IN THE WILDERNESS

*"...in order to humble you, testing you to know what was in your heart, whether or not you would keep his commandments." **Deuteronomy 8:2***

The experience of Wilderness taught Israel nearly as much as her blessed state in the land of Canaan and ask experienced Christians if their hard times taught them anything they can now count on. If you were to ask people like Paul, now that they are through their "sore years" if it was worth the trouble, they're liable to say to you, "What trouble?"

In the Wilderness God taught Israel assurance. Yahweh was able to provide their every need (Deuteronomy 8:1-5). He was able to guide them through the trackless desert and bring them safely home. He was able to extort blessing from curse and make flinty rocks bring forth water and stony ground to feed their flocks.

In the Wilderness God taught Israel that sin matters. They shouldn't have rebelled; they shouldn't have violated the covenant when it was hardly out of God's mouth. They shouldn't have whined in distrust because conditions were hard. Wasn't he who made a

141

wilderness out of Egypt the Lord of wilderness? Couldn't he who redeemed them from Egypt bring them safely to Canaan? Their prolonged stay in the Wilderness underscored the nature of their trustless peevishness.

In the Wilderness God taught Israel trust. It isn't usual to see the Wilderness experience in this light but Jeremiah 2:1-3 brings it out. Here's what it says: "Go proclaim in the hearing of Jerusalem: 'I remember the devotion of your youth, how as a bride you loved me and followed me through the desert, through a land not sown. Israel was holy to the Lord, the firstfruits of his harvest; all who devoured her were held guilty, and disaster overtook them."

That text depnds on Israel's firstfruits festival. When the crops began to appear Israel would choose out the best of what had already shown and offer it to God as a confession that *all* is his. They were not to eat of the firstfruits—that would have been displeasing to God. In the Jeremiah 2 text God pictures all the nations as the crops he had sown and so belonging to him [compare the last phrase of Exodus 19:5] but he saw Israel as his firstfruits.

Israel was more than the rebels who were purged from the heart of her; she was more than a collection of grumblers. There were those who turned from Egypt to face the Wilderness and didn't shrivel in distrust because of what they saw. There were those who took their loving Husband's hand and said, "Where you go, I go". It's true there was a generation left lying, bones bleaching in the sun, but there were others who survived that generation and had to endure the wandering. These who bore the judgment along with the guilty held to God in trust and the Wilderness experience for them was the occasion and the birth of walking by faith rather than sight.

In the Wilderness God taught Israel discipline. "As a man disciplines his son, so the Lord your God disciplines you" (Deuteronomy 8:5). That's why he led them through the Wilderness (8:2), to make disciples of them; "disciple" and "discipline" are immediately connected. They were to be tempered by the absence of soft conditions in the Wilderness before they entered the promised land which produced so abundantly. In either place they were blessed! How was that possible? Because behind bread, behind

142

the physical needs lie the great Provider whose purpose is not to bind them to prosperity but to *him*! It was by the word of God they would find themselves in a place of abundance where they would live and prosper but how is it that they could live and prosper in a Wilderness? By the same word of God! It isn't where they are that ultimately provides life, it's who they are with wherever they are that makes the difference. It isn't a land that provides; it's a God! A God who name is Yahweh.

That is a hard lesson to learn. And who learns it perfectly? It's simple enough to believe that we can live when we are capable of earning, have a job that brings in what is needed, possess the brain-power (or whatever) to compete in the market-place. It's tempting at such times to believe, "My power and the strength of my hands have produced this wealth for me" (Deuteronomy 8:17). No, God says (8:18), "Remember the Lord your God, for it is he who gives you the ability to produce wealth, and so confirms his covenant, which he swore to your forefathers..." These words make the point again that they live by the word, the promise of God. No farmer thanks the plough though it is his instrument to gain a harvest—the farmer brings in the harvest. Moving that truth to its proper conclusion—it is God who provides even as he has promised.

...the Wilderness theme speaks

to us most powerfully...

34

THE NEW TESTAMENT CHURCH & WILDERNESS

And the woman fled into the wilderness, where she has a place prepared by God, so that there she can be nourished for one thousand two hundred sixty days. **Revelation 12:6**

The NT Church for all its differences is the organic continuation of God's People (Israel) so Israel's history is hers. The theology of that history is hers also. NT literature is permeated with the truth and Church hymns bear witness to the same truth, that the NT People have found much sustenance, challenge and conviction in and from OT experiences.

The NT repeatedly calls on the Wilderness experience of ancient Israel to shape the lives of individual believers and the life of the Church. 1 Corinthians 10 makes full use of the OT Wilderness experience and events. Hebrews 3—4 develops the theological meaning and importance of what happened to Israel. Rev 12 speaks of the Church's Wilderness experience as she goes through her great trial under the Roman oppression. There we're told she is carried into the wilderness (which speaks of testing and trial) but while there she is sustained by God (see Deuteronomy 8 and the experience of Elijah during the three and a half year drought in the days of Ahab).

It's in our "pilgrimage," between the time of our calling and election as the People of God and our finally reaching our inheritance in a day yet to come that the Wilderness theme speaks to us most powerfully.

Once more, if someone were to "pan the world," in the midst of the chaos and wilderness of the nations, they would finally come to notice a "new creation" (see 2 Corinthians 5), a people, a holy nation (1 Peter 2), a peculiar treasure belonging to God. They would see order, life, worship, joy, purpose and fruitfulness.

They would also see other things not so pleasing. They would see the Church fail as Israel failed and they would see the Church under judgment from the God who dwells in the midst of her. What Israel was physically and theologically in the Wilderness of Sinai, the NT Church is in the wilderness of social, political and national affairs.

As the Head of the Church faced his personal (and representative) Wilderness experience so the NT Church, his Body, endures hers. She is called to show herself trusting toward God no matter how difficult her circumstances. She is called not to bitterly demand special treatment that would exempt her from hunger just because she has a special relationship to God. She is not to seek the kingdom of glory so desperately that she will get it by any means. God is her benefactor, he will give to her the kingdom and the glory and the Church must resist Satan's call to worship him on the understanding that he will give the Church the glory of the kingdoms. The Church must not make demands on God that he will bless her projects and schemes to prove that he is with her. See Matthew 4 and the texts from Deuteronomy and Exodus 17 quoted by the Master in the face of trial.

And, of course, individual disciples have experienced this ordering work of God. Many of them knew lives of utter fragmentation, barrenness and chaos until God had his way with them and things changed from formlessness and conflict into

146

paradise and harmony. The process is ongoing and will not be completed until that day when they gain their full inheritance.

Israel was not simply another nation—it was a nation chosen and shaped by God and representative of all the nations of the world under God. Sinful, weak, self-serving, oppressive, vengeful and self-righteous but God took her, made a covenant with her and gave her form, destiny and made her a model for the world to watch.

The joy, prosperity, holiness, integrity and selflessness (which Israel was to exhibit) were to be an appeal to all the world. Israel was not only to speak light to the nations it was to *be* light to the nations. The NT Church which is the present phase of the elect People of God has the same role as ancient Israel and brings the conflicting nations to peace with God and one another.

It's clear that while all isn't blessing for the human race, all isn't curse either. There is the witness of Psalms 67, Matthew 5, Acts 14 & 17 that God continues to pursue humanity, blessing it and bringing it to greater blessing, to Himself! It would be a mistake to think he supplies only the physical necessities—the qualities which humans in their better moments prize most (honesty, fidelity, kindness, sacrifice, love and the like) are also the blessings of God who gives humans life "and everything else"—Acts 17:25. What God gave and promised to give to Israel and the NT Church down the centuries he offers to humanity at large. His redemptive purposes are as wide as his creation purposes and he doesn't limit his holy generosity to his elect people.

How could Israel eat in the

wilderness? Because Yahweh

was there!

35

THE SMITTEN ROCK AND AMALEK

Moses replied, "Why do you quarrel with me? Why do you put the Lord to the test?" **Exodus 17:2b**

The place was called Meribah and Massah because it was there they insolently tempted God and picked a quarrel with him—"was he with them or not?" Can it be bad to complain when you're thirsty? When your family is hot and thirsty? Surely not—unless, unless the complaint is a mark of character (and that is for God to know and judge).

They picked a quarrel with God by picking a quarrel with his messenger (Exodus 17:2-3). I think we get the sense of 17.3 if we hear the people implying that it was Moses who brought them out into the wilderness and because it was Moses, it was spiteful of him to lead them all to their death. It wasn't disappointment speaking, however, it was rage because they were in a mood to stone him, Moses tells us.

The God who made an Egyptian garden into a wilderness by ruining its water (the Nile) would make a garden out of a wilderness by bringing water out of a smitten rock (17:5-6). How could Israel eat in the wilderness (Exodus 16)? Because Yahweh was there! How could they drink in the wilderness (Exodus 17)? Because Yahweh was there! How could they defeat Amalek in the wilderness (17)? Because Yahweh was there! This is a major lesson of the wilderness—the presence of Yahweh makes the difference!

What nation was so privileged? What God was so tempted? What God was so patient? With bread, meat, drink and victory supplied in the wilderness, why was it that so many died and left their bleaching, crumbling, bones in the desert? Because God was displeased with them, said Paul (1 Corinthians 10), because of their unbelief, said the Hebrew writer (3:7—4:2). They wanted to know if Yahweh was present with them after all he had done? Their spirit went beyond the natural plea for food and water and rest—at least that's how God saw it. They had cried for generations for God to come and free them from Egypt and when he came with manifest tokens of his presence, leading them out and toward home, they picked a quarrel with him. "Are you really with us?"

The rod that struck the first blow against their Egyptian captors is thrust before the leaders' eyes as Moses smote the appointed rock and brought forth water for an unbelieving nation. Every mouth that drank up water, every animal that slaked its thirst, every man that cooled his brow was a visible witness to the presence of Yahweh. The God who brought them out of Egypt, whose envoy was Moses and whose scepter was a shepherd's staff had not deserted them and in spite of their insolence he provided.

On a later occasion, even though he was told to take the staff with him Moses is expressly told to *speak* to the rock but strikes it in unbelief (Numbers 20:8-12). God rebukes his lack of trust but still honored Moses in the sight of the nation by bringing water from the rock. Perhaps Moses had come to trust in the symbol of God's power rather than the God behind the symbol and was afraid to speak since he normally depended on the staff. Be that as it may, he acted in unbelief and was chastised.

Paul takes "the rock" from which Israel received water and likens it to Christ (1 Corinthians 10:1-5). Though struck in Numbers

20 in unbelief the rock still gave life-giving water for unbelieving people. So it was with the Christ who was smitten in unbelief and brought life (see Acts 2:23 and elsewhere).

And who would protect them against their hardened enemies? Were Israelites better warriors than their enemies? Had they sharper swords, longer spears, sharper vision, quicker reflexes? Perhaps, but it wasn't in these that victory lay. Armies would carry their banners into battle as assurance to themselves and defiance of the enemy and on a hill sat the despised Moses with the staff of God in his hands, high above his head for a banner. It reminded the fighting Israelites that the battle, in the end, was not theirs, but Yahweh's and though they needed courage to be involved in the war it was the sight of Yahweh's symbol, his banner, that reminded them of his presence and therefore of their ultimate victory. Yahweh-Nissi spells it out—"The Lord is my Banner" (Exodus 17:8-15)!

In 17:14 Moses is told to write in a scroll so that a permanent record would be kept of Amalek's fierce purpose against Israel. Since they opposed Israel, they opposed God's purpose to bless the world through Israel and the Messiah. God's purposes permanent judicial hostility toward that nation but the Amalekites made their own vows of hostility and many centuries later we find a world-ranking Amalekite who sought the extermination of the Jews. See the story told in the book of Esther.

...he would be pleased to hear of the good that Abraham's God had done...

36

REUNIONS IN THE WILDERNESS

How very good and pleasant it is when kindred live together in unity!
Psalm 133:1

A series of reunions in 18:1-12 strike a pleasant note after the fierce word from God about Amalek in 17:8-16. There are some reasons to believe chapter 18 is out of chronological order and actually occurred after the giving of the covenant Law. This will hardly bother us since we see this from the beginning to the end of Jeremiah (in Daniel, Isaiah and others) that chronological sequence isn't as important to biblical scribes as to us.

There was the glad reunion between Moses and his hospitable and wise father-in-law who sent word ahead that he was coming. There was the reunion between Moses and the two sons, Gershom and Eliezer.

There was the reunion between Moses and Zipporah. He had "sent her away" (18:2) and her father "received her". Had he sent her away because of a rift that had developed with the mysterious incident at the inn in 4:24-26? Maybe the fact that her father "received her" gives support to that idea. And 1-7 seems to breathe an air of stiffness, polite stiffness that seems to melt later (vv. 8-9). Perhaps this is due in part to a coolness between Moses and Zipporah. On the other hand he might have sent her away with his sons because he was about to undertake an absorbing and perhaps dangerous job. There is barely a mention of Zipporah and the boys but we're told by scholars that that wouldn't be surprising in an ancient and eastern setting. When Jethro left, it appears he left without the boys and Zipporah (18:27).

The main character in the reunions (18:1-12) is clearly Jethro who is described in a glowing fashion. He sends word ahead of his coming as would be expected for several reasons; courtesy being one. He reacts with enthusiasm when he hears Moses confirming what he had already heard ("Jethro was delighted"). He is treated as the senior figure by Moses who bows down to him and he offers open praise of Yahweh for his righteous deliverance of both Moses and Israel from Egypt. Jethro follows his confession and praise with sacrifices to God and is the host of a special meal, that is, a meal consciously eaten as people who know they are "in the presence of God".

The trigger for his visit was the story which had spread throughout that part of the world about what Yahweh had done to Egypt and for Israel. Jethro being a Midianite, was of the seed of Abraham (see on 2:16) and being as fine a man as he is shown to be he would be pleased to hear of the good that Abraham's God had done to his descendants and therefore to Jethro's kin and not just his son-in-law. The celebration meal the Midianite had with Israel (represented by their elders) was a nice touch. Any contribution to the healing of any wounds must surely bring us pleasure in a world that permeated with divisions.

37

LEADERSHIP AND WISDOM

"For by the grace given to me I say to everyone not to think of yourselves more highly than you ought to think, but to think with sober judgment..." **Romans 12:3**

There Moses sat from morning till night. There they stood from morning till night. He made decisions, gave teaching, spoke the mind of God, as much as he knew of it and settled disputes (18:13). And he must have done it in a hurry, or tried to do it in a hurry or he wouldn't have settled many cases. Didn't he know it was unwise? Did he not know he was not only wearing himself out but that he was wearing out the people who had to wait and wait and then wait (18:17-18)?

Perhaps he did, but the pressure of the situation shoved aside his better judgment. We've all known occasions when even if only for a little while we knew we were in over our heads but felt there was no one else to deal with the things that needed dealt with.

There is the temptation of course to fall in love with "calling the shots" because after all no one else is wise enough to handle things.

Then again, it's nice to have the reputation of being the wise one, the indispensable one. The whispers that go around when we enter a room or conference building ("That's him/her, nothing moves around here without...") can be addictive. Ill health and death have a blunt way of curing us of that addiction—cold turkey!

Jethro obviously watched all this for the day and 18:14 opens his remarks. He isn't looking for information. I think we should read the words with a tone of incredulity as though he said, "What on earth are you doing...?" and read Moses' response with the I-can't-help-it tone, "They come with problems and I have to deal with them."

There's no doubt that Moses meant well but his father-in-law thought it was benevolent blundering. What you're doing isn't good, he told him, you're serving neither yourself nor the people in this way. This was a brave step on the part of the Midianite priest. He had just come to realize fully (what he may have known earlier), that Yahweh is God of gods (Psalms 135:5, 15-21) and he speaks to the special envoy of Yahweh in this fashion?

It was more than that. He was telling a well-intentioned man that his bone-wearying work wasn't good or wise; it was hurting rather than helping. It's one thing to rebuke deeds or enterprises which are done with wicked intentions; it's another thing to speak against what is done by the well-meaning. For doing the first we may be regarded as heroes. For doing the second we might hear, "Yeah? And what are you doing? That's the trouble with you people, when someone decides to do something you come along with nothing but criticism." This is a possible response. Another is silent sulking and a withdrawal from that arena. When asked if the withdrawal is the result of the criticism, we're tempted to rationalize and deny it when we know full well that that is precisely why we've resigned from the role.

Of course, there are those who do nothing but criticize. They're good at the destructive part but have nothing to do or say of a constructive nature. Jethro wasn't like that. He offered something better (18:19-23) and he offered it in the name of God.

Jethro is clear in his criticism, Moses is over-worked and over-worked people are not at their best. The people are denied a hearing and people denied a hearing soon become a discontented people (even if they weren't at first). And the nation is robbed, Ellison reminds us, of the wisdom and willingness of others (18:12).

A great leader was told he was well-intentioned but wrong and he recognized the truth of it...

38

LESSONS IN LEADERSHIP

But Moses said to him, "Are you jealous for my sake? Would that all the Lord's people were prophets, and that the Lord would put his spirit on them!" **Numbers 11:29**

None of the complex questions about life have simple answers; we would just like it to be that way. One of the reasons Britain and South Africa down the years have dragged their feet on granting nations and peoples political power and/or independence was, "They aren't ready for it; they don't know how to exercise it." After all, "We made something out of these countries, invested our lives, toil, wisdom and made them prosperous—you can hardly expect us to allow people who know nothing about the exercise of authority or the running of a country to take over and bring it to ruin." That makes sense—of a sort.

"You should have seen this country when we came into it! You don't know the sacrifice our people made over the centuries to build this great state and nation so it's easy for you outsiders to say we should hand over the reigns of government to those who are incompetent and who benefited from us and our toil. We work to build and make it great, you tell us to hand it over?" That makes sense too—of a sort.

But nothing's that simple. How wise can we be if we don't raise up wise leaders from the people with whom we live? How shortsighted we are not to see that one day, if we don't give them a voice, in some honorable and wise manner, that they'll be sorely tempted to seize power from us? That people are not ready for independence or the honorable exercise of democratic and/or moral power may be because we did not prepare them for it.

A great leader was told he was well-intentioned but wrong and he recognized the truth of it (Exodus 18:18; Deuteronomy 1:9-12). He was offered wise counsel and took it. With the cooperation of the people (Deuteronomy 1:13-15) he chose leaders who were competent, honest and devoted to God and the people. They shared the burden of government with him (Ex 18:22) and everybody benefited. [This tells us that Moses didn't have to bear all the burden of governing the people alone—there were helpers all over the place.]

This is another section that makes it clear that Moses was no power-hungry tyrant. As soon as he realized the wisdom of the counsel, his love of the people and his recognition of his own limitations led him to implement it (18:24). He didn't feel he had to hog the power and would have been glad if the whole nation were prophets (Numbers 11:29). That wasn't just talk—which is easy—that was walk, as we can see from this section.

There's something else about this section worth noting. The wise counsel came from an "outsider". Precisely where Jethro stood with Yahweh isn't clear from the texts, but he could hardly have been an ignoramus since he would have heard truth from Moses down the years, since he was a descendant of Abraham and since he had heard the story of what Yahweh had done to Egypt. But he wasn't an Israelite! And what is a non-Israelite doing offering lessons on statesmanship to the leader of Israel?

God has more than one way of speaking to humans, more than one way to teach them. Sometimes it is done in what we call "special revelation" and at other times it is done by what we call "the school of hard knocks". With special revelation as a basis we can then do some reasoning on and from nature (see this in Romans 1). With special revelation as background and realizing that all our good gifts come from God, we can go through life learning. The "Wisdom" literature makes this clear to us.

Proverbs 1:8-9, 6:20 and other texts insist that we should listen to the teaching of our fathers and mothers. Much of what is in Proverbs is the kind of thing we learn by living. This too is the teaching of God. It is God who gives the farmer wisdom says Isaiah 28:23-29, esp.26, 29. *And do we think that means only Israelite farmers? Israelite fathers and mothers? When we pray for men and women in high office and ask God to bless them with wisdom, are we asking him to pour verses into their heads? Do we not pray for foreign rulers that God and his wisdom might influence them too? Or do we ask wisdom only for our own?* See 1 Tim 2:1-3.

It shouldn't surprise us that a Midianite priest (Reuel—"friend of El"), though an "outsider," had wisdom from God. Nor should it surprise us that many people in political office, though they have no personal relationship with Jesus Christ, have integrity and wisdom from God. What kind of God would God be if he was so grudging with his blessings? Everywhere we look, in every face we look we see or have reason to believe we would see, God's gifts "strewn like sands upon the great seashore" and Acts 14:16-17 and 17:24-28. Instead of denying their existence we ought to thank God for them and tell these gifted people who they should thank for their giftedness.

It is part of a great leader's character to acknowledge his or her debt even to those "outside". It's part of the humility of a great leader to allow himself/herself to be taught the wisdom of God by whoever has it. We have enough special revelation to work with, as a basis of judgment on what is or is not wise, but God didn't only give us a Bible, he gave us gifted people. "outsiders" as well as "insiders" to teach us.

He gives gifts to all so that all

may contribute to the blessing

of the Community

39

POWER SHARING

*And the twelve called together the whole community of disciples and said "It is not right that we should neglect the word of God in order to wait on tables." **Acts 6:2***

*T*he sharing of power is the will of God. The Midianite priest appears to say he is relaying to Moses the will of God (18:23) and Moses certainly implements it as the will of God. To say power-sharing is the will of God is a truth, but it is only one truth.

The leaders of God's People do not have the right to hog the power, elect more leaders without dialogue with the Community or refuse to develop leaders (and so hinder the Community and frustrate the larger aims of God in this world).

The sharing of power is made possible by the work of God. He gives gifts to all so that all may contribute to the blessing of the Community (in this case, Israel). You can see this view of the matter expressed by Paul in 1 Corinthians 12, especially vv.6-7. If God hadn't invested and nurtured the noble qualities in the Israelites

163

(see 18:21) there would have been no one for Moses to share authority with on behalf of the nation.

The sharing of power is regulated by God. He does this, first, by assuming that people acknowledge him as the ultimate vision and authority, whose word is to be obeyed rather than debated and whose image is to be reflected in them. He then designates the people and/or the literature that mediates his will to those who hold him as supreme (18:19). He gifts people with the qualities and capacities needed to achieve the purposes he has in view, calls on the people to acknowledge these in such persons and submit themselves where appropriate to them, to achieve the divine goals.

In the Exodus 18 setting, the men with whom Moses shares authority are marked out by 1) their acceptance and understanding of the Torah; 2) their God-fearing lives; 3) their trustworthiness; 4) their honesty; 5) their willingness to serve; 6) their willingness to serve as decision makers; 7) their willingness to accept their own limitations and 8) their love of the nation. Be sure to read Exodus 18:20-22. And see from important major texts both in the OT and the NT that this is the consistent pattern for choosing leaders rather than an exceptional occasion.

In saying "yes" to such men, Moses was saying "no" to men unlike those. He was following the will of God. For one man or a few men to hog power when there are others gifted by God to serve is monstrous—for many reasons—but to hand over decision-making power to men thoroughly unqualified is equally monstrous. What God regulates must not be thrown up for grabs. *The People of God have no right to choose as leaders those whom God has rejected.*

We need to note from Deuteronomy 1:9-18 that the leaders were chosen with the help of the entire community. See also Acts 6:1-6.

Covenant under Yahweh: 19:1—24:18

The covenant God enacts
includes his commitment to
bless but it also involves his
creating something new in the
world—a People who will
practice God-imitating
righteousness

40

THE NATURE AND FUNCTION OF THE TORAH

Oh how I love your law! It is my meditation all day long.
Psalm 119:97

Scholars aren't agreed on how the Hebrew word "Torah" should be rendered; they're still working on it. The one thing that modern scholars are agreed on is that our English word "law" doesn't work well as a translation—it's too narrow and too loaded with notions of what is "legal".

"Teaching," "instruction" and words of that nature are suggested but there is still dissent. The word certainly doesn't mean "suggestion" or "advice"—it may not denote "legal law" but it isn't a "see-what-you-think-about-this" production. The arguments will continue on the meaning of the *word* and we should expect them to because word-studies, while they are essential, are still very limited and linguistic fallacies are still plentiful despite what James Barr did to them in 1961.

The word is used to speak of the first five books of the Hebrew Bible, it is used to speak of the covenant material of the Pentateuch, it is used for the entire OT [when viewed from a specific angle]. In the OT it is used in the plural of various covenant responsibilities [laws, commands] so to say our word "law" isn't correct as a translation is not correct.

But once more, to interpret the Bible "word by word" as if words had "meaning" *independent of* context or the writer's intention is clearly untrue. Even if we rightly call [and we do] "the Ten Commandments" ten "laws" we're not to forget that they are part of a narrative, they are part of a record of the mighty acts of God who is keeping his covenant promises to Abraham. These ten commandments are spoken to a specific people under specific circumstances and with a specific purpose [note Exodus 20:2 which spells this out for us]. To abstract them from this historical and narrative setting is to change their character, to reduce them to "statements of law" is to rob them of their richness and relational quality.

We're to bear in mind that in delivering Israel from "the house of bondage" God purposed to set up an alternative kingdom; something entirely different in character and origin from the empire of the Pharaoh. The covenant God enacts includes his commitment to bless but it also involves his creating something new in the world—a People who will practice God-imitating righteousness.

Israel can never be God or do what God did but in their worship and way of life they can bear witness to what he has done and the nature of his way—they can be his "witnesses". The covenant requirements [the laws] profile the character of God [as the house rules of sadistic parents will reflect the character of the parents] and they shape the People so that they are equipped to bear witness to Yahweh and so glorify him while they bring light to the nations [see Isaiah 43:9-12; 49:6 and elsewhere].

God's laws remain God's laws, of course, but there's a way of looking at laws that makes them nothing but "decisions handed down by the boss". This is certainly not how God's laws function in the Torah. But this shouldn't surprise us because in our more lucid moments we know that rules and regulations don't work that way even in human structures or homes. Speed limits may be cursed as a plague and as nothing more than arbitrary laws set up by bureaucrats but giving them their best face they're enacted to shape a safer place for children, the elderly and the vulnerable and for other important social reasons.

Then there's the case of Franky and Jennifer. They grew up together; they went to the same school, shared some of the same classes, outside interests and became good friends. They not only admired and respected each other, they began to miss each other when the other wasn't around, and to worry when the other was sick. Nobody was surprised when the two close friends announced they were going to get married.

They had talked a lot about what they wanted out of life and high on the grand list was a warm, loving family. How would they achieve that? Well, they'd both been part of families that gave them clues-positive and negative-how to go about it; they were reasonably well read and though they were young, they weren't dumb. They'd seen and heard much that would act as groundwork on which to build. So they set up home.

A few years later the babies began to arrive. For all the best reasons the two of them found a lot of pleasure and deep joy in the children and, of course, they were committed to holding, feeding, clothing, bathing, loving and providing them with what they needed.

The babies earned nothing, they didn't need to—the parental love was unconditional and unashamed.

As the time slipped by they laughed and rejoiced at every sign of progress in the children. Progress they nurtured and encouraged. There was David's first time to hold the spoon for himself (even got some food to his mouth); Rachel's first tottering steps, Andrew's successful (and unaided) first read. There was the tying of shoes, the brushing of teeth, the making of beds, the putting on of socks, a bath all by one's self (with nervous parents calling in every thirty seconds, "Are you all right?") and other social challenges which grew more difficult and more complex as the years slipped by.

There were house-rules, of course! No one was allowed to play around with electric sockets or sharp knives, scream at someone, use bad language they heard at school or maybe on TV. There was bed by 8.30 and lights out by nine, there was homework to be done (usually) before a favoured TV program was watched and there were chores to be done-before or after play didn't matter-but they had to be done.

The rules weren't created to enslave, narrow or deprive the children. The opposite was true!

The children learned the behavior that pleased or displeased their parents but it never entered their minds that Franky and Jennifer loved them because they kept the rules. And it never entered their minds that when the rules were sometimes broken the parents stopped loving them. If someone had suggested that their parents only loved them when and because they kept the house-rules, the children would have scoffed! They knew they sometimes disappointed or displeased their parents; they even knew what it was to be disciplined but it was utter rubbish to suggest that Franky and Jennifer loved them only when they did what they were told. That may have been the case in other homes—but not in this home!

The two older children noticed that the "lights out by nine" rule didn't apply in Rachel's room when she developed a real fear of the dark. That made sense. The lights out by nine rule was for their benefit, to allow them to get enough sleep but since Rachel had become terrified of the dark, she wasn't getting any sleep at all. In Andrew and Robert's room the rule still applied because it was achieving for them what the parents were aiming at.

One response to Rachel's fear might have been, "Rules are made to be kept no matter what the circumstances, so, nightmares, cold sweats and endless tears notwithstanding, the lights go out at nine." But that would be a poor response.

Franky and Jennifer would insist that "the law was made for the child and not the child for the law." They would leave the light on while they tried to help eliminate the anxiety.

Since the law was introduced for the child's benefit the parents assume that the child is more important than the law. To insist that the rule be kept when it is clearly contrary to the child's welfare is to regard the rule as more important than the child and it would violate the parental purpose for the child.

170

It wouldn't help the other children either to see their brother or sister mauled by a law which was supposed to be a blessing. Parental credibility would be under siege and the relationship under threat.

This helped the kids to see that the rules weren't the fundamental realities; that behind the rules was the will of the parents for each child's good. They were learning not only the importance of rules, by a wise application, the parents were teaching them the place of rules.

As they grew older the parents changed the 'to bed' and 'lights out' times. That made sense to the children as well. At five, in bed by 8.30 seems sensible but at fifteen, it isn't geared for their age and maturity. (A maturity which had been helped along earlier by rules such as an 8.30 bed time and the children's glad submission to them.) They couldn't always understand why some of the rules were made, even when they asked and the parents explained. But the children trusted Franky and Jennifer and supposed that they would understand better later.

And there were times when the rules didn't suit, even when they did understand the why and wherefore of them. Sometimes they broke them and paid the price of discipline. For example, any eating was to be done in the kitchen at meal or snack times and there was to be no eating done in bed. (Too many children had nearly choked while they ate lying down.) No one was tarred and feathered if they didn't resist the temptation to a snack in bed but there was some sort of discipline ranging from a stern rebuke to loss of privileges.

There were other house rules that hardly needed mentioned because they would have been such a radical departure from family values and aims. Physical abuse of one another, marked verbal or emotional abuse would all have been taken as serious crimes against the family. This was clear from the way persistent squabbling was handled, squabbling that led to some pushing and unbridled speech. It was made plain too by the frequent discussions about some TV programs, news and fiction, as well as experiences at school.

The very idea that someone in a fit of temper would set light to someone's room or hit them with a sharp instrument made coming in fifteen minutes late or smuggling some biscuits to bed appear to be mild transgressions indeed.

This showed that while all house rules were to be kept, some were more important than others. It would have been nonsense to view every house rule as of equal importance. The parents made it clear to the children that there were more important matters in "the law of the house".

I could easily leave you the impression that what the Wilson family did was spend their lives thinking about rules and laws. This is far from the truth!

The proper response to the rules of the home is a wise loving commitment to the family and that's what was nurtured in the Wilson house. They didn't go about thinking of "rules". They didn't always consciously think of their being a family-they simply understood that they were, and much of the time they lived out their place in this loving family without analyzing the situation.

The rules were seen as servants to the family unit. They were seen as protecting, promoting, defining and revealing what it meant to be a loving family.

I mentioned earlier that a generally wise rule was set aside when Rachel's need was not only not being met by it, she was being injured by it. And the change of bedtime and lights out was made when the rule no longer reflected the conditions/age of the children.

Only the rules changed—the aim was maintained. If the rules were contrary to the family's well being, they wouldn't have been made in the first place. If due to changes in circumstances the wise rules no longer gained what the parents aimed for, they were either altered or removed. But as long as the rules served the grand purpose, for which they existed, they stood and were gladly obeyed by all the family.

The rules didn't determine the over-arching aim, the rules were there to support and help achieve the over-arching aim: fullness of life for all within a loving family relationship.

Because life within a family unit had change and difference written into it, many rules were understood to relate only to specific sets of circumstances.

David, the older son, noticed that his parents held him more strictly accountable than his brother and sister. He would hear Franky say to him on occasions when all three of them had been disobedient, "You should know better than them." At first he didn't understand or like this, but as he got older he understood, and though he smarted under it at times, he felt good about it. It meant they saw him as more mature and so expected more of him. (He was also pleased because his maturity brought privileges with it. He was free from some of the restrictions the younger ones were still subject to.)

Andrew noticed that while they all had so many things in common, each of them had their own roles in the family. For example, David wasn't the dad and wasn't expected to carry that responsibility. Rachel wasn't the mother and she wasn't David. And dad wasn't Andrew so he didn't have schoolwork to do. Of course there were jobs that the whole family pitched in to do, jobs that weren't exclusively assigned to anyone (dishwashing and clearing up would illustrate the point) and it was OK for David to give Rachel advice, as Jennifer would do. Just the same, while there was plenty of dialogue and everyone got a fair hearing, it was clear that some responsibilities couldn't be passed off to someone else.

There was no competition in the home to see who kept the most laws or who kept them best. Nobody assessed himself or anyone else on the basis of the number of laws kept or broken. That would have been too simple and it would have missed the whole spirit of the family. Franky and Jennifer would have been appalled if the children ever felt that that was what the parents wanted.

"No," the parents would have said, "if we gave you that impression we've misled you. The keeping or the breaking of the rules is not the bottom line here. The final issue is: are we committed to each other in love, seeking one another's joy and best interests?"

If Rachel came to Franky and Jennifer every day with a 'laundry list' of rules kept and broken, seeking approval from her parents and seeking to be seen as "child most committed to the family"—if she did that, they would set her down and made some things clear.

Because there could never be enough rules to cover every conceivable life-situation, where guidelines were needed, the parents made new rules. For example, when they went on vacation, they faced new conditions (crowds, fairgrounds, river rides, and the like) so new rules were created that weren't necessary at home. In a large fairground Franky said, "If we get separated for more than thirty minutes, we go to the entrance of that big marquee marked CENTRAL."

This was a new rule but it served the same purpose that all the other rules served: the protection, enrichment and care of the family. And because this was true, the whole family willingly subjected itself to the new rule. Nobody wanted any member of the family to get lost or hurt or be subjected to needless anxiety.

Safely back home that rule was forgotten while family commitment remained as fresh and vital as ever.

The fact that new rules had to be created because they were on vacation confirmed to Franky and Jennifer what they had always realized: it isn't possible to have enough rules to cover all situations—even if that were desirable.

Having enough rules would mean there would have to be rules on how to apply rules.

Let's suppose, one of the rules is: you will be back in the house no later than 10 p.m. On winter evenings. If unintentionally one of the children came in at 10.05 that would be one case but what if one deliberately chose not to make it home by 10? He arrives back in at 11.15 to worried parents who are about to verbally reprimand him and he tells them of a friend who was hit by a passing motorcyclist and needed to go to the emergency room. He could have made it home by ten but deliberately chose to ignore the 'curfew'.

Franky and Jennifer would be pleased. That sort of decision could be fitted into the spirit of the family. It shows the maturity and compassion that the parents are aiming to create in the children. In this case, the breaking of the rule honored, and was intended to honor, the parents and the family ("my parents would want me to do this").

To deliberately choose to break the rule to spite the parents, to exercise pride, to 'do what I want to do' would have been a different kind of decision altogether.

It was in areas like these that Franky and Jennifer realized with special clarity that they were shaping hearts and lives and not just handing down laws. There were occasions when the children were older that the parents were away and decisions had to be made without their input.

How could the children know, know for sure, what the parents would have wanted under some serious circumstances? Well, they couldn't know for certain just what they would have said, but they had been shaped by their spirit, wisdom, values and overarching purpose so that the decisions they came to by themselves weren't completely without parental input. There were some options, which just weren't possible for the children in the light of their raising. Of course they could have physically carried them out, but they couldn't have done it and thought they would be pleasing to their parents.

And while people who didn't know the Wilson family perhaps could have suggested other sane options if they had been given the facts, they wouldn't have been as well qualified to know what would please Franky and Jennifer and fit in with the spirit of the family.

The Wilsons learned as they grew together as a family that life wasn't a static 'thing'—it was dynamic, it was a relationship, not something you could take in your hand or set on a cabinet and admire; not something 'finished'. Being a family involved the biological connection (they were all related by 'blood') of course, but it meant being committed to one another, seeking one another's highest good. It meant giving and receiving, adjusting or standing firm.

It was loving one another!

'Love' wasn't simply an emotion; it was a bias in favor of each other, a loyal commitment to one another, which showed itself in different emotions depending on the circumstances. Sometimes they cried because the others were crying, sometimes they laughed for the same reason. All the emotions that are part of being human and which are constructive were exerted toward each other.

Behavior and emotions were tested by their relation to the overarching meaning of what it meant to be a loving family. They sometimes mistreated each other, forgave and/or confronted each other. The wrongs committed were wrongs that could (and were) gladly tolerated as 'within the covenant'.

But there were wrongs that were immediate violations of the family covenant. These involved not only the nature of the acts but the attitude that went with them.

Physical violence was always frowned on but this had to be worked out in light of the foundational values and commitment of the family. A slap in anger would have its consequences but prolonged sly beatings or some form of inflicting pain would be in a wholly different category. A disrespectful word against the parents was unacceptable but a day after day stream of obscenities would be something else.

David in his very late teens got caught up in wrong behavior and the wrong company. He became addicted first to booze and then to cocaine. It was the beginning of a nightmare. The whole family pleaded and worked with him over an extended period, tears were shed, practical help was given, money was spent, abuse was endured, advice was sought but all to no avail. It came to a head after about two years, with David seriously injuring Rachel and holding a knife to his mother's throat, demanding money.

You understand, it wasn't just what David did that turned harmony into chaos, it was his disposition and attitude toward the parents and the children. The wrongs were not only of a foundational nature; they were done in a spirit that demonstrated that the family meant nothing to him.

With sorrow in the hearts of the two children, the parents removed David from the home as someone no longer capable of/willing to live as part of the family. (For two more years he would come back, abusive, smashing windows, ripping tyres and threatening the family.)

What had been lost was more than the willingness/ability to abide by 'the rules' of the family—what had been lost was loving commitment to the family.

No one was pleased at the loss of David! Every member of the family felt the pain of the loss and wished things were different.

Now and then they'd sit and look at each other. Jennifer, in particular worried about their excluding David. Franky assured her that what they did was not loveless. They owed something to Andrew and Rachel as well as to one another. A 'conflict of interests' had arisen. Love toward the other children meant offering protection to them and it was that expression of love that led to David's exclusion. David wasn't excluded because he was hated or that the family didn't wish him well or had easily grown tired of him. And it certainly wasn't that they had lost all feeling toward him. (Even as they discussed the situation they felt pity toward David and wished things could be as they once were, as they had sought them to be.)

As Franky and Jennifer reflected on the way they pursued family joy and enrichment through the years, they knew they didn't do everything right. They had made some rules they thought were useful but with hindsight they realized they hadn't been. But their intentions had always been good; their motivation had always been for the blessing of the family as a family.

As deeply as they loved the children they could never have made rules that were purposed to narrow or hurt or cheat them. Both parents and children knew that love was not without content. There were certain types of behavior that love wouldn't approve—there were things love wouldn't do! On the other hand, there were things love could not avoid doing. It was more than a feeling, it was a commitment and a purpose and it was shaped by a vision of what a deep, rich, full life was.

Later, when the children left home and had families of their own, they would follow the loving guidance of their parents. This wouldn't mean they would do everything the same way, have the same number of rules, the same emphasis and the like. Their family would be a different family with different needs, dispositions and temperaments and while families would always have things in common and have the same over-arching purpose—changed circumstances would require a different approach to things.

In order for them to remain constant they would have to change!

41

CHOSEN

"And you did not chose me but I chose you..." **John 15:16**

Israel wasn't different in and of itself, it was made different (holy) by being chosen (19:5-6). They didn't choose themselves (compare John 15:16) nor did they work themselves into a position of such spirituality or moral grandeur that Yahweh could hardly have been faulted for choosing them. There was nothing in their "person" that made them especially worthy of being elected (see Acts 10:34, Deuteronomy 9:4-5).

Israel's election, that is, being chosen, is a model of the electing work of God. It is true that on occasion God will choose a wicked man, say Pharaoh (see Exodus 9:16), to gain the purposes of a righteous and gracious God while dealing with those bent on oppression but that isn't characteristic of the teaching of the Scriptures on it. Just the same, what I've just said is true. There's no need for us to apologize for God's bringing judgment on a person bent on wickedness and using that judgment to bring himself glory as a God who cares for the oppressed (9:16b). But the broad teaching concerning election looks in the other direction.

Election speaks of God's redeeming work. It's normally in the context of God setting things right, restoring the world to himself that election is discussed in Scripture, even when the word itself is not used.

Election speaks of God's sovereignty. It's never the humans who take the initiative in the matter of reconciliation or setting things right. It is always the work of God. If there is merely human initiative, it is sinful and tends to the estrangement of the humans from God, which is no doubt why Paul tells us the wages of sin is death and that eternal life is a free gift (Romans 6:23).

Election speaks of blessing. Related to God's redeeming work is his intention to bless because he loves (Deuteronomy 8:6-9). Those chosen are not dispassionately called out as though they were mere instruments to do God's will. No, humans count with God. He means to bless because he loves; so we aren't to see God's relation to Israel or to us as a surgeon's relation to his scalpel.

Election speaks of purpose and responsibility. Everywhere you find the teaching of election mentioned or implied, in that text or in the context, you find God has chosen unto blessing and mission. Abraham is chosen to be blessed and to be a blessing (Genesis 12:1-3). Israel is to be blessed and to bring light to the whole world (Isaiah 49:6 and elsewhere). In the NT, God chooses people to salvation and holiness (2 Thessalonians 2:13-15, note the 'so then" of 15), to bring forth fruit (John 15) and to bring honor to God who called them (1 Peter 2:9). Election relates to God's universal purposes and centers in the chosen One, Jesus Christ (Luke 9:35). Each time we hear the word "called" or any word in that semantic domain, we're hearing about "election".

Election speaks about "difference". It is one of the offences the world must face that these people, whose conduct or speech is not always exemplary, who often distort the image they are to bear—it is an offense the world has to bear that these people are 'the elect". And it is a reproach God has to bear, that those who profess to be his own, those he professes to be his own, are the source of derision which falls on him. But he is willing to bear that reproach as he works with his People, molding, chastising and working through them to reconcile the world to himself. The Elect are different because they have been adopted by a gracious God and they are to be different because they live in the presence of the electing God. The difference in their lifestyle is laid out in covenantal terms (see Exodus 19:5-6). If they live in covenant loyalty before God they will indeed be what they have been chosen to be.

Election speaks about community. Election often relates to individuals, of course, but it never stays at that stage. It always has a Community in mind. Even when the Messiah is the Chosen one, God chooses him with a Community in mind. We weren't created to be isolated, to be loners. Humans were created a plural unity, a human "community"—male *and* female, not male or female. Election can result in temptation to arrogance and varied sins but since it places a person in a Community, it can put purpose, power and certainty at the core of a person or a nation. The Elect are bound together and in this there is blessing and empowerment. To lovingly criticize the Church is an obligation; to bitterly curse her is self-destructive. (There are some whose experience of the Church is *so* horrendous that their bitter response is almost to be expected. I have no criticism for such people. How could I who have been so blessed by the Church know what these poor people have been through? But there are those who only *think* they have been treated badly.)

And if you got it as a gift from someone, why are you strutting as if you earned it?

42

TEMPTATIONS OF THE CHOSEN

Already you have all you want! Already you have become rich! Quite apart from us you have become kings! Indeed I wish that you had become kings, so that we might become kings with you!
1 Corinthians 4:8

The elect always found it hard to remember that what she was, she was by grace. Hadn't God said she was his peculiar treasure out of all the nations, even though he had the pick of the whole world (19:5)? How could they help it? A boy tells a girl that if he had the pick of the whole world he would marry her and proves it by marrying her. Why wouldn't it go to her head? Why wouldn't she say, "He loves me above everyone else there I must be special in myself"? (Of course, if Israel had been the loveliest, smartest, strongest, most righteous nation around, she might have had more grounds for saying what our girl could be understood as saying. None of that was true.)

What is it in us who are richly blessed that seduces us into believing that our blessings are the result of or, at least, the reward for, our goodness or our brilliance? "Where do you differ from another?" Paul wanted to know from the bragging Corinthians. "If you are different, who made you different? If you have anything, who'd you get it from? And if you got it as a gift from someone, why are you strutting as if you earned it?" (See 1 Corinthians 4:7.)

"Ah, but I know I didn't earn it. I am a sinner saved by pure grace. But don't I repent magnificently? My quickness and willingness to repent justifies God's giving me so many blessings". Ah, when are we going to learn? Ever?

The elect are tempted to self-centeredness. The sense of who we are, the joy of knowing who we are is such a pleasing, comfortable, warming and satisfying experience. Like snuggling up in a lovely warm bed on a bitterly cold day or toasting ones toes at a beautiful open fire. "All this and heaven too!" The privileges and joys creep up on us, we pull the warm blanket a little higher or shift our chair a little closer and drift off into a pleasant sleep while millions pull their threadbare clothes tighter around them, trying to keep out the winds that blow in the icy, empty, darkness of the world they live in. "God bless them," we mumble as we turn to a more comfortable position.

The elect are tempted to self-service. There aren't many things, in our better moments, that distress us more than the awful state much of the world is in. To see the pain, degradation and injustice that goes on around us. One doesn't have to be very noble to feel pain at the heart in the face of all this. "The world is going to hell" is a truth. It's equally true that something of that hell is what we see around us. And our response to this? The good news is: our response isn't always bad. The bad news is we often feather our own nest, the Church, and damn the world.

Our churches can become forts, castles of righteousness. On a regular basis we have forays into the world, capture a few and bring them back into our castle where they, by the grace God has given them, make our community life richer and warmer. We isolate these socially useful people from the society that can ill-afford to lose them. We gain the benefit and the world goes the more quickly to ruin. The temptation is to hoard, to gorge on life-giving truth while a billion Lazaruses are lying all around us. The temptation (and it's real and powerful) is to see the world only in terms of an enemy to be put down (either by the ballot-box, political power or other). Either they will live our way in this society or they won't live in it at all! We will make this world safe for our children (and how can that be wrong?) and in the course of it all, we lose sight of God's love for them and we lose sight of the truth that part of the reason he elected us is because he loves them and wants them in.

The elect are tempted to self-sufficiency. The ceaseless repetition of the Story is so crucial here. As soon as we being to leave the Story behind and begin to stress some other truth, some other necessary elements of living (interpersonal relationship skills, church growth studies, as examples) we begin to lose touch with our roots and its our roots that make sense of anything we're involved in. All these other studies only make sense because we are the People of a Story. Where leadership studies, counseling skills, biblical exegetics and the rest are divorced from (even by accident, unintentionally, by default) our foundational Story, we are thrown back on to ourselves. Our plans, brilliance, projects, keen insights, scintillating logic, passionate concern, shrewd analysis, statistical evidences take on them a life of their own and, while it's true God is the Great Controller, he's lucky to have us to get the job done. Now who would ever say such a thing? Not one! Who would ever consciously think this much less endorse it? Not one. But it isn't at the conscious level that our greatest temptations come. It's a mark of human sinfulness, and a scar that the Elect bear as surely as the rest, that our skill and success often results in our drifting from or our tearing ourselves from dependence on God (see Genesis 3).

...they are not all independent priests; they all make up a single community or nation and it is a priestly nation...

43

A NATION OF PRIESTS

Like living stones, let yourself be built into a spiritual house, to be a holy priesthood, to offer spiritual sacrifices acceptable to God through Jesus Christ. ***1 Peter 2:5***

Exodus 19:6 declares that Israel is a nation of priests. That should mean every man, woman, boy and girl was a priest. This would hardly be a problem for those who understand the NT to teach "the priesthood of all believers". In fact, one of the major texts of the NT which teaches the priesthood of every believer is 1 Peter 2:5,9 and a glance at that shows it is taken from Exodus 19:6.

It is a problem for some, however, to reconcile the idea of a special priesthood confined to the family of Aaron, as in Exodus 28:1, 30:30 and elsewhere, with the priesthood of the entire Israelite community.

Perhaps the major difficulty lingers in the background. Unhappy with the notion that there is a special priesthood in the NT Church and not wanting to allow any room for support of such an institution, some might not want to acknowledge the priesthood of the whole OT Church and a special priesthood within that priesthood. But we need hardly worry about that since there were a number of institutions in the Mosaic economy we've allowed to vanish without concern. That there was a special priesthood within the universal priesthood in the OT arrangement need not mean there is one today in the NT Church. Such things have to be determined by the teaching of both covenants.

Despite the fact that Peter adopts the LXX rendering of Exodus 19:6 and applies it to the NT Church, meaning they were all priests (see his 2:5), it is still fiercely debated that Exodus 19:6 has that in mind. Many suppose it to mean it is *like* a priestly nation and others that it is a nation *headed up* by its priests rather than kings or politicians. Perhaps it's best to hold it is a nation of which every member is a priest and its business is to stand before God for all the nations and to stand for God before all the nations. But in saying that, I'm not suggesting that we think every Israelite is a free-standing unit—they are not all independent priests; they all make up a single community or nation and it is a priestly nation. In other words, the priestly nature of the nation is *corporate*; it is like one body with many members as is the NT Church. It is the **nation** that is priestly.

It's certainly true that believers under the Mosaic covenant understood that they could offer sacrifices to God without going through the Aaronic priests. They knew they could offer the sacrifices of a broken spirit and a contrite heart (Psalms 51 and see passages such as Psalms 40:6). They understood that they could offer themselves willingly and that while some expressions of worship could only be carried out through the Aaronic priesthood there were vast areas of personal worship and communion with God carried out within in Israelite fellowship.

Whatever else is true, the special priesthood reflected and probably represented what the whole nation was to be before the nations and before God. The nations were to see YHWH as present among humans and served by humans and this was the vocation of Israel *as a whole*. In being and doing this, Israel would be a light and salvation to the Gentiles (compare Isaiah 49:6) and in this they would be offering to God that which was a sweet aroma to him (compare Paul's use of priestly terms in Romans 15:16 for the idea).

The relationship which existed between God and Israel was a covenant relationship

44

THE DECALOGUE

Owe no one anything, except to love one another; for the one who loves another has fulfilled the law. **Romans 13:8**

A few preliminary remarks are in order before glancing at the specific commandments of the Decalogue.

Though there are dangers involved in the new stress, there is a healthy growing realization that "family" carries with it more than biological connection. A "family" is as a family does. There's a dynamic aspect to the "family," a relational element which says that people within that unit commit to each other and to one another's welfare on the basis of foundational values. The physical/biological parent who is committed to oppressing the child and creating continuous misery is repudiating an essential element of what "family" should mean. The child that devotes him/herself to using and abusing the biological parents is, in practice, repudiating an essential element in what "family" means. Nothing will change the fact that there is a biological connection between parents and children but, at some stage, there must be a commitment to living the meaning of "family". (The same would be true, of course, where adoption has taken place.)

So while keeping the "house-rules" (laws) to perfection doesn't establish the relationship at some point there must be a commitment to the family unit for each member to be part of the "family" in a real sense, one that goes beyond the word. The parent or child who is bent on destroying the relationship or serving a program which is the denial of all that "family" means is begging for exclusion from that family. The denial I'm here speaking of is the denial of foundational values where the word "family" becomes just that, a mere word.

This is true in relation to God and Israel. Flawless obedience to the house-rules didn't create the relationship but a commitment to some foundational truths that shape and guide the "family" we know as Israel was essential to the existence and continuation of the relationship which was grounded in the initiative of a God of love and grace.

"You shall have no other god beside me" is just such a foundational requirement. Without it no relationship could exist between God and Israel.

The relationship which existed between God and Israel was a covenant relationship. While it was initiated and nourished by God's grace, it required Israel's yes to the "image of God" and the kind of attitude, purpose and behavior that would grow from that. This made a relationship with such a God possible. It's generally agreed that the Decalogue expresses the core of how Israel's ethical and religious life would express itself.

Everything we learn about the "ten commandments" marks them out as different from what follows them in the text. (In spite of their exalted status, however, it would be wrong to suggest that the Decalogue was intended as an exhaustive listing of foundational requirements on which life should be based.)

God spoke them, we're told, and added no more (Deuteronomy 5:22). The rest of the laws were given through Moses but these were delivered by the voice of God to all the people.

192

They were stored in "the ark of the covenant" which was placed in the most sacred spot in the camp in the wilderness—the Holy of Holies, in the Tabernacle. Later they were placed in the holiest place in the whole of the land of Canaan, that is, in the sanctuary of the Temple.

They are alluded to again and again as core material in places such as Hosea 4:2, Jeremiah 7:9, Leviticus 19:3-4; Ezekiel 22:1-12.

It certainly appears to be the Decalogue that Jesus is glancing at when he speaks of the two great commandments that summarize the whole law and the prophets (Matt 22). The "two tables" of the Decalogue which speak of Israel's response to God and neighbor are embraced in the "love commandment" by "love God" and then, "love your neighbor". The "sermon on the Mount" treats the Decalogue in a thoroughgoing fashion as something central to the whole Judaic system.

Paul (Romans 13:8-10 and Gal 5:14 where one "word" fulfils the Decalogue's last six "words") treats the "10 Commandments" as something apart and it appears that his Romans 13 echoes Christ's "love commandment". And he doesn't hesitate to use the Decalogue form when calling Christians to behave uprightly and in a way that would place Christ.

All of this and more makes it clear that the Ten Commandments are not peripheral teaching or on a par with many of the cultic rules and regulations. Anyone who thinks Christians have nothing to learn from them and have no need to take them seriously in life needs to think again.

Farrar has a helpful summary of the "two tables" of the Decalogue. Here's what he says, "...the first commandment means, Worship God exclusively; the second, Worship God spiritually; the third, Reverence Him in your words; the fourth, Reverence Him on His day; the fifth, Reverence Him in every form of sacred authority...So that the summary of this first table is that life is worship...turning to the second table, we see that the sixth commandment is the law of kindness; the seventh, the law of purity; the eighth, the law of honesty; the ninth, the law of truthfulness; the tenth, the law of contentment. So that the summary of the second table is that life is love."

Since the covenant is of God, the neighbor's rights under God are only secure as long as God is given his rightful place—hence the first four commandments and "the first great commandment". Under God the neighbor has a right to rest, a right to a secure society, a right to live, a right to own property, a right to justice and a good name, a right to the good will of his/her fellow-citizens of the theocracy. The Decalogue is laid down to secure all these things.

Kaiser and Birch point us to Steve Kaufman's work, which shows that the book of Deuteronomy (12—26) is structured on the basis of the Decalogue. See Birch's chapter 5, "People of the Covenant".

A life in Christ that takes seriously this profound teaching would bring honor to God and itself and blessing to everyone around.

45

YOU WILL HAVE ONE GOD— ME!

Little children keep yourselves from idols. ***1 John 5:21***

Israel's origin, according to the Bible, is the Exodus (with the whole corpus of events connected with it). It was at that point God began the process of fulfilling his promise to Abraham (Acts 7:17). Israel became a nation unto and under Yahweh at that time (Exodus 19:3-8; 24:3-11). The signs and wonders in Egypt were the hand of Yahweh to whom Israel made a covenant commitment and he became their God (Hosea 12:9; 13:4).

This new nation did not create, define nor direct itself. If the Exodus really happened and if the nation's interpretation of it was true, they owed their existence, shape and destiny to Yahweh for no other god stepped in to rescue them or have compassion on them in their dire need (Isa 43:11-12). In light of the words of Moses who contextualized the Exodus, this series of stark historical events were the womb in which Yahweh brought Israel to birth.

When Israel turns to idols she becomes a people without reason! The Exodus couldn't have occurred! Her history is sheer fiction! Or if indeed the events of the Exodus occurred, they were stupidly misinterpreted. Mindless chance conspired to produce the devastating series of events that led to her liberation. She was lucky! A God named Yahweh didn't send Moses—Good Luck did! Moses, if he existed, was deluded. With a brain baked by the sun in the Midianite desert he imagined a divine commission. In from the desert he wandered, this mad dreamer, raving about (what's the name again?), Yahweh. And the irony of it all? By sheer chance, the deliverance he spoke of came true! All this or something like this, Israel must believe in order to turn to idolatry. It becomes a people without sense. Idolatry with its awful lifestyle, as Hosea would have it, makes them brainless (4:11; 7:11).

When Israel turns to idols she becomes a people without roots! Assuming the nation's tradition was in any way true, it clearly isn't true in any way that puts Israel's existence on a sure foundation. In an unknown way she became a nation. If it was just sheer good luck and chance that gave Israel her origin, it could be just sheer bad luck and chance that could destroy her. If Chance "rescued" her then Chance could bury her. Her connection with Yahweh is inextricably tied to those historical events. Deny them and Israel is rootless! Deny them and her origin is shrouded in mystery. Was she ever a slave nation? Did a god ever adopt her? Was she ever delivered from anything?

When Israel turns to idols she becomes a people without a destiny! To deny the Exodus is to deny her election for it is only in the context of history that her (alleged) destiny is brought to light. She is no light-bringer for the world. She is just another of the nations, like her predecessors in Canaan, who for a while cast their shadows on the earth on their way to oblivion. All the power that comes into the lives of those driven by a sense of mission will decay because with no reason to believe she has been chosen and commissioned she will behave as a nation without a mission and begin to drift rather than live, she will begin to rot rather than be salt to the world. Not being shaped by a divine commission, a sense of mission she will be shaped by the restless, drifting nations around her whose national strength, like the desert sands around them, is scattered and dispersed by every passing wind.

46

NO GOD BUT YHWH?

Little children keep yourselves from idols. **1 John 5:21**

Why should Israel have no other God but Yahweh? It was the claim of the Messiah, Jesus of Nazareth (John 17:3) that Yahweh is 'the only true God" and to "know him" was to have eternal life. If we want "eternal life" (as distinct from "endless existence") we will want to "know" God who can and will fill us full of life, real life. A life of honor, joy, nobility and bravery. If Israel wanted to have the quality of life which alone has the right to be called eternal, life which is part of but transcends the temporal and passing phase of things here and now, they will have Yahweh and no other God. The same is true for all of us.

Why should Israel have no other God but Yahweh? Because Yahweh commanded it!

Yes, yes, I've heard the gripe that raw power is a pathetic substitute for persuasion and that appeal is the morally correct way to go, that ordering people around is simply bullying and that a divine bully is no more acceptable than a human one. If all we knew of Yahweh was raw power this gripe would have more to commend it. And if humans were all sweet-spirited people who eagerly listened to persuasion that calls them to honor, justice and compassion, I'm sure God would have more patience with the gripe. But they aren't!

But beyond that, this Yahweh doesn't come to us with his cap in his hand asking for our pity, awkwardly shuffling his feet as he stands at the door of our hearts, timidly, almost apologetically asking us if we will give him the time of day. This is the sovereign Lord of the universe! Whether we like it or not, he comes demanding. A slow and thoughtful reading of Isaiah 40 is an education. We don't negotiate with a God like that—we pay attention or pay the price.

Somewhere in the middle of all this pleading for God that ministers do (and a good thing too!), there must be an announcement that the God who condescends to plead is the one who measures oceans in the hollow of his hand, who puts the mountain ranges on scales and sees the nations as fine dust on a grocer's scales. A God of endless sweetness and light becomes a god of froth and weakness. When the world is quaking beneath our feet, when nations clash in brutal earth-threatening duels, when disease rages across the world, when economic gloom deepens and Man has come to the end of his tether—in a world like that, a world like this one, we need a God big enough and powerful enough. To offer one who comes grovelling, wringing his hands, apologizing for intruding into our lives, a weakling who fears the criticism of the latest psychological or sociological fad—to offer one like that is monstrous. Well, whether we will or we won't, whether we like his message or not, God, however unfathomable his love for us, doesn't come crawling!

A God without judicial anger, a God who whimpers, a God who is at the mercy of every individual on the planet, a God who is straight-jacketed by the latest pop-psychology or the current number one on the bookshelves calling us to "self-actualization"—a God like that is no good to us. More to the point—*that's not the one we've got!* The one who buried rebellious Egypt that he might bless the world through Israel is the one we've got to deal with. Thou shalt have no other gods before me!

And this may be Torah, but it isn't merely advice! Or wise counsel! Or simply "for our own good". This is command!

"You will have a God;

Me and no other!"

47

NO GOD BUT YHWH? (2)

Little children keep yourselves from idols. **1 John 5:21**

Why should Israel have no God but Yahweh? Because he commanded it! And however we balance that truth with the other truths, we aren't to ignore or deny it.

But Israel was to have no other God but Yahweh because he earned that place!

This was no stranger! (Well, not wholly a stranger.) This was no unknown quantity! (Well, at least not completely unknown.) This God had acted on their behalf. They had been a handful when they entered Egypt. They were hungry and all at sea. An awful famine had hit the world and God arranged a refuge for them. While there he had blessed them (Exodus 1:7, cf. Genesis 1:28) and when their host nation (who owed them so much—as so many host nations do today to those aliens they allowed to settle in their land) turned against them this God had come to their rescue and was leading them to a home of their own which he had been preparing for them for centuries. This God had shown his love to them and their fathers.

If to others he was unknown (see Exodus 5:2), if to others he had not been gracious—though he had been gracious to all, even when they didn't know it—if to others he had not been gracious, he had been so to Israel. Who else had cared for them when they were hungry? The gods of Egypt? The gods of Canaan? Who had come to their aid when murderous minds hatched plans to smother them? Who cared that whips cracked over their backs and they were made no better than beasts of burden? Who would they put in his place?

If they had delivered themselves things might be different. If they had plotted rebellion and Joshua or someone like him had killed the guards, seized the palace, defeated the Egyptian armies in battle by wise strategies, brave rushes and daring deeds—if that's how their history had been we would have a different picture. Then they might have said to this Yahweh who came demanding: "You will have a God; Me and no other!"—they might have said to him: "Where were you when we needed you? Where were you when we called for you—for anyone? You wait until we by our own power and courage have delivered ourselves and now you come claiming we should recognize and serve you? Away, we are our own saviors and have no need of you!"

Such a temptation is real! Never more real than in modern times. Was there ever been a time when people felt more sure that they strive alone against the universe, the disease, evil and want that exists in the universe? Who finds the medicine to cure the disease? Who comes up with the social reforms that feed the poor? Who discovers the natural resources to feed, warm and clothe humanity? Man does, humanity by itself does! And should we now allow some God or other to step in and claim the right to be worshiped when we have answered our own prayers? Rescued, enlightened, secured and nourished ourselves? We see no God rescuing us! We see ourselves with our own brain and brawn doing it all. If we worship at all—we will worship ourselves!

We're more tempted to think this way when we're well and prospering. The temptation to believe we're our own deliverers is so intense and when we are involved (even under God) in our own rescue we often shut him out. Because the thoughts occur in us, because the wonderful dreams occur in us, because the brilliant discoveries become known to us, because the sharp eyes and steady hands belong to us we often believe that God has not been behind and in the uncovering of the theories and the discoveries.

And the temptation can often—not always—be more severe on those who languish in suffering, unblessed by the Western advances and discoveries, and so they are led to curse the gods they believe in and despise themselves for believing in any gods at all. Yahweh knows about all this and Yahweh knows how to right all wrongs and defend his own reputation. But whatever these endlessly hurting people say, whatever the "enlightened" westerners say—Israel wasn't part of them!

They had experienced rescue. They had seen his hand at work. They had felt the utter helplessness of a nation without military or economic power. They had known desperation and despair. Then came Yahweh! He cursed the gods of Egypt and punished the power of Egypt and led the slaves to freedom, calling them—wonder of wonders—"my son". When Yahweh said, You will have me as God and no other! they knew they hadn't saved themselves, they knew they hadn't been utterly abandoned and they knew that Yahweh had earned the right to claim their exclusive allegiance. And Christians? What shall they say?

...in response to his faithfulness and his gracious past rescue and future promises, they gave their word!

48

NO GOD BUT YAHWEH? (3)

Little children keep yourselves from idols. **1 John 5:21**

Why should Israel have no God but Yahweh? *Because he commanded it.* It was a non-negotiable demand from the Sovereign of the Universe. *Because he had earned the right to that position.* Who else was worthy?

But despite his awesome power and majesty and despite the fact that he had earned their trust, Yahweh still put it to them in such a way that they must choose to say yes to his covenant offer and they did (20:19 and Deuteronomy 5:27).

Israel should have no other God than Yahweh because they said they would!

They gave their word. In response to the majesty and awesome power of God, in response to his faithfulness and his gracious past rescue and future promises, they gave their word! And because they gave their word they should stick with it. To do that was to do what was right. They owed him and they said they would pay. They didn't bribe him or he them; he hadn't freed them from Pharaonic slavery to make them wheedling and servile crawlers to him. He called them openly and was willing to receive their heartfelt commitment (cf. Deuteronomy 5:27-28) even when he knew their limitations. And they gave it!

"Duty" has become a dirty word in some circles. In the religious realm it has had such a connection with legalism than one hardly dare mention the word without expecting a raking over the coals of criticism. "Never mind duty, let's talk of grace." Because of the heresy of legalism a fine word, and a noble conception has been made an outlaw. Anyone who would make "duty" the ultimate for the life of a disciple of God misses the mark, misses it by a long way but anyone who has so "matured" as to despise duty has missed by a long way too.

It's all right to recognize that we owe and because we owe we feel the debt and wish to respond in kind. We wish to earn nothing for grace and our own evil have put that out of the question but we don't want teachers to rob us of the "hero in our soul"; don't want them to rob us of the deep sense of obligation we feel when we give our word; don't want them to steal from us that motivation which at some level of our lives and in some areas of living never vanishes— "I gave my word and therefore it is my duty". No one will say that "duty" is the only or finest motivation for our behavior but we get weary when we hear people becoming too precise and too sophisticated when describing real humans. If we were God we would do thus and so for thus and so reasons; but we are not God, we are we and sometimes we act out of motivations which, while they aren't the highest, they aren't evil. We need to stand in our place and do what we said we would do whether we have the consent of our emotions or not. A black poet of years ago hit it dead-center when he wrote:

There's a king and a captain high
And he's coming by and by
And he'll find me hoeing cotton when he comes.
You can hear his legions charging in the regions of
the sky
And he'll find me hoeing cotton when he comes.

There's a man they thrust aside
Who was tortured till he died,
And he'll find me hoeing cotton when he comes.
He was hated and rejected
He was scorned and crucified
And he'll find me hoeing cotton when he comes.
He'll be crowned by saints and angels when he comes.
They'll be shouting out Hosanna to the man that men
denied
And I'll kneel among my cotton when he comes.
No one will (or should) gain our respect who while he rightly
proclaims God's full and free grace without apology
undermines what we feel in our bones is right: Love doesn't
despise the letter of the law—it fulfils it.

...he was offering God who is

their life. Nothing less than

God himself, his living

presence with them,

is what he offers

49

GOD OR THE WIZARD OF OZ?

*Even to your old age and gray hairs I am he, I am he who will sustain you. I have made you and I will carry you; I will sustain you and I will rescue you. **Isaiah 46:4***

Having Yahweh as their one God was not negotiable; the God who said this commanded it and he had earned the right to command it. At the time Israel gave their word, whatever their personal and national limitations, they meant it (Deuteronomy 5:27-29). At a national Level they later reneged but their initial commitment was sincere—at least it appears that God thought so.

Connected with all of that but going beyond it, *Israel should have no other God but Yahweh because otherwise it was self-ruin.* God was thinking of them when he laid down this law. It was to their advantage he spoke. He narrowed them to the worship and service of one God (himself), not to narrow their lives but to deepen, enrich and ennoble them. Just prior to leaving them, Moses assures them (Deuteronomy 31:19-20), "This day I call heaven and earth as witnesses against you that I have set before you life and death, blessings and curses. Now choose life, so that you and your children may live and that you may love the Lord your God, listen to his voice, and hold fast to him. *For the Lord is your life...*" I've emphasized the last phrase to make the point that Moses wasn't just offering life, he was offering *God* who is their life. Nothing less than God himself, his living presence with them, is what he offers. The blessings that would result would be signs of his personal Presence with and among them and continuing indicators of his character and his purposes toward and through them. No wonder we hear God musing, as it were, in Moses' presence, "Oh that their hearts would be inclined to fear me and keep all my commands always, so that it might go well with them and their children forever" (Deuteronomy 5:29). See Isa 48:18-19.

Was he capable of giving them freedom? Capable of feeding and clothing them? Capable of protecting them? Capable of ennobling them? Had he not shown it even before he thunders out "No One But Me"? And was he willing to do all these things? To continue to do all these things? Had he not kept his word to the patriarchs?

Why wouldn't they then gladly give him exclusive allegiance? Who else would they go to? They would worship someone! That was never in doubt. But who would they worship? The Egyptian gods that determined and rejoiced in their enslaved state? The gods they saw judged in Egypt? The gods Yahweh would judge in Canaan? And when moderns smile at all this and dismiss worship as a weak man's choice, have they ceased to worship? Is intellectual/moral/spiritual anarchy better than Yahweh? Have the Hedonists who worship ease and pleasure offered us better? Have the Existentialists who worship choice improved on Yahweh's offer? "Will you go away also?" asked the Christ. Said Peter, "Lord, where would we go. You only have the words of life eternal". No, if they're going to talk us out of serving our Lord, they're going to have to offer something better.

There were those who fought their way through tough times and down painful roads, making their way bravely to their central shrine, their citadel—and found it empty, deserted, dusty, weed-grown. They had heard the word, "Lo here, lo there...here is God, there is God, that is God" and they were deceived. They hadn't heard the word: I AM GOD! Like Dorothy and her friends, they followed a yellow-brick road, half-afraid, half-believing. They saw the smoke, heard the boom, the awesome voice, were fittingly frightened but when the curtain was thrown back, they found themselves thrown back on themselves. Their future hung on a dithering little man who had nothing more than a dithering little man has to offer. How can we do it, century after century? Humanity continues to patrol the graveyards looking for a Savior.

"There is no God apart from me, a righteous God and a Savior; there is none but me. Turn to me and be saved, all you ends of the earth; for I am God, and there is none other" (Isaiah 45:21-22).

The second commandment

forbids the making of images

and likenesses.

50

NO GRAVEN IMAGES

For all the gods of the nations are idols. **Psalm 96:5**

The first commandment despite the general terms in which it's couched commands that Israel have YHWH and no god but YHWH. It didn't matter at that point whether Israel was monotheistic in the full sense of the word, whether there were gods or lords many, Israel was to worship one, and one only.

The second commandment (Exodus 20:4f) forbids the making of images and likenesses. It seems clear in light of the instructions given in the building of the Tabernacle that this prohibition was not an absolute, since God instructed them to make likenesses of various things. No, it wasn't sculpture or art that was being forbidden, it was sculpture or art with a view to worship by means of it. "You shall not bow down yourself to them nor serve them" seems to confirm that.

Any form of polytheism would subsequently be put to rest and so any idolatry which would be in the service of any other gods (presuming they existed) would be condemned. But what was wrong with making an image to "represent" YHWH and use it as a

213

"point of contact" through which to worship YHWH? It isn't difficult to ignore the scriptures themselves and come up with "ideas" and argue from there but maybe God's objections to the making of images and bowing to them can only be discerned from the Bible itself. Just the same, whether we can deduce the good reasons behind the prohibition or not, God did forbid them. So while it can't be a bad thing to seek God's reasoning on the matter, it would serve Israel well to obey even if they don't fully understand.

But because "blind obedience" is not characteristic of God's call to serve him maybe the incident of the "Golden Calf" (Exodus 32) can give us some clues as to why it is a wise prohibition.

Idols are the creation of humans.

Idols depend on the worshipers for their movement and power.

Idols are under the control of the worshipers.

Idols (images) identify the god with natural/physical forces.

Idols locate the god and promote rival sanctuaries and so division.

Idols in some sense controlled the god.

Idols in some way confined the god—limitation and immanence. Consider how actual animals became manifestations of the gods.

It's clear from these observations (which seem well grounded) that whatever god it is that idols reflect—it isn't the God of Israel. There seems no getting away from it that the use and worship of images promotes and defines a god other than the God we"re confronted with in the Bible therefore the God of the Bible who is a jealous God (Exodus20:5) will not tolerate their existence or use in worship.

51

IN IT THOU SHALT DO NO "WORK"

But the seventh day is a Sabbath to the Lord your God.
Exodus 20:16

"Remember the Sabbath day to keep it holy; in it you shall do no work..." There! That's plain enough. Is it? And what does "work" mean? Any physical activity! So people had to lie prone during the Sabbath?

A farmer was forbidden to plow or harvest on the Sabbath (Exodus 34:21) and merchants were chastised by Nehemiah for trading on the Sabbath (13:15-22) even though guards *worked* to enforce non-trading (19,22). Jeremiah (17:19-27, esp. 22) opposed the carrying of a burden on the Sabbath (compare John 5:10 and elsewhere in the NT).

A "worker" who did the bulk of his work in his head and with words, gaining and exchanging information, would he have been allowed to "work" on the Sabbath? Let's compare a farmer with, say, a stockbroker who lies watching the TV information or reading the newspaper for material germane to his business or 'discussing business" with friends to gain insights or close deals.

Here's a doctor who works at healing people for a living. Someone with an ailment wants cured; someone with a serious ailment wants cured, someone with an excruciatingly painful (though not life-threatening) ailment wants cured. Is he allowed to heal them on the Sabbath? Here is someone with a life-threatening ailment, is it permissible to heal him on the Sabbath? (Compare NT instances of people watching to see if Jesus would heal on the Sabbath.)

Well, obviously everyone knows that the commandment isn't to be followed in a life-threatening situation. Where do we get this "obviously"? You shall do no work on the Sabbath!

What if the situation is a family-threatening situation? What if the storm is coming that will destroy the farmer's crop and put his family in the workhouse? Is he allowed to harvest the crop on the Sabbath?

The people put their animals to work for the family. The ox to tread corn, the donkey to carry burdens and the chicken to provide eggs. You shall do no work on the Sabbath, neither you nor your animals. The ox is tethered in the sun, the donkey has fallen in the ditch and the chicken has just laid an egg—all on the Sabbath. Can the ox be led to shade, the donkey rescued from the ditch? Can one lawfully eat an egg laid on the Sabbath?

Charges of nit-picking make no sense to those who are serious about the command. These are serious issues! This is a question of breaking or not breaking one of the ten commandments given by the voice of God. "Be careful to do what the Lord your God has commanded you; do not turn to the right or to the left."

Whatever else is true, the word "work" needs interpretation! The Jewish debates down the centuries were debates by people who were serious about their relationship to God and this God of theirs was an earnest God!

But if God was so earnest, why were things left undefined? Why wasn't an exhaustive blueprint given? Why was debate necessitated? What if people, well-meaning and deeply committed people interpreted incorrectly? What if the rank and file, who depended on the teachers in Israel, unknowingly accepted a wrong interpretation? Desperately seeking to please him they seek the wisest counsel and are misled. What then? Why wasn't work exhaustively defined?

Or is there something more basic, more important, than always having the precise understanding of the rules?

Yahweh created, shaped, harmonized and blessed creation—including the human race—in six days and ceased

52

THE LORD RESTED THE SEVENTH DAY

Israel's week was laid out as it is—like a creation week!
Every week had the same pattern—work six days
and rest one. Creation was remembered.

Why did God require Sabbath observance of Israel? (The question could just as truthfully be framed, Why did God give Israel the Sabbath?) There was more than one reason, as numerous texts make clear. As recorded here in 20:8-11, it is related to creation and God's work in creation.

Yahweh created, shaped, harmonized and blessed creation—including the human race—in six days and ceased. On the seventh day he "rested and was refreshed". Because that was the case, God blessed and made holy the seventh day. The question as to when he made it holy (the creation week or at the beginnings of his work with Israel) is a matter for another time, that he blessed it and made it holy is expressly said.

Yahweh worked six days and showed by resting the seventh day that all had been done, all had been provided and all pleased him (Genesis 1:31-2:3).

The creation (including humanity) did not create itself; it did not perfect itself or cause itself to flourish. It was God who said, "Let..." and it was so. Wherever one would look, land, seas, sky, fields, flocks, even a specific area—the garden (Genesis 2:8)—all of it, the completed work of God. Unaided by anyone or anything, the sole creator and blesser was Yahweh. The humans arrived where they were and enjoyed all the blessings of where they were as a result of the loving labor of someone other than themselves.

This is why Israel's week was laid out as it is—like a creation week! Every week had the same pattern—work six days and rest one. Creation was remembered. No, *the Creator* was acknowledged and proclaimed. They were to act out the conduct of God and remember that their very existence under God, their blessed state in a blessed environment is the work of him who created them. They have their place of fellowship with God because of God's creative activity, their prosperity and blessedness because God (without their help) provided for them. In this truth they were to rejoice!

Israel was given a pre-covenant rehearsal of this in chapter 16. Without their help and in the face of their total dependence God provided what they could not provide for themselves. Everything about the manna supply is geared to convict Israel of their utter dependence and the needlessness of worrying. The great Provider does and will provide. He rested only on the seventh day because he had done all that was necessary to create and sustain his creation. The seventh day makes that point with great plainness and the rules about gathering manna underscored it. They gathered and ate under strict provisions and when they tried to "manage" or control the supply out of fear or greed it became wormy.

For Israel the Sabbath is a grand confession that they owe all to Yahweh and have no need to be anxious or shoulder the concerns of tomorrow.

The God who ten times said, "Let..." in Genesis 1 as he exercised himself in loving creation spoke ten words at Sinai in Exodus 20 and creates again. (See the use of the language of creation applied to Israel and her environment in the prophets and in relation to Israel's experience with God in the wilderness.)

We are reminded often of the truth that Israel is a new beginning, another Adam—who only came to full and obedient disclosure in Israel's Messiah, Jesus of Nazareth. And it isn't difficult to see that Israel is a model of mankind as a whole (in blessing and curse, in success and failure). Israel was to instruct the nations of the world and lead them into life and blessing with Yahweh.

In joyfully keeping the Sabbath and devoting it to God, they were not only making their own confession they were speaking to the world. The message of the Sabbath, looking at it from a creation angle, is as much for mankind as it is for Israel. So, in that respect, whether it was sanctified for Israel or mankind as a positive ordinance might not matter very much. The truth it taught to Israel is a truth it teaches through Israel to humanity.

Repeatedly Israel has to be warned that God is the provider; that they were to eat and enjoy his blessings on his terms and to devote the seventh day to him as a witness to all this.

Sounds easy. But what if it is Friday, the harvest is still not in and a storm is gathering which will destroy the crop by Sunday? What if there are debts which must be paid and can only be paid by this harvest? What if, when Israel becomes more and more a nation of merchants, there's a deal which must be but isn't quite completed and the Sabbath is coming on? The family's immediate future hangs in the balance—what then?

Should they have said, "the Sabbath is made for man, not the man for the Sabbath"? Should they have developed a caring community that when the storm came or the critical moment for the deal was missed that the honest people were taken care of by their creditors or their neighbors? What if carers were a scarce commodity?

The Sabbath was God's gift to Israel but even as it was Israel's, it was the Lord's Sabbath

53

THIS SHALL BE A SIGN

*Remember that you were slaves...Therefore the Lord your God
has commanded you to observe the Sabbath day.*
Deuteronomy 5:15

The Sabbath pointed Israel back to her divine origin. Exodus 31:13 says, "You must observe my Sabbaths. This will be a sign between me and you for the generations to come so you may know that I am the Lord, who makes you holy." So you may know. There's the purpose clause.

As they rejoiced and rested they were given the chance to absorb the truth that Yahweh, not some god or other, some army or other, some stratagem or other, some hero or other, redeemed and blessed them. No, Yahweh made them different. It wasn't their brains or brawn that made them different from every other nation on earth—it was Yahweh.

The Sabbath was God's gift to Israel (compare Exodus 16:29) but even as it was Israel's, it was the Lord's Sabbath (31:13— "my" Sabbaths). All space, all life and all time are the Lord's. When he

223

chooses to take to himself some portion of that all it stands as a witness that all belongs to him. Whether it is the firstborn of animals, the firstfruits of crops, a piece of ground, a number of special priests from among a nation of priests or a particular nation among all the nations of the earth (cf. Exodus 19:5). Numerous texts affirm this. See Leviticus 23:3; Isaiah 58:13 as two examples from many.

But in this text, the Sabbath functions as a witness to the relationship between Israel and God, a sign of the covenant, of their election and consequent holiness. In Sabbath morning liturgy, concerning the Sabbath, devout Jews pray,

"For thou has chosen us and sanctified us above all the nations, in love and favor has given us thy holy Sabbath as an inheritance...You did not give it to the nations of the earth, nor did you make it the heritage of idolaters, nor in its rest will unrighteous men find a place. But to Israel your people you have given it in love, to the seed of Jacob whom you have chosen, to that people who sanctify the Sabbath day."

Such a prayer shows a fine sense of appreciation for their heritage. (I don't think, by the way, that's there anything "anti-Gentile" about it. I don't see why distinctively Christian prayers should be viewed by Jews, as it is by some, as anti-Semitic.)

The Sabbath marks Israel out as a "having-been-given-rest" people. A people whose rest was given and a people whose rest was given by Yahweh with whom they were in covenant.

There is great power in ritual and ordinances. They draw people together into a community with the power that that fellowship brings. Isolated individuals are weaker than the community, the faith of an individual is more likely to swing from one extreme to another. To be part of a community is to make the history of that people one's own. Its ordinances and rituals remind each person that their identity is bound up with the identity of the community.

The Christian community knows what this means when they think of people being immersed into union with their living Lord and sharing their Lord when they engage in Holy Communion. Christians are marked out as different from other decent and upright people by the faith they confess and commit to and this Faith is reflected in the ordinances just mentioned. A weakness in the view of many who practice believer's baptism is that they view it too much from the angle of an individual personal response (which it is and must be). It's Community aspect is often missed. It's as though baptism (immersion) was nothing more than a matter for the individual—it is not!

The Sabbath and Sabbath observance, above all other things, Jews tell us, are the marks of their difference from the rest of the nations. Circumcision was a once-in-a-lifetime act, the Passover once a year, the Sabbatical Year every seven—these are unlike the weekly Sabbath and don't have for the devout Jew anything like the power of the weekly Sabbath. Temple worship required a specific place but the Sabbath could be observed anywhere. A reading of the literature on the Sabbath from a Jewish viewpoint is enlightening indeed.

Biblically, the Sabbath is a sign of Israel's election by the God who creates, reveals, redeems and blesses.

"I'm glad you asked, have a seat and let me tell you a story..."

54

YOU WERE SLAVES IN EGYPT

Remember that you were slave and that the Lord your God brought you out of there with a mighty hand...Therefore the Lord your God has commanded you to observe the Sabbath day.
Deuteronomy 5:15

Israel had multiplied in Egypt and a fearful ruler had begun to enslave and exploit them (Exodus 1). For at least eighty years they were under the threat of the Egyptian power, working at hard-labor seven days a week and watched over by task-masters who weren't reluctant to whip the workers. Centuries of alienation and generations of oppression came to an end when the God of the powerless strode into Egypt with a man called Moses as his representative.

Now they're in the plains of Moab, just about to enter the long-awaited land they would call home (Deuteronomy 1:1) and Moses preaches the covenant in their hearing.

"Remember that you were slaves in Egypt and that the Lord your God brought you out of there with a mighty hand and an outstretched arm. Therefore the Lord your God has commanded you to observe the Sabbath day." (Deuteronomy 5:15)

They had been enslaved and God rescued them, therefore (and that's why) they were given and were to keep the Sabbath.

A stranger to an unenlightened Jew, "I see you have a lot of things needing fixed and done and I see your servants and your family sit around doing nothing. Why is that?"

Unenlightened Jew: "That's just another of the rules handed down to us from above. Rules are rules. We do it because we're told to do it and that's that."

That'll hardly do. A stranger to an enlightened Jew, "How is it you don't work today even when there is so much to do?"

Enlightened Jew: "I'm glad you asked, have a seat and let me tell you a story..." And he would tell the stranger that once the people had lived in a land of bondage where they were worked like animals, seven days a week, with never a rest. They had cried unto the Lord and the Lord had come to their defense and rescue. "We rejoice in a day of rest," he might say, "because it is God's gift to us, his gracious gift to us. And each day of rest reminds us of a time when we were defenseless and exploited and were given no rest. And as we rest and enjoy the freedom from toil, we remember who it is that freed us and give him our thanks by giving this day to him."

"And your servants and animals?" the stranger might ask.

"The God who rescued us from a life of slavery when we had no rest would not be pleased with anyone who worked people or animals without rest. Why, then, we would become the slavers and tyrants who crushed us until we begged for deliverance from injustice and enslavement. This God, Yahweh is his name, won't tolerate tyranny from us or anyone else."

It is enough that God commands something to be done for us to know it much have great benefit attached though it isn't always necessary to see precisely what he has in mind. The lover of God will obey but the lover of God will also seek the spirit behind the rule that he or she might drink of it and be shaped by it. Not to seek the heart behind the rule is sub-Christian as well as sub-Judaic.

55

HONOR THY FATHER AND THY MOTHER

Honor your father and your mother. **Exodus 20:12**

I t's a lovely commonplace to hear writers, from ancient times up to now, remind us that under God, the authority invested and acknowledged to be in parents is the beginning and source of all other authority in the world around us.

And how damaging, how damning these philosophical and consequent sociological theories about "universal human rights" and how to achieve them have proved to be. This benevolent bungling is killing the West—no, it's killing people!

When belief in the gods began to weaken in ancient Greece, endless debate, cynicism and sophistry became the order of the day. In France, the motto of the revolutionaries was "equality, fraternity and liberty" but a "reign of terror" and anarchy developed. The loss of a universally recognized authority has terrible results even if the authority has not been particularly benevolent. (Which would be fiercely debated by those in some non-Western countries. For cases like those there are other truths which must be told but only those in the West who are subjected to that kind of crass governmental violence have a right to protest this: Anarchy is even worse than bad government.)

God has been rejected as the supreme moral governor in the West and morality, for various reasons, has been severed from revealed religion. In its place we were offered a rational (non-religious or non-revelational) basis for moral authority which even those who offered it, when they offered it, knew—it can't and won't and doesn't work. (See the confessions of men like Russell, Sartre and Nietzsche and Kaufmann.)

But if 'moral authority" cannot be established then the authority of parents over children (or teacher over pupils) cannot be established.

That's where governments step in. Their honorable aim is to ensure that every person gets full "human rights" and so, to maximize the personhood of every human, they introduce "citizens charter" legislation. They stress that under them everyone is equally a citizen and therefore has a right to what everyone else has a right to. The government will see to it that each citizen has an equal voice and equal share in whatever is available.

A citizen is a product of "the state" and since 'the state" (duly elected in democratic countries) has authority over all the citizens, it has the right to make decisions about parent/child (and all other) relationships because these are first and foremost—citizens.

Of course the State has no moral authority, its authority is legal. In addition to this, it is contractual authority. It has been given to them and can be withdrawn from them if the citizens see fit. Those citizens who reject the will of the majority of the citizens, as expressed by the government, are penalized (imprisoned or fined and so forth).

This rejection of God as the supreme moral governor (and the Bible as his special instrument for his special People for making that God known) has resulted in the creation of a Western society of citizens who are all equal in the eyes of the law and whose relationship hinges on contractual authority rather than moral. Across the table from each other at breakfast each morning are fellow-citizens.

The well-meaning government, following the latest fashion in psychological, political and sociological theory, wishing to abolish the abuse of children (and parents!) and to secure for children (and parents!) the best possible family, does what? Does what? It abolishes the family in all but name and creates citizens!

We put the parent/child (and all other relationships) under the authority of the government. In this way we deny authority to parents over children. The government will allow the parents great freedom in this area, of course. This is due to the government's inability to do for the child-citizen all that needs done and because it is incapable of enforcing many laws it might like to enact. But in a home like this, what authority parents have is "contractual" and "legal". It is given or withdrawn depending on how the child sees the parent fulfilling his/her needs and wants.

To deny and dismiss moral authority while depending on the citizens to possess and exercise lovely moral qualities makes no sense. Even civil contracts (say, between a builder and a house-buyer) can only be "honored" if there is honor in both parties. The government can (and should) punish the covenant-breaker, of course, but it can't force him to keep the covenant so it depends on him to possess and express the qualities of honor and justice.

The way to gain voluntary submission is to encourage and nurture the qualities which lead us to want to submit to the needs and rights of others as well as our own and that's where "honor your father and mother" comes in with peculiar power.

If we stress that each person is a "citizen", that the government is "by the people and for the people" and that there is no universal moral standard we are inviting people to moral, social and psychological "individualism" that breeds social fragmentation and selfishness. The groundwork is laid for parent/child and teacher/student problems.

The parents may grow frustrated with the "child-citizen" who does what he wants, when he wants and insists on claiming his legal rights. The teacher may become frustrated with the "student-citizen" who tirelessly questions his/her authority. Both parent and teacher when they lose the heart for the task which really calls for loving commitment offer only the legal minimum.

If we should add to that a strong emphasis in school, college and university teaching that "self-fulfillment", "self-actualization", "self-esteem" and "self-awareness" are the central needs of the "citizens" then we have a recipe for increasing tragedy. If we are convinced that there is no universal moral law and that the only authority over us is the authority we decide to give (because it's in our interests), and if we"re convinced that the central need of humans is to be self-fulfilled how could we honor father or mother muchless become "other aware"?

[This piece does not intend to deny that the People of God live under a peculiar covenant with God in the Lord Jesus. The speech in this pieceabout a "universal moral law" needs development and clarification.]

56

NOT MERELY OUR NEIGHBORS

*Honor your father and your mother. **Exodus 20:12***

One of England's most eloquent preachers of any generation, F.W. Farrar, reminded his hearers a long time ago, "Our parents are not merely our neighbors; they stand to us in a unique, in a divine, relation." He saw the need of this reminder well over a hundred and fifty years ago but, as sensitive as he was to the world's pain and loss, I wonder if he would not have gone out of his mind if he had seen what has happened to the 20th and 21st century societies?

There is a brand of pious twaddle that says we should relate to all people alike. If we have Christian love (agape), we're assured, no one will mean more to us than another because we are to love everyone in the same way. Agape, you see, is the great leveller and obliterates the distinction between our families and the world at large, all relationships are homogenized. How like Christ, it is said to be, to love and feel toward all people what we feel toward our families.

We're assured the relationship with brothers and sisters in Christ goes deeper than the relationship with our flesh and blood families. Without doubt! And we move from that truth to muddy the waters. Our parents are set out there in the crowd, on the same level as our nodding acquaintances or casual friends and even strangers, people on the other side of the world we've never even seen much less met.

Didn't the Christ, we're told, repudiate his mother and family when he said his family were "those who do the will of my Father" (Matt 12:48-50)? And with half-baked notions of precisely what he had in mind we obliterate what God not only created but jealously guards—the family structure. Jesus taught us that we cannot appreciate our earthly (but divinely-given) family structure until we see it within the context of our relationship to the heavenly Father from whom every family in heaven and on earth is named. But in teaching us this he wasn't undermining the family—he was securing it!

Of course we're not to exalt our physical/blood/social ties above those we have in God through Christ! But it doesn't follow from that that there are no blood/social/familial ties. One of the crimes laid against the sinful world in Romans 1 was that it lacked "natural affection" ('storge"—v.31). That is, the tender feeling and disposition which humankind, with good reason, has come to expect from parents toward children and children toward parents (cf. 2 Tim 3:3).

It is witless nonsense to regard parents as just another two neighbors. A parent is a neighbor but not just another neighbor. They are not "my peers"; not just my friends; not "my pals" in that ugly egalitarian way in which all wise, healthy and wonderful distinctions are dismissed as old fashioned, or worse, unjust. Even pathetic Stalin who initiated the destruction of family ties to suit his political and personal agendas soon realized that without healthy parental/child relationships there was no affection and therefore no moral authority. And without moral authority there is moral anarchy and society becomes ungovernable. The immoral scoundrel changed his tactics.

I've no doubt whatever that there are families where the children can call their parents by their first names without serious damage to the family. Of course! But they have to be the exceptions to the rule. "I don't want you as my girl-friend," one daughter sobbed to a mother who offered herself as that for years, thinking she was very modern and up to date with the latest pop-psychology, "I want a mother!" Do we have to pretend we're all on the same level, all equal in every possible sense of the word, all equally, intimately related, for us to have a just and joyous world?

Do we really think we raise the level of affection in the world by undermining the affection we feel for our parents in particular? Do we really think we raise the level of submission to wise and compassionate authority by downgrading the wise and loving authority of our primary authority figures—parents? Isn't it true that it's by seeing how loving fathers live affectionately and justly with the mothers that children learn how to live with their husbands or wives? Isn't it by lovingly honoring our own mothers and fathers as we honor no others that we can understand how others feel about their parents? Isn't it in such a relationship of loving respect, humble submission to wiser people that sympathy, humility and tenderness is spread throughout the world? They are not merely our neighbors!

We can't help but love our parents and children above all other parents and children and we shouldn't be made to doubt that that is as it should be. What nonsense it is to undermine, in the name of Christ or Scripture, the uniqueness of our family relationships and substitute for them a vague humanitarianism toward everyone. Not only will it not work—we aren't built that way—it wasn't meant to work—He didn't make us that way.

In a peculiar way he calls us to "honor thy father and mother"

"so that you may live long in the land the Lord your God is giving you"

57

HONOR THEM BECAUSE...

Honor your father and your mother. **Exodus 20:12**

G.K. Chesterton said that if democracy reminds us that every person has a right to a hearing from us because he/she is our brother or sister, tradition reminds us that those who went before us have a right to a hearing from us because they are our mothers and fathers.

In this commandment to honor our fathers and mothers we move (but not really) from our responsibility toward God, set out in the first four commandments, to our responsibility toward our fellow-humans, laid out in the final six.

Here, said Paul, is the first commandment with a promise attached—"so that you may live long in the land the Lord your God is giving you". The promise has a peculiar force for Israel and the land of Canaan but it's still interesting that God didn't append this promise to each of the commandments. It's easy to give good educated guesses as to why that's so, but in the end, that's what they are, "guesses". But not wild guesses.

It isn't hard to see that when people sink so low as to despise loving and wise parents they are rotting at the core. If there is no "natural affection", perversion has set in, reprobation is on the way. If a house built on sand or a nation built on dirt cannot stand, neither can a world built on scorn and despising. No matter how rich or educated or acclaimed a man, if he has despised wise and loving parents he is a dead-beat, a loser and we can stamp FAILURE across his life and chisel it on his tombstone. And where a nation has become characterized by its refusal to honor its aged, its fathers and mothers, the rot will lead to ultimate loss of all that we call blessed in life; home, family, contentment, security, peace and hope.

Land being what it is in the OT meant more to Israel than most of us. It was a symbol as well as real estate, it was a sign as well as turf, it was a sacrament as well as a location. If Israel would show itself to be a nation of righteous, loving men and women, sons and daughters under Yahweh, living with God in the land God gave them, it would be seen with special clarity in how it treated its parents. And if they showed themselves faithful to Yahweh in this way then they would indeed be a sign to the nations around of the reign (kingdom) of Yahweh. To honor their parents would not only bring glory to God, it would bring honor to themselves and a prolonging of their days in the land of Canaan. When they began to dishonor and despise their parents it would be a sign of their corruption and the beginning of their exile from the land. If the degree of their wickedness became so pronounced that they no longer reflected the reign of Yahweh he would remove them from the land.

The temptation to the young and strong to despise their aging parents who are being left behind by technology and the information explosion is an ancient one. It isn't for nothing that we hear Israel warned over and over again against despising or dishonoring their parents (Ex 21:15,17; Deuteronomy 27:16 are examples).

And what is it to honor them? It means to esteem and prize them. To view them as people of substance and "weight". The

238

Hebrew word has a wide range of meaning. It is used (Childs reminds us) of a right response to God (Psalms 86:9), a response that is close to worship and in the Leviticus 19:3 call, Israel is told to "reverence" or "revere" (NAS,RSV,NEB) the parents, using a word normally reserved for God. Some of Christ's most scathing words are reserved for those who undermined this command to revere or honor parents (Matt 15:3-9).

But what if our parents are not honorable? If we owe someone something, it is still a debt even if that person is a drunkard. And difficult as it might be, the consciousness of our own sins should keep us from being 'too" judgmental.

Honor your parents because you have learned more than you have discovered. Honor your parents because they have shown you how to love your family and friends. Honor your parents because they introduced you to the love of God, the Bible, the Church and humanity. Honor your parents because only they are there all the time to live with your changes, your moods, your selfishness and whatever else you are afflicted with. Honor your parents by gently but firmly opposing the dishonorable things that are part of them. Honor your parents because on top of all that, God said, Honor your parents!

Honor your parents because before long they aren't going to be around for you to honor.

"Think how closely your earthly parent takes after that Divine Father..."

58

THE IMAGE OF GOD IN PARENTS

Honor your father and your mother. **Exodus 20:12**

In giving us the genealogy of Jesus, Luke takes us all the way back to Adam, "the son of God" (2:33). God was the father of Adam and Eve and he (as it were) "begat" children in his own image. Though the OT rejects the idea that God is the Father of anyone in any biological or mythological sense, it does speak of him as Father to elected people (Mal 1:6; 2:10) and it implies this of elected persons (such as kings—see Psalms 2:7). The twin ideas of God's "fatherhood" and "creator-hood" occur again and again in the later Isaiah chapters and Mal 2:10 asks: "Have we not all one Father? Did not one God create us?" When God created humans, he didn't simply create "creatures"; he created 'sons" and 'daughters" so the ideas of creation and fatherhood are closely associated in God's history with humans.

With this and Genesis 1:26-28 and 5:1-3 in mind we can better appreciate the words of J.Oswald Dykes. "Think how closely your earthly parent takes after that Divine Father, whose sacred title he wears. In the mysterious origination of a new life, derived yet separate; in the no less mysterious communication of personal qualities, begetting a son in his own likeness; in the responsibility that sits on him to nurture, provide for, and educate his child; in the power and authority which belong to parents to legislate for their children, and to enforce their legislation by penalty and reward; in the peculiarly strong love which nature inspires into parental bosoms, and in the unlimited sacrifices which such love can prompt: in all this consider how closely human parenthood resembles the heavenly."

With this as background, is it any wonder that Deuteronomy 27:16 will say, "Cursed is the man who dishonors his father or mother"? Or that one of the words uttered by God at Sinai is, "Honor your father and your mother..."?

I know that parents who are everything they're not supposed to be and nothing they are supposed to be—I know they tempt the oppressed children to sneer at the description given above. For children wickedly oppressed I have nothing to say at this point. The very idea that God wouldn't care if parents abused their children is a denial of all that he has shown in his own "fatherhood". Of course he cares! But those who aren't suffering under these circumstances, for those whose parents are having an honest shot at making the best of their children as they provide the best they have for them—for those the word from God comes with clearness and power--Honor your father and mother.

This word from God is the foundation of submission to all legitimate authority in life. Those who will not gladly take their place under God-ordained and honorable authority in the home will find it tough in the world of business, in school, in the Church and in every other phase of life where we must allow ourselves to be governed. Parents mustn't be expected to be sinless. Only two children had a flawless father—Adam and Eve, the rest just stumble on as best they can, making mistakes but truly aiming to please God as they act in his image to bring all that they think is good for their offspring. We wouldn't humiliate strangers the way some children humiliate their parents.

But it isn't just "authority" that's in view here. Involved in parenthood is the sacrificial, the giving, the denying of self. Parents are, in the words of Kipling, from another setting,

People who set aside their Today,
All the joys of their Today
And with the toil of their Today,
Bought for us Tomorrow.

In the face of warm, caring and giving people whose lives have been spent in bringing God, life and joy to us, surely it isn't too much to ask that we give them credit for living up to the image of God to the degree his grace has enabled them. If we were guests in the home of some kind and generous stranger we would ask for less than what we sometimes demand from our parents. Of course parents who go on and on about what they've done for their children ("since we've done all this for you we have a right to expect...") are shaming themselves and make it more difficult for children to strike the right balance. Of course! But that test is for children who have parents like that, it is no refuge for those who parents are not like that and who still won't offer the appropriate response. I know from personal experience of parents who impatiently dismiss all talk of sacrifice on their part. They seek no endless praise for doing that which they insist should come naturally to them and in showing this spirit, we honor them all the more.

And one of the fundamental ways in which we honor those who are in the image of God, parents in particular, is to honor and not worship them. To give them their place as the image of God rather than truly God.

"You are not your own" is to believers a fundamental truth and so they seek to live their lives shaped by that truth.

59

DO NO MURDER

*You shall not murder. **Exodus 20:13***

You shall not murder, God thundered! That is, you will not "unlawfully" take life. That's what murder is. But at this point he doesn't say what murder or unlawful killing is. Later legislation gives guidelines which help to "define" the word but there's nothing exhaustive about the guidelines.

There were those who, as far as God was concerned, forfeited the right to live so he ordered their execution and authorized certain people to take those lives. When that happened, there was killing but there was no murder. This was true even in cases which involved the destruction of cities in war. In the final analysis the issue was: "Did God authorize the taking of the life and was it done according to God's instructions?"

(The death of innocent children in the process makes the question more complex but "punishment" and the innocent suffering with the guilty must be seen as two distinct categories. When a judge today sentences a criminal to imprisonment, it often places hardship on his wife and children. Everyone with a heart anguishes over the suffering the innocents bear but no one views it as punishment on them. But God who, in the cases we're speaking of, ordered the destruction knows how to right wrongs in relation to innocent victims. And he'll do it—Genesis 18:25.)

It's wrong to commit homicide because it's a blow against the image of God! It's wrong to murder because its grasps a godlike power that we have no right to want much less exercise. It's wrong to murder because it takes from a human without authorization what God has given to them and so violates God's will. It's wrong to murder because it robs the victim of his/her ultimate treasure—life, and whatever potential for joy and creativity is there. It is wrong to murder because it undermines the very fabric of society by showing that might makes right—that power is the answer—and so brings every neighborhood and street under the threat of ruthless people. It is wrong to murder because it breeds fear and bitterness, gangs and warlords, reprisals and counter-reprisals. It is wrong to murder because it destroys the boundaries of legitimate anger and justifies hate, it is the ultimate rejection of self-control.

Between the execution of an impenitent and brutal murderer on one end of the spectrum and the torture and slaughtering of an innocent child on the other there is the taking of life under numberless circumstances. Killing in war, killing in "self-defense", killing under the pressure of day-in-day-out verbal/physical abuse, aborting developing humans or euthanasia. The wife of a devoted husband of fifty-five years is suffering from an inoperable brain tumor, she has been in agony for months on end, she hourly begs an overdose of sleeping pills, he finally and with heart breaking gives her the lethal pills. Whatever else we'll say about that, and I'm persuaded we have to oppose it, we won't put it on the same level with the savage beating to death of an elderly woman by a gang of boys two streets away.

It's a funny old world. It's commonplace to hear groups advocate the humane killing of a new-born baby who is mentally retarded or seriously handicapped and to hear the same groups oppose the humane killing of a sadistic murderer as barbaric. We hear the point made of "scarce resources" when it comes to seriously handicapped

246

children but not a word about it when the nation is called to house murderers in prisons built and run like an Acapulco hotel. We kill developing humans by the millions because they get in our way of self-actualization but our toes curl at the thought of capital punishment for someone like Jeffrey D. We insist that life (ours) is so precious that it mustn't be interfered with even by the growing human we helped bring into existence. So we first downgrade and then obliterate the life of that human.

We insist that capital punishment should be absolutely rejected because there is no proof that it is a deterrent but we don't insist on the absolute rejection of imprisonment when not only is there no proof that it is a deterrent, there is "proof" that imprisonment leads to re-offending. Prisons are now widely regarded as "colleges for prisoners", a place where they learn how to break the law without being caught. Many years ago Mott Osborne, the one-time Governor of Sing Sing said:

The prison system endeavors to make men industrious by depriving them of work; to make them virtuous by removing temptation; to make them respect the law by forcing them to obey the edicts of an autocrat; to make them farsighted by allowing them no chance to exercise foresight; to give them individual initiative by treating them in large groups; in short to prepare them for society by placing them in conditions as unlike real society as they could well be made.

We insist that the death penalty is inhumane but lock men and women away for a lifetime. Only recently two serial killers (one in the USA and one in the UK) died while in prison (one bludgeoned to death and the other a suicide). One of the angry and agony-filled parents of their victims screamed, "He didn't suffer enough". She didn't want him to die, a lifetime in prison, locked away, she thought, was a more severe punishment than a quick death. Similar feelings were expressed in the UK about the prisoner who was allowed to "escape" by suicide.

We insist the death penalty is inhumane but create movements to allow doctors and others to humanely kill those whose "quality of life" has fallen to a certain low.

Maybe our response to mental retardation, severe handicaps, congenital illness and the like shouldn't be, "Let's put them out of their misery" ("their misery" or "our misery"?). Maybe it should be renewed efforts to eradicate the causes of such illnesses while we care for those who presently suffer from them. Maybe we should band together, support the brilliant researchers in all these fields in every way we can instead of having them work to make already rich people richer by working on less pressing matters. Maybe we should recognize that our greed and apathy lead us to virtually ignore the prevention and healing of such diseases. We need to see that the problem does not begin with the Downs Syndrome baby but with us who enjoy good health for most of our lives. We need to see that killing the babies is advocated because it costs us less in terms of money, energy, resources and commitment.

There are those who verbally punish others because they believe that punishment should be administered to law-breakers. But people are more afraid of anarchy than of tyranny so, in a world of sinful people, there will always be the need for punishment/chastisement of some kind. Even if it's only a verbal one.

For believers, what constitutes murder is determined by the will and character of God as mediated to them by the Hebrew/Christian scriptures. If God has called for the death penalty under such and such circumstances, then it cannot be murder and it cannot be inherently immoral (though it may be a concession under those circumstances which, if the circumstances were different, he wouldn't call for).

Some say, "that's a cop out, you bring in a God you can't argue against to settle things for you. That's no way to establish moral norms!" In the place of "God" these people bring in the great god, "Reason" or 'Truth". They take "Reason" as a given and confess they can't go behind it. Believers take "God" as a given and insist they can't go behind God. God has purposed a kingdom in his own image and they seek to follow his thinking as they reason on what he has revealed. Though there are complexities and difficulties for the believer, they don't see these complexities and difficulties as proof that their over all stand is self-contradictory. They accept as central the claim that their lives and behavior are to be under God and lived in light of his claim on them. "You are not your own" is to believers a fundamental truth and so they seek to live their lives shaped by that truth.

Those who live their lives outside that Story aren't working from the same moral premises as those who live within it so why should it surprise us that there's disagreement? Even those who live within the Story often disagree on "How then shall we live?"

Whatever the complexities of life, some things are clearly immoral. You will not murder her love by treachery. You will not murder her purity by seducing her. You will not murder his reputation by lies or spreading his shame. You will not murder her right to speak by screaming abuse at her. You will not murder his growing hunger for truth by your bigotry and intolerance. You will not murder the church on the altar of your adored opinions. You will not murder the feeble by deriding their efforts. You will not murder his sense of honor by involving him in what is cheap and mean. You will not murder his hope with malicious cynicism. You will not murder her desire to serve with a dismissive sneer.

You shall do no murder!

"At the resurrection people will neither marry nor be given in marriage"

60

NOTHING TO DO WITH ME AND MY WIFE

You shall not commit adultery. **Exodus 20:14**

I love what I read of Charles Kingsley. He didn't like Matthew 22:30 but he didn't know how to make it say other than it said. It is a word from the Messiah saying, "At the resurrection people will neither marry nor be given in marriage; they will be like the angels in heaven." Kingsley knew what it said and it looked too plain to controvert but he adored his wife and couldn't bear to think of himself not married to her, ever. "All that I can say about that text," he twittered, "is that it has nothing to do with me and my wife." Atta boy, Kingsley! Wouldn't surprise me a bit if Christ had smiled when he heard that remark.

Marriage is one of God's finest blessings for humans during this phase of their history. It seems clear that the Messiah says the union doesn't exist in the future phase of human living. (He doesn't say that human male/femaleness ceases to exist!) Kingsley knew that, but the feeling his undying love for his wife generated had to be

251

vented, so he said, "that text...has nothing to do with me and my wife."

Monogamy? That's the teaching which says: one man for one woman in marriage. "That's not monogamy" gasped Fosdick, "monogamy is two people so loving one another that all their lives they don't want to love anyone else in the same way."

"Marriage," says Landon Saunders, "is two people looking deep into each other's eyes and saying: 'Others may come and go in your life but I never will. If you get sick, I'll care for you, feed you, bathe you; I'll do anything for you except leave you. I will never leave you.'"

Marriage isn't all froth, sweetness, candlelight dinners and endlessly whispered sweet-nothings; but it isn't all tough times, stiff-upper lip, "I've given my word and won't go back" grimness either. I haven't seen many marriages in close but the good ones I've seen at close quarters over a long period have been covenants between friends who were lovers as well. Adultery was a theoretical possibility but that was about the extent of it—practically, it was so remote as to be impossible. That was because, for them, adultery was not (simply) a sexual sin, it was a base betrayal, the betrayal of the closest friend either of them had in all the world.

Their knowledge ("adultery is sin") was well-grounded but they had so exercised themselves in loving loyalty to one another that the knowledge had the consent, no, the active support, of their powerful emotions. It was more than that their intellect rightly said, "that would be wrong," their heart said, "that would be dishonorable and treacherous." A lady once said to me, "Not only would I not wish to do what would dishonor my husband, I wouldn't knowingly want even to embarrass him." Bravo!

The ultimate safeguard against sexual betrayal—besides other important but not quite central matters—is the nurtured friendship of two lovers. Somebody said in a lovely exaggeration that people don't act on what they believe, they act on how they feel about what they believe! Scholars assure us that "emotion" and 'motivation" (motive) have a common Latin root—to move (out), that which moves. The linguistic information is interesting, the psychological truth revealed in the information is even more interesting: shape and nurture the right feelings with the aid of truth and our behavior follows our feelings. For some lovers, adultery is not only physically out of the question, it is unthinkable for they are driven by the depth of their feelings for their lover

It is wrong to give the

impression that the OT called

for anything other than

monogamy!

61

YOU SHALL NOT COMMIT ADULTERY

You shall not commit adultery. **Exodus 20:14**

Adultery was taken seriously in the ancient world and the Bible shares that view. In Genesis 20:9-10 even the Philistine, Abimelech, rages against Abraham because he put him in great danger of committing "a great sin" that would affect his kingdom. He wants to know what on earth led Abraham to do such a thing.

It's a common view among scholars that: "According to the Jewish view of marriage, adultery could only be committed by the wife. The husband was permitted extra-marital relationships since, in a polygamous system, every woman was a prospective wife, unless she was married. That is, a husband could not violate his own marriage".

By "Jewish view" this writer meant not only the teachings of the rabbis in later Judaism, it included texts from the Pentateuch. But only a wife could commit adultery? Is this seventh commandment,

255

then, only addressed to women? Does not Leviticus 20:10 speak of men committing adultery with other men's wives?

Childs (page 422) and Birch (page 170) quote the Stamms and Andrews work with approval: "the man can only commit adultery against a marriage other than his own, the woman only against her own".

John Kitto (in 1870) made the point that an "adulterer" was a man who had sexual intercourse with a married or betrothed woman not his wife. An "adulteress" was a woman who had sexual relationship with any man other than her husband.

Remarks like these are commonplace. Hauck (TDNT, 4.730) says, "Adultery is the violation of the marriage of another...Hence a man is not under obligation to avoid all non-marital intercourse...Unconditional fidelity is demanded only of the woman, who in marriage becomes the property of her husband." As long as he doesn't have sexual intercourse with another man's wife (a betrothed or married wife), he is allowed to have sex with any woman he likes (prostitutes and all unmarried women). An interesting view that. Hardly one that takes Genesis 2:24 seriously. At least, not as seriously as Jesus seems to take it in Matt 19 or Paul in 1 Corinthians 6 and Ephesians 5.

It seems to me that a number of things are very clear. The "polygamous system" was no creation or part of the Mosaic covenant nor was it any part of the life to which the covenant Law called people. One didn't break the law by being monogamous. The covenant didn't *require* the people to be polygamous. If we mean that polygamy was a cultural reality in the world the ancient Jews lived in, we should say that.

It is wrong to give the impression that the OT *called for* anything other than monogamy! Polygamy, concubinage, "divorce for any cause"—all these at best, were tolerated as existing evils and the laws that governed them were intended to regulate those existing evils.

When critics of Jesus came to test him on the divorce/remarriage question they made use of Deuteronomy 24 as if it were God's heart's desire. ("After all, it's in the Torah.") They debated who had the right view of that text and moved from that to self-congratulation since they lived their lives in line with "a correct interpretation" of that legislation. The Messiah insisted that they couldn't regard themselves as spiritual giants if they lined their lives up with this piece of legislation because it was a concession to hard-heartedness. To take advantage of a concession to hard-heartedness is no act of a spiritually mature man. If they wanted to brag about their spiritual maturity they should line up with Genesis 2:24. God's heart's desire was Genesis 2:24, what he tolerated and regulated was revealed in Deuteronomy 24. To present what was tolerated as if it were God's unchanging desire is hardly excusable.

Had a man come to Jesus Christ to ask, "Is it lawful to have more than one wife?" Jesus might well have said, "that depends on what you mean by lawful. If you mean are there texts in the law which regulate polygamy or are there men of faith who took to themselves more than one wife, the answer is yes. If you mean does the Torah call people to polygamy or does it view the practice as wholly acceptable to God, the answer is an absolute no. Have you not read Genesis 2:24?"

The covenant Law had a civil thrust as well as a moral/spiritual dimension.

At the civil/criminal level adultery was treated as a threat to the whole nation (that's why capital crimes were capital crimes). The importance of family and inheritance in early Israel can hardly be overstated. To get an idea of how important, we need to listen to people like Christopher Wright and to note crucial texts in the OT. Look, for example, at Numbers 27:1-11 and the whole of Numbers 36. Read through the book of Numbers and get the feeling there, see the case of Ahab and Naboth and see Wright's discussion on Torah law in regard to land.

Adultery threatened this whole arrangement. The children of a woman's "lover" might well inherit all that belonged to her husband's family. For a man to lie with a prostitute or an unmarried woman was no threat to the stability of society from *that* perspective since if either of these became pregnant, no inheritance of family or tribe was at risk. But this doesn't deal with adultery from the moral/spiritual perspective. To speak of adultery in these texts as if that's all the OT taught about it is misleading. It's only half the story. And to conclude from half the story that the man "was permitted extra-marital relationships" because polygamy was a social reality is hardly fair to the biblical evidence.

The man had no obligation to his wife? Hauck thinks not because the woman "in marriage becomes the property of the man." Even if that were what the Torah taught, what would that settle? A man had an obligation even to his ox or donkey! He had an obligation to an animal in trouble even if it was the property of someone he "hated". But no obligation to his wife? Had Genesis 2:24 nothing to say to these people?

At best, to say a man couldn't commit "adultery" against his wife and his marriage covenant is *technically* correct, legally correct. The same might be said today of murder and other crimes. At one level the courts have nothing to do with the morality of acts, only their civil/criminal nature. A jury isn't asked to bring in a verdict that the act is immoral no matter how they feel about the act from that perspective. To deal with the covenant Law of Israel this way is surely unacceptable. To abstract the civil from the religious, the legal from the ethical, especially in major matters, matters that are expressly named in the Decalogue is hardly wise.

The foundational teaching on marriage is Genesis 2 and its form is monogamous. God, said Jesus Christ—speaking about how people should understand the Mosaic covenant Law—never changed his mind about that! The wisdom literature calls on men to live with one wife and Paul gives us 1 Corinthians 7:1 and the analogy in Ephesians 5. Job insisted that the lustful look and loitering with intent was wrong before God (31:1,9). The idea that only the legality mattered is wrong. Joseph saw that fornication with Potiphar's wife was an outrage against God as well as Potiphar (Genesis 39:8-9).

The scholars admit that later in the OT, in numerous passages, the line between adultery and fornication is obliterated. See Hauck in TDNT.

Adultery in the OT is "illicit sexual intercourse" which had its civil and criminal aspects as well as its moral, spiritual and religious dimension. When it showed itself between two married persons, it carried the death penalty as a maximum punishment. When it showed itself in a married woman, even with an unmarried man, it carried the death penalty (since it undermined the whole inheritance system). Beyond the civil ramifications it was unrighteousness, a violation of a covenant made with one's spouse, an act of treachery against one's companion and against God (cf. Malachi 2:10-14).

To endlessly take when you could also give is to steal

To endlessly take when you could also give is to steal

62

YOU SHALL NOT STEAL

You shall not steal. **Exodus 20:15**

"Steal"? To steal is impossible unless someone has the moral right under God to say, "this is mine." But in Israel, to say, "this is mine" isn't enough—"this is mine because God has blessed me with it" is required. Of course, even that, isn't enough. "this is mine because God blessed me with it and calls me to use it to his glory" is even better. Just the same, "this is mine!" is perfectly legitimate before God because God gifted the person with it and so he thunders: You shall not steal!

There were poor among Israel but the covenant Law was geared by God to see they were provided for and behind the Law was the person of the Lord God. And as Chris Wright has pointed out, God took land off the market as a commodity so there could only be the leasing of the land and not the outright buying of it. This was part of the insurance against land barony, which would lead to permanent landlessness and poverty for the poor.

In parceling out to each clan and family their inheritance God was recognizing ownership with stewardship in relation to these persons. So, "don't steal" from them is essentially, "don't steal from them what God has given them and made them stewards of". If you steal from him you will not only deny him what he has a right to by God's grace, you will be robbing all those he feeds, clothes, shelters. You will be robbing the priesthood of the tithes needed to sustain the ministry and you will therefore be robbing God!

Stealing takes a multitude of forms.

To endlessly take when you could also give is to steal. To live off society and to give nothing in return is to be an enemy of society, it to steal. If you can't give money or goods back to society, what can you give? To live off society but not to live for it is to steal.

To make a living by doing what undermines society, what robs it of a God-ward vision and a deep commitment under God to society, is to steal. Tertullian wrote on Idolatry. In his opening remarks he speaks of fraud which he defines saying, "the essence of fraud, I take it, is, that any should seize what is another's, or refuse to another his due; and, of course, fraud done toward man is a name of greatest crime. Well, but idolatry does fraud to God, by refusing to Him, and conferring on others, His honors..."

He critiques not only idolatry, but those who make their living by making idols, statues and such things. Then he addresses some excuses these tradesmen make. One of them is, "I have nothing else whereby to live," to which Tertullian replies (in Glover's translation), "must you live?" His point was, the only *must* there is, is faithfulness to God. If it's a choice between faithfulness or death, he says we must choose death, otherwise, we live by our own laws and not God's. If that's the case, we are not God's people, but our own! But if God's, then it isn't true that we must live.

The cheating of the tax man and the knowing grin: "A man's gotta make a living!" The selling of a vehicle we know is worthless and the careless shrug: "A man's gotta make a living!" Taking advantage of someone who is desperate. Knowingly offering much less than what they're selling is worth, doing it when we could easily do otherwise and then the that's-life look: "A man's gotta make a living!"

> A man must live? We justify
> Low shift and trick to treason high,
> A little vote for a little gold,
> a whole senate bought and sold,
> by this self-evident reply: A man must live.
> But is it so? Pray tell me why
> Life at such cost you have to buy?
> In what religion were you told
> a man must live?
> There are times when a man must die,
> Imagine for a battle cry,
> From soldiers, with a sword to hold—
> From soldiers with the flag urolled—
> This coward's whine, this liar's lie—
> A man must live.

And will we rob God? Speakers who will not speak to his honor but to make a reputation for themselves while speaking in the name of him who made himself of no reputation?

Will we enjoy his many blessings while we speak and act as though they were our own creations, withholding praise and thanksgiving from him? Attributing our prosperity to our own hard work, our personal skills, or shrewd management?

That we're redeemed from putting our hands in other peoples' pockets, is something for which we should offer thanks but the word of God still thunders,

- You will not rob him of his reputation and maybe, as a consequence, of his friends. You will not, by this, rob him of his peace of mind or of the joy his usefulness brings which makes a hard life more bearable. You will not leave him lying at the side of the road robbed of his good name, bleeding from invisible wounds and now an untouchable.

- You will not rob her of her honor and leave her marked as one who gave away, as if it were of no consequence, what is a precious gift, filled with mystery and wonder when offered to God and the one who has a right.

• You will not rob them of the word of forgiveness for which they beg and without which they cannot live.

• You will not rob her of her dignity as a person; you will not rob them of their friends by monopolizing those friends and wooing them away; you will not rob them of the praise that is due them and for which they hunger; you will not rob him of the credit due him for his work, claiming it as your own; you will not rob her of the tender words you owe her; you will not rob him of your presence at his side in his pain when he has earned that presence down the years; you will not rob your parents of the noble spirit of thankfulness and respect which is the wages they'd never claim.

Thou shalt not steal!

63

THOU SHALT NOT BEAR FALSE WITNESS

You shall not give false testimony against your neighbor.
Exodus 20:16

Most of us would immediately insist that to deceive in order to hurt or to take advantage of someone is morally repugnant. Where wickedness of some kind is the motivating factor we have little trouble is saying that lying is unvarnished evil. Where deception is carried out to gain "a greater good" (maybe justice for an oppressed person, or an advantage for the vulnerable over the bully) we begin to have doubts—doubts we shouldn't apologise for.

Questions that truly deal with exceptional circumstances cannot be dealt with by general considerations. They introduce other complex questions, don't you see. Questions like, do moral duties ever compete with each other in a sinful world? Are we sometimes compelled to choose between two moral evils? [Should we agree to pay income tax? Should we agree to pay income tax even when we're told that much of it will be used to further projects that we think are morally reprehensible? Should we purchase more expensive clothes with the very little money the family has to cover many other needs or should we buy cheaper clothes that are made by underpaid workers in distant sweat-shops? Should we boycott goods made in sweat-shops because the workers are paid a pittance or even when the boycott puts those poor people out of a job they must have if their family is to be fed?]

Morally mature people will honor truth but they will also honor other moral obligations that must exist if truth is to have any virtue and if a person is to be an evenly and well-developed moral person. They'll take into account the virtues of compassion, generosity, forgiveness, wisdom and insight and they'll want their lives to be shaped by those as well as the virtue of esteeming truth. Sometimes two truths compete for our attention and it takes wisdom and other qualities to make the choice between them.

It's clear—or so it seems to me—that much of the disagreement between passionate people is less about "the facts" than it is about the weight we give to the different "facts" we're faced with. The kind and impulsive person wants the poor family catered to "this very hour" and the kind but more thoughtful person wants to know how best to help the poor family. Those that are markedly tender-hearted tend to think that those that are not as emotional as they are lack feeling. It isn't surprising then that you hear anguished protests levelled against doctors or lawyers or government officials who try to balance the demands coming from various directions. Experience tends to calm our emotions. A surgeon doesn't panic when he or she sees an artery spewing blood but the patient's loved ones or an inexperienced nurse might climb the walls. It isn't that the surgeon is unfeeling or even less sensitive than the others—she has seen this kind of thing hundreds of times and knows that the best way to deal with it is not to climb the walls. The surgeon and the new nurse both see the same "facts"—blood spewing from an artery, but the weight given to the facts is not quite the same though both take it as critically serious. Fear affects how we assess what we're faced with.

Often it's the case that lies are the expression of an evil heart that seeks a wicked advantage or seeks the hurt of someone. Right-thinking people won't hesitate to brand such lies for what they are.

Since we're all sinners we tend to tell the story before us in a way that suits us. This can easily lead us to use lies ("white lies" or ones that gain us only a small advantage) to benefit us. This is part of a downward moral spiral. It's clear that to go through life working with a "moral dilemmas" model is nonsense. Clearly the better approach is to concentrate on character formation and this will affect our responses—we'll "see" better and ethics is a way of "seeing" things before it's a way of responding. This too needs careful development because we will want to ask what it is that we'll rely on for "character formation". The Church of God has committed to some non-negotiable truths revealed in and as Jesus Christ. For Christians some questions may already be answered in Jesus Christ no matter what other people think.

Often it's the case that telling a lie gets a person out of a difficult predicament that his or her prior immoral behavior got them into the first place. A man lies in order to cover up the fact that he embezzled. He doesn't wish to be arrested and convicted because it will cost him his job and his family will suffer. Now he lies to "do good" (that is, continue to provide for his family). Or a woman lies about her sexual immorality to spare her husband and family the shame and hurt. Right-thinking people will condemn the plainly evil but will have sympathy with the desire to ease the pain of the innocent even if that attempt involves a lie and even though the innocent should have been thought of earlier.

Defence lawyers and those that work in research enterprises will give their word to publish nothing that will injure their client's/employer's interests. In practice they will withhold important information which, if made known, will hurt the people to whom they owe fiduciary responsibility. It's clear that in withholding such hurtful information that they aren't lying *in the formal sense* but they do deliberately remain silent even when they know that the whole truth is not being served and that false information is being accepted and acted on. They do this not because they are *liars*, because in their daily lives they esteem truth as much as the next man but because they keep their word—thus maintaining integrity—to a prior commitment.

It can be argued that to begin with they should never have agreed to withhold information that is injurious to others. But since the clients or employers are paying for the research they do, the information really belongs to those that paid for it. This point needs developed. Then you have the doctor/patient confidentiality where, say, the husband and wife and children are all patients with the one GP. The husband contracts a serious venereal disease but doesn't want his wife to know. So when the wife comes saying she wants to have another baby with her husband and wants to know if the doctor knows anything that would lead her to postpone or abandon the notion. What then? Build your own illustrations from life— they're easy to find since they're all over the place.

When we begin complex discussions like this with a definition already agreed on things are so much easier. But it's precisely there that a major difficulty lies. What precisely do we mean by "a lie" or by "murder"? If we settle for a legal definition, we still have some difficulties, but it's certainly easier to work our way through the discussion than if we want to include the moral element.

So when we ask if it's ever right to lie the answer's no *if* we mean... When we ask if it's ever right to murder the answer's no but we need to be sure that we know what *murder* means.

This commandment involves "lying", of course, but it is more specifically dealing with *perjury*—that is, lying under oath. It speaks of bearing false witness "against a neighbor".

The sin/crime in view here is the undermining of the possibility of justice in the courts. All acting or speaking to deceive generates problems in one way or another but lying so as to subvert the possibility of justice in a court setting is viewed as profoundly more serious because it undermines the foundation of community justice. An act of perjury may well be personal in its aim but it makes use of the judicial system to gain personal ends and so contaminates and weakens the possibility of justice for all.

We have a clear and horrifying illustration of the corrupting and cruel power of perjury in the case of Naboth and Jezebel [see 1 Kings 21]. Ahab wishes to purchase Naboth's desirable property but the man doesn't wish to sell or trade and the king sulks in grief. His

268

ruthless and domineering wife [who frightened even Elijah—1 Kings 19:3] sent letters in the king's name to the leaders in the city of Naboth. These leaders arranged for two "worthless" men to perjure themselves in bearing witness against Naboth and he was stoned to death. In this case the judges of the city are in on the cruel deception up to their necks and they suborn perjury. What chance has anyone like Naboth in the courts when these administers justice?

If here is nothing precious enough in the life or thought of a witness on which he can/will swear then the jury is hindered in seeking a right verdict because they have less reason to be sure of the truth of what he says. Human judges are obviously very limited and need all the help they can get to come to a satisfactory verdict so when someone will swear to nothing or stake his claim to truth on nothing the jury is left guessing. It's for this reason [in part] the governments punishes those who commit perjury. The fear of severe punishment is used to "make" them tell the truth that they might otherwise pervert.

Note Ezekiel 17:11-19 where Zedekiah under oath made a covenant with Nebuchadnezzar and then broke it and allied himself with the Egyptian Pharaoh. God insists that he will overthrow Zedekiah for not only did he break the covenant he made with an oath, he had sworn in the name of God. Nebuchadnezzar took it that if he had sworn in the name of Yahweh that he would certainly keep his word but since he broke it, it was clear that the name of Yahweh can be despised even by his own worshipers.

But *behind* any legislation against perjury the OT depends on the heart that speaks the truth—in or out of court but if hearts are evil they will find ways to subvert the truth in court or "good reasons" to lie out of court.

Jesus spoke to the matter of truth-telling when he said his followers must say "yes" and "no" and leave it at that. They were to speak the truth without being compelled by some judicial oath [see Numbers 5:19-31, a strange text]. This is part of what Jesus had in mind when he said, "Swear not at all" [Matthew 5:33-37 and 23:16-22]. It was common enough [and still is] for people to underscore their daily speech with oaths [see Jeremias' *New Testament Theology*, page 200] to give it added weight. Jesus said, "Speak the truth; that's all you need to do!"

Here in Exodus, the law depends on people with good heart but iot nevertheless says:

Do not bear false witness against your neighbor!

64

THOU SHALT NOT COVET

You shall not covet. **Exodus 20:17**

Henry Sloan Coffin was speaking of covetousness when he said, "No man is entitled to set up his private opinion that it would be better for him to have that which is now another man's, and better for the other man to be without it." With his characteristic no-holds-barred speech he said this also, "The desire to possess and enjoy what is another's is the same dirty desire whether the object be another man's wife, or his position, his fortune, his reputation, his business."

A right thinking follower of the Decalogue would have agreed with that and would have added that the person who has the "possession" has it because God gave it to him. (Yes, this needs balanced when given certain other factors, but the truth of it stands.)

I'm taking it that coveting is an unhealthy and an unbridled desire for anything. Biblical word study will show that the word itself may or may not speak of an evil desire but our established use of the word has left the good use of it behind. In the Decalogue we're not to covet what belongs to another but the full teaching of the Torah makes it clear we're not to have an unhealthy and an unbridled desire for what is "our own". See the piece entitled *Giving As Worship* which shows how Israelites were to use the blessings God gave them—generous compassion was to be a hall-mark of Israelite life.

When Paul (speaking as a representative Israelite who reflected the nation's experience under the Torah) wanted to show how sin had thoroughly damned the nation's soul he said sin used the Torah and produced in him "every kind of covetous desire" (Romans 7:8). There, so to speak, is the true denial of God rather than some confused theology. The New Testament repeatedly teaches us that covetousness is idolatry and so it is the violation of the first and second commandments, it is the violation of both the first and greatest command and the second. Romans 7:7-11 speaks of "having life" until sin worked covetousness and "I died!" I was alive—I coveted—I died!

Covetousness is fed by polluted steams and while it is one of those sins that John Watson used to call "respectable sins" it stinks to high heaven. Feeding it are all the foul desires we can imagine. The truth is that the feeding is mutual; covetousness feeds the dirty desires and is fed by them. The lecherous person wants his addiction fed and so he slyly plots and goes after whatever and whoever he thinks will satisfy that greed. But the greedy are never satisfied and the envious never know what happy peace is. The scriptures consistently associate covetousness with unclean sexual behavior and the love of money (which is the love of power).

Spenser in his *Faerie Queene* has a unsettling description of repulsive lechery, greed and envy all of which are first cousins and incestously related to covetousness. I've adapted some of his spelling to make it easier to read.

> Inconstant man, that loved all he saw,
> And lusted after all, that he did love,
> Nor would his looser life be tied to law,
> But eyed weake wemens hearts to tempt, and prove
> If from their loyall loves he might them move;

Which lewdnesse fild him with reprochfull paine
Of that fowle evill, which all men reprove,
That rots the marrow, and consumes the braine:
Such one was Lecherie, the third of all this traine.
And greedy Avarice by him did ride,
Upon a Camell loaden all with gold;
Two iron coffers hong on either side,
With precious mettall full, as they might hold,
And in his lap an heape of coine he told;
For of his wicked pelfe his God he made,
And into hell him selfe for money sold;
Accursed usurie was all his trade,
And right and wrong alike in equall ballaunce weighed.
His life was nigh unto deaths doore placed,
And thred-bare cote, and cobbled shoes he ware,
Ne scarse good morsell all his life did tast,
But both from backe and belly still did spare,
To fill his bags, and richesse to compare;
Yet chylde and kinsman living had he none
To leave them to; but thorough daily care
To get, and nightly feare to lose his owne,
He led a wretched life unto him selfe unknowne.
Most wretched wight, whom nothing might suffise,
Whose greedy lust did lacke in greatest store,
Whose need had end, but no end couetise,
Whose wealth was want, whose [plenty] made him poor,
Who had enough, yet wished ever more;
A vile disease, and ache in foote and hand
A grievous gout tormented him full sore,
That well he could not touch, nor go, nor stand:
Such one was Avarice, the fourth of this faire band.
        And next to him malicious Envie rode,
Upon a ravenous wolfe, and still did chaw
Betweene his cankred teeth a venemous tode,
That all the poison ran about his chaw;
But inwardly he chawed his owne maw

At neighbours wealth, that made him ever sad;
For death it was, when any good he saw,
And wept, that cause of weeping none he had,
But when he heard of harm, he waxed wondrous glad.

The Christ said we can't serve God and money. He said that life isn't made up of our possessions or the things we lust after. No man can serve two masters, he taught us, he will either be loyal to one or another. So whether we're lusting after someone's reputation, success, possessions, position or family we're engaged in a dirty, filthy business and God is being denied.

To those of us who are covetous the world and everything in it becomes our servant and we its lord. Everything is to be used, it's value is determined by what it (or they) can do for us. We become self-worshipping, self-indulgent, self-centred, self-promoting, self-bound, miserly and miserably self-absorbed excuses for real and vibrant humans beings.

Thou shalt not covet!

65

A FEW PRELIMINARY REMARKS

*God liberated the nation but he didn't work moral magic and turn
them into a nation of sinless people*

It won't hurt if we keep in mind that we are working here with
covenant laws that God is laying down for his chosen people.
He has liberated the nation but he hasn't worked moral magic and
turned them into a nation of sinless people whose only desire is to
please their Lord. He is dealing with a sinful people and he knows
well that that's what he is doing. He knows they have been sinful in
the past and that they will break his heart and his covenant
generation after generation. If there is to be faithfulness in this
covenant union it will be God and not the Jewish nation.

We need to pay special attention to this truth because God has
given Israel a place and a mission in the world—they are to be his
witnesses before the nations. But they have been, are and will
continue to be a sinful people; *his chosen People are not disqualified
as his witnesses because they are sinful.* When they so sin that he

chastises them severely he nevertheless remains faithful to his commitment to them *and* to his purpose to bless the world through them.

This truth needs developed and balanced but we must acknowledge it as we work with it. The "success" of God's overarching purpose does not lie in the moral excellence or faithfulness of his chosen ones but in God himself. We're not to say that his chosen ones have nothing to do with his "success" but we are not to check God's health and effective power on the basis of how well his People are doing.

The presence of all these laws take it for granted that the chosen nation needs them and that they will sin against God and one another. We mustn't act surprised that God's elect [OT or NT] continue to sin as they pursue holiness by walking in the light. As a People God will hold them accountable for their sinfulness, of course, and when severe chastisement is required he will render it [**Revelation 3:19**] but through them he *will* gain his eternal and overarching purpose to bring a human family to glory in the image of the Lord Jesus.

66

THE BOOK OF THE COVENANT

Then he took the Book of the Covenant and read it to the people. They responded, "We will do everything the Lord has said; we will obey." Exodus 24:7

Exodus 20:18—23:19. The circumstances of the giving of the "Book of the Covenant" are these (20:18-21). The people are terrified by the roped-off, quaking and burning mountain, the trumpet blasts which increased in volume and finally the voice that shattered their nerves. They no longer need the ropes or Levites to keep them from the mountain, they might well have picked up their heels and ran but Moses, himself frightened (**Hebrews 12:21**) but under control, urged them not to panic. God's way of approaching them would be a sure cure for over-familiarity and could be good medicine for the future (**20:20**). Moses himself gives an Example of bravery by bringing his fear under control and walks into "the thick darkness were God was" (**v.21**) to receive further instruction from the God with the voice.

This "Book of the Covenant" (**24:7**) contains specific laws about a Numbers of specific cases. Many of them have the form "If...then..." (see **21:2,7,18** etc). These are given as illustrative of how one is to behave under these circumstances *and* as models that point the direction they were to go when working out community judgments.

There is instruction about worship, about violence and injury (fatal and otherwise, intentional and otherwise), instruction about property disputes, about faithfulness to God, family and society and teaching about the sacred Seasons and Festivals.

Idolatry and the making of images are again forbidden and this is probably connected with the instructions on the altars they were to build in the Wilderness (**20:23-25**). The instructions about altars in their wanderings function at several levels and one of them has to do with God choosing to manifest himself in particular places; there they were to make earthen altars. Or if a more substantial altar were needed then one of stone would be permissible so long as it avoided ornamentation. It would be something in keeping with their environment and their status—as pilgrims in the Wilderness (**20:24-26**). God was not only willing to wander in a Tent with his people; he wanted no elaborate altar in a place where such a thing might suggest the desert was their home. They were not to live as Bedouins for God had promised Abraham a land.

Whatever is to be said for the temple of Solomon [in the promised land] and God condescending to manifest himself in it—in the Wilderness "an altar was not to be a proud structure" that might seduce the worshiper from its God. When they worshipped, clothing mattered; nothing was to shock or be crude or reminiscent of frenzied pagan worship (**20:26**). The minds and wills as well as the emotions of the people must be on their God.

67

I LOVE MY MASTER

I love my master...and do not want to go free. Exodus 21:5

"If you buy a Hebrew slave..." says **21:2**.

To compare "biblical" slavery with the rest that goes under the heading of slavery is to compare apples and oranges. One is designed to regulate already existing evils and to produce responsible citizens (biblical) and the other is sadistic and in some modern cases, masochistic muck connected with the S & M fraternity.

"Slaves" are divided into several categories. There were Hebrew slaves who became servants to fellow-Israelites perhaps as a way of repaying something they'd stolen, or because they had been irresponsible and got into serious debt or because their crops failed and were left with honest debt that still needed to be paid. (See **Exodus 22:3** and other places.)

Covenant governed and protected such people but we're not to think of them all as poor pathetic beings who suffered unavoidable misfortune. Still, they were released at the end of seven years and the master sent them away with enough goods to make a new beginning (**Exodus 21:2-6; Deuteronomy 15:12-18**). The master was to remember that he had been a slave in Egypt and to treat his servant in that light (**Deuteronomy 15:15**). The treatment might be so good that the man who came as an unwilling servant is persuaded to remain in his master's employ permanently (**Exodus 21:5**).

Not every person who became enslaved would be genial or cooperative. There are people who are rebellious and lazy. We see different kinds of prisoners in modern jails that are there because they owe a debt to society [yes!]. Some of them are willing to acknowledge and pay the debt others are the reverse. In ancient times there were rebellious servants who were to be punished if they wouldn't work or committed crimes but the covenant law regulated the punishments (**21:20-21; Leviticus 24:17,22**).

Placing irresponsible people in slavery aimed to rehabilitate them. It's no help to a woman and her children if the man continues to be irresponsible so that they suffer. A wise master does the entire family a favor if he does whatever is loving and wise in the area of punishment and demand in order to rehabilitate the wrongdoer.

The slave wasn't sent to a five star hotel or sunny Acapulco. It was *meant* to be demanding and meant to be seen as a consequence of his theft or irresponsibility or whatever. He was taught to work, to obey, to be responsible, to act as one on whom others in the society depend. In short, he had to pull his load (though, see **Leviticus 25:43,46,53**). To deal with people otherwise (in particular those who have need of discipline) may seem pious and loving but there's so much high-minded bungling and benevolent incompetence. It would appear that we think the abuse of slaves or prisoners is corrected by sickening sweetness and spineless submission to intimidation. Hardened prisoners snigger at this and rub their hands together in delight. It not only hurts the wrongdoers, it also dishonors those to whom the debts are owed. I'm *not* saying we should grind their bones to powder because they're "criminals". Note **Deuteronomy 25:2-3**.

There were slaves who were foreigners bought from slavers or gotten at war (**Leviticus 25:43; Numbers 331:12; Deuteronomy 21:10-14**). Note the laws that governed them, in regard to marriage, punishment and the like and see how different the biblical handling of "slavery" is from what happened under Stalin, Hitler, in Asia, Africa, as well as North America and the British colonies and in some 20th century prisons.

H.R. Mackintosh, with that lovely way of his, in his book, *Highway of God*, broadens the picture when speaking of those who have found freedom in Christ. Throughout their lives, he reminds us, they get many offers to leave their Master and go back to the old "freedom". "Freedom is good," he says, "and Christ gives it abundantly; but freedom without Christ, freedom rather to put Christ away, is evil through and through. Freedom is sweet, but what are all its joys if to taste them we must leave our best friend?"

Another side of his point relates it to our husbands/wives/children/parents/friends and fellow-humans. Freedom is sweet, but what are all its joys if to taste them we must leave our best friend(s) crippled, scarred and lonely for a lifetime? No, to the offer of freedom that isn't freedom there must be a resolute, "I love my wife or husband or parents or children/friends or neighbors, I will not go out!"

"We are to seek that which is
appropriate—that is, both
good and possible—in a
society
not yet ripe for the full and
free exercise of the ideal life"

68

THE REALIZABLE BEST

"Love sees not only what it could do if the conditions were favorable, but also what it can do under conditions as they are".

"But if there is serious injury, you are to take life for life, eye for eye, tooth for tooth, hand for hand, foot for foot, burn for burn, wound for wound, bruise for bruise" (Exodus 21:23-24).

There is much in this "book of the covenant" that sophisticated moderns are tempted to smile indulgently at, if not to sneer. It's too easy to live in a society created and shaped by the Hebrew-Christian traditions and Scriptures, thoroughly blessed, and from that privileged position to stand in judgment on them. It's like so much that is modern and sophisticated, it's a shallow and thankless response.

Away from the Scripture (and yet, not away from it) paramilitaries and other gangsters curse and rage against the law, break and malign the law, kill and plunder in spite of the law and then, when they're caught, they insist on being treated fairly under the terms of the law they abominate and destroy. If the law were as bad as they profess it to be, why on earth would they want to be judged under it? Why would they want authorities to abide by it? It must have something going for it when they prefer not to be judged by their own standards but by the law they despise and rage against.

There are those who respond in this way to the biblical Law about which they are so ignorant. Ignorant not only about what it actually says and means, but about its ultimate goal, the understanding it shows not only about the situations it faces but also about the people it is dealing with in those situations.

T.E. Jessup instructs us well when, speaking of ethical pursuits, he says, "We are to seek that which is appropriate—that is, both good and possible—in a society not yet ripe for the full and free exercise of the ideal life". Yes, yes, I know we aren't to water down the will of God but, again, as Jessup has rightly reminded us, "Love sees not only what it could do if the conditions were favorable, but also what it can do under conditions as they are". This is precisely what the Scriptures say God has done.

And G.A. Chadwick insists: people of goodwill and critical ability will recognize that public laws and institutions curb, educate and elevate societies (providing, of course, they are wise and good laws). He also rightly insists "legislation must not move too far in advance of public opinion. Laws may be highly desirable in the abstract, for which communities are not yet ripe." *Many of those who sneer at the biblical laws (as codified) know in their bones that they themselves help to enact laws that don't go nearly as far as they would wish.* They recognize that the truth behind a law may be wondrously deep and rich and that the statute will carry people in that direction even though the people are not yet up to the full measure of that underlying truth.

Are we to take "an eye for an eye" (21:24-25), rip it out and isolate it from a covenant founded on grace, sustained by grace and culminating in grace? Are we to suppose that this nation, which was created and shaped to nurture a spirit of generosity, kindness and forgiveness, is *urged* to *demand* burning for burning and eyes for eyes? No, these were public sentences to be carried out if and when administrative justice and the needs of the situation required it. There *were* criminals in Israel as there are criminals in modern society. Like it or not, the innocent and law-abiding need protection and if the law will not defend them, God help them! (And he will!) Were circumstances ideal in this life and in human society there would be no need for laws or punishments dealing with deliberate crime or willful negligence. As long as our situation isn't ideal "the realizable best will be given cheerful precedence over (the unattainable) ideally best".

God's heart's desire was never the rupture of a marriage union or the practice of polygamy, but evil entered human relationships and abuse with it. Since these evils entered, laws were given to regulate them so that the lives of the vulnerable—divorced women very often— did not become intolerable (Deuteronomy 24:1-5). The seduction of young girls might well result in their being unable to marry later so the seducer of a virgin was required to marry and provide for her (Exodus 22:16 and other texts on caring for wives).

Laws of retribution not only persuaded the victims that they mattered, they put a limit to the punishment that could be handed out. They saw to it that a hungry man didn't have his hands cut off merely for stealing a loaf or that an angry man wasn't executed for slapping a fellow-citizen. They placed the exercise of judgment in the hands of recognized authorities and sent a signal to other would-be offenders that criminal behavior wouldn't be tolerated (21:24-25).

A close and fair look at all the covenant texts in this area will show that the OT has much to teach those "benevolent bunglers" in high offices whose "over-Christianized" views lack contact with reality about punishment and how to rehabilitate. *I now and then think that those entering political office should be required to have training in Biblical Ethics, especially OT ethics and jurisprudence.*

The covenant law is filled with teaching about compensation rather than a mechanical doling out of teeth for teeth

69

CRIME AND PUNISHMENT

The legislation is also given to ensure justice for the offender. Let me repeat it won't do to sever a man's head because he knocked out somebody's tooth.

"Eye for eye, tooth for tooth, hand for hand, foot for foot, burn for burn, wound for wound, bruise for bruise" (**21:24-25**). What a law! "A quick way," said one critic, "to a toothless, sightless world". Witty, but is it useful?

If these were the only words in the OT covenant law maybe we could be forgiven for treating the words that way. Since they aren't, there isn't much excuse for such talk, especially from a serious Bible student.

It's this needless superficiality that leads unbelievers in *their* ignorance to critique the Scriptures. If the Bible's friends do it such dishonor why should we be surprised if its enemies do the same? But only on the surface does the OT look like Shylock's handbook— demanding its pound of flesh. The Pentateuch is not only filled with teaching about being merciful, generous, kind and gracious it is filled with wise counsel on *civil* response to *civic* offenders.

It was the Master himself who insisted that church-leaders were missing the more important matters in the law—mercy, justice, love and faithfulness (**Matt 23:23; Luke 11:42**) and he was echoing the OT in passages like **Micah 6:8**.

I've elsewhere mentioned that an individual wasn't *forced* to take an offender to court (compare the Master in **Matthew 5:25**). It was all right to *forgive* personal wrongs. **Exodus 21:24-25** didn't *have* to be carried out. It wasn't written to *promote* litigation or encourage vindictiveness but it *was* written for a society that like our own knew plenty about people who abused power or were quick to lash out in violent retaliation.

Again, we aren't supposed to take the text with slavish literalness. The covenant law is filled with teaching about *compensation* rather than a mechanical doling out of teeth for teeth. In **21:26-27** we hear of a servant having his eye or tooth knocked out. The judges are not required to gouge out the eye of the master in return or select the same tooth in the master's mouth and knock it out. *No, the servant is given his freedom.*

(And it won't hurt to note that this is a *servant* who is given freedom for a lost tooth. Here's another proof that Israel's slave laws were absolutely nothing like those of other ancient nations. Contrast that with the case of a Roman slave whose master was being attacked by a wild boar. The slave grabbed a spear from one of the master's companions, bravely fought the animal off, saved his master's life and had his arm cut off for daring to seize a weapon!)

This provision, like so many others, is given for the protection of the vulnerable. If modern societies spent more time legislating on behalf of the victims rather than the offenders they'd move much closer to the spirit of the OT *and* they'd show a sense of *realism* that would keep them from much "benevolent blundering". If those given to violence were assured that the persons of their potential victims really mattered, that their rights would be regarded as paramount, that some form of punishment, one that suited the crime, *would* be carried out—if all that happened, some of the possible offenders would be deterred.

But the legislation is also given to ensure justice for the offender. Let me repeat it won't do to sever a man's head because he knocked out somebody's tooth. **Deuteronomy 25:2** offers this piece of legislation, "If the guilty man deserves to be beaten, the judge shall make him lie down and have him flogged in his presence with the Numbers of lashes his crime deserves..." The number of lashes *his crime deserves* is important at this point. Punishment is approved but to *degrade* a person by punishment is not only bad for the person it is bad for the society that hands out the punishment. "But he must not give him more than forty lashes. If he is flogged more than that, your brother will be degraded in your eyes" (**25:3**).

It's true that many wince at the very thought of a public flogging. They call it barbaric but if prisoners were asked which they would prefer—jail time or a flogging and be done with it, there's no doubt in my mind that they'd choose the flogging. To be isolated for a long time from a [somewhat] healthy society and made to live with hardened criminals under threat and abuse of all kinds is no easier punishment than a flogging.

It's time the friends of Scripture "took the cure" for their overly sensitized and Christianized sensibilities and sat at the feet of the Old Testament covenant law.

They spread discontent throughout the nation, they spread disloyalty toward Yahweh, and they taught and practiced lies as well as fraud.

70

THE KILLING OF WITCHES

The word, "warlock" comes from an old English word that means "oath breaker". In theocratic Israel that was quite literally true.

"Do not allow a sorceress to live" (**Exodus 22:18**). "A man or a woman who is a medium or spiritist among you must be put to death. You are to stone them; their blood will be on their own heads." (**Leviticus 20:27**)

Strong medicine! Not the kind of thing our modern society would approve of, where the idea of punishment *of any kind* has to fight for its very life. Of course not! But then our modern society isn't the biblical theocracy called *Israel*.

Could witches and warlocks *really* contact the dead? You couldn't prove they could by the OT scriptures. The incident in **1 Sam 28** seems as much a surprise to the witch as to anybody else. But if they couldn't really *do* anything why were they threatened so? *The effort was rebellion!* Whether they could or couldn't, they *try*.

Consulting spirits was the rejection of the Torah and the providence of the God who created the world, elected the patriarchs, rescued, guided, protected and sustained Israel. To proclaim his inadequacy by turning to others to achieve one's purposes was to fly not only in the face of the facts, the gracious facts, it was a violation of the covenant oath these individuals made to Yahweh as part of the People of God. To turn from *his* revealed and being-revealed purposes was to choose purposes not known to be his. To deliberately choose that which is without God's approval is itself an evil choice. (Even to choose that which you *think* is an offence to God (even if, in itself it is not) is an offence against God. See **Romans 14:23**. Some people believed eating meat left over from idol worship was sinful. Under peer pressure they were tempted to eat it anyway. Paul says the heart that would choose what it thinks offends God is a sinning heart. "I believe it offends him but I will do it anyway because others are doing it" is a decision made by someone *willing* to offend God. That makes the choice sinful.)

Israel was not even allowed to turn to other nations, much less their gods or spirits or the dead. Such turning from the Torah and those appointed by God to teach the Torah was a breaking of one's covenant oath. The word, "warlock" comes from an old English word that means "oath breaker". In theocratic Israel that was quite literally true.

These people were subversives in the deepest sense of the word. They spread discontent throughout the nation, they spread disloyalty toward Yahweh, and they taught and practiced lies as well as fraud. They proclaimed the power of spirits and the dead over the elements and over daily life; they seduced the fearful, the sorrowful and hurting into giving money for what wasn't true or helpful and they weakened their faith in their Lord and redeemer.

In older times passages like these were used by the cruel and stupid to bring torture and death to the old, the ugly and lonely and there are those today who lay the blame for all that at the feet of the Bible. What rubbish. Might as well blame it for the entire lynch law and mob rule that has gone on down the centuries because it urged the execution of murderers.

These people stole more than money, they stole faith! They stole people with their mumbo-jumbo, their potions, veils and magic cloths. See **Ezekiel's** scathing denunciation of all this (**13:17-23**). It was heartless lies, it dishonored the people, it was treason against God, and it fed on pain and loneliness and fear—on the vulnerable! Even sophisticated moderns believe that con men that deprive the vulnerable of money and peace of mind should be punished. The punishment in Israel's circumstances was severe because the crime had even deeper ramifications than these humane considerations— which are important in themselves!

And witches knew the punishment! They didn't have to be part of Israel. Had they wanted they could have withdrawn from that Community and lived apart from it as many others did. Israel wasn't called to execute non-Israelite witches. What witches couldn't do was take an oath to obey the King, share in all the benefits of that Community while acting treacherously against both King and Community. *Modern nations are death on "treason" but refuse to see that this is exactly what the OT is getting at when it deals with witches.*

But we see this modern and western reaction against severity in other ways. Between Singapore and Maylasia there are huge signs that essentially tell everyone: *If you bring drugs in here and we catch you, we'll take your life. That's the punishment!* Westerners smuggle them in anyway, get caught, are sentenced to be executed and we go wild, screaming about the punishment being too severe. That the drugs produce countless deaths and immeasurable suffering to countless families doesn't seem to matter. We're so humane, don't you understand, so kind and compassionate. Compassionate to whom? Kind to whom? Those who doom and damn countless families! Shouldn't we be kind to the victims? The law *against* witches was a law *for* the vulnerable!

But most of the religious response against passages like **Exodus 22:18** is one of condescension ("they were ignorant, we're advanced"). We can understand those poor ignoramuses speaking in those terms, modern society knows better. What rubbish this is too. Modern society buries its millions of noses in the astrology columns, millions believing, that this vague nonsense, poured out of computers by "astrologers" who *do* know better—believing that their lives *are* guided by the stars. Advanced? The OT teaching proclaims better than that. It would be Moses and his peers who would snigger if they knew what millions are grabbing for each day in the newspapers. And even now, it is the lonely, the fearful, the bewildered and hurting who are used by these frauds. (And now astronomers have just told us that the whole astrological chart is phony—there are *thirteen* constellations we pass through, not twelve. Good grief!)

Here's something for God's people to think about. "I will set my face against the person who turns to mediums and spiritists to prostitute himself by following them, and I will cut him off from his people" (**Leviticus 20:6**). It wasn't just the mediums God was mad at. He was angry at all those who financed and supported these charlatans. He was angry at those who trusted these crooks and rejected him as the source of assurance and truth.

It wasn't a matter of a divine sulk—this treason, this moral and spiritual stupidity affected the entire society, influencing children who would later influence their own children. No wonder the agnostic T.H. Huxley got angry at those who dismissed the OT, thinking it useless and outdated.

71

WHO OWNS EVERYTHING ANYWAY?

The consecration of the part is a confession by Israel of the justice of God's claim to all of it. And the acceptance of the part is a kindness from God who justly makes the claim.

"Do not hold back offerings from your granaries or your vats. You must give me the firstborn of your sons. Do the same with your cattle and your sheep..." (**Exodus 22:29-30**).

"Bring the best of the first fruits of your soil to the house of the Lord" (**23:19**).

For the ancients the "firstborn" son was the promise of the future as to family, the firstborn animal and first fruits of crops, grapes and olives were the promise of future prosperity.

These were all to be offered to God. The firstborn of clean animals was to be sacrificed, the firstborn of unclean animals (say, a donkey) was to be redeemed or killed and the firstborn of humans was to be redeemed with silver.

But why were they offered to God? It was *a confession* that everything belonged to God, he was the creator and giver. Eve confessed, "With the help of the Lord I have brought forth a man"

295

(Genesis 4:1; Deuteronomy 28:1-6; Leviticus 25:23). It was *a token of gratitude* for what the Lord had done and promised to do. It was *a signal for celebration* when, having confessed and expressed thankfulness, they gave themselves over to joy (**Deuteronomy 26:1-11**).

There is in all offerings by Israel this confession that God rightly claims ownership of everything. Instead of demanding that *everything* be handed over which would mean the end of life for the people, he accepts a representative part of it all. Whether it's time (Sabbath), people (priests and firstborn), animals or crops, money or property (a site for the tabernacle or shrine—see **3:5**). But the consecration of the *part* is a confession by Israel of the justice of God's claim to *all* of it. And the acceptance of the part is a kindness from God who justly makes the claim.

God's absolute ownership is made clear during the plagues on Egypt. He is able to control, to curse or bless, land, sea, air, crops, herds, water and weather, light and dark. He is Lord of people also. Beginning with the plague of flies he makes a difference between Israelites and Egyptians that people might know he is Yahweh in the midst of the earth (**Exodus 8:22-23**). He makes the hail and electric storm cease "so you may know the earth is the Lord's" (**9:29**). He makes a distinction between the land of Goshen where Israel lives and the rest of Egypt; he makes a difference between Israelite and Egyptian animals and crops. No, the entire world is God's, people and things and when the first fruits are offered, if they are offered with understanding, they are a confession and a thanksgiving.

There are no self-made men or women, and for humans, there is no absolute ownership. This is a standing truth we learn from the Covenant Law of Israel and highlighted by our deaths. We are stewards of all the good that God has brought our way. *Of course* people like Ted Turner, the media magnate, will laugh at that but that's because they don't believe our *Story*. What's said here only makes sense within the parameters of *the Story* we believe and tell. It isn't surprising that others don't see it our way. That they should and one day will is true but in the meantime it's for us to live *the Story* (and thus become a part of it) and tell it (which is part of living it). If they hear *the Story*, maybe they'll believe it. One thing is certain, "how can they believe in him of whom they've not heard?"

To eat in a certain fashion, to eat only certain things and to avoid eating others was part of telling the Story

72

DON'T SHARE A TABLE WITH FLIES

Under normal circumstances, when an Israelite sat down to eat, the Story was being told, about him or her and about Yahweh.

"You are to be my holy people. So do not eat the meat of an animal torn by wild beasts; throw it to the dogs" (**Exodus 22:31**). See **Leviticus 11:39-30**.

Non-Israelites who dwelled with Israel as "resident aliens" were permitted to eat what died of itself if it is *given* to him or it could be *sold* to a foreigner (**Deuteronomy 14:21**). It would obviously be edible; but Israel was not permitted to eat it. They were "different" and these laws marked them out as different and *that* was an important element in the giving of these laws.

There were some animals and insects forbidden to Israel under any circumstances. They were "unclean". There were birds that lived off carcasses, shellfish and sea creatures without fins, things that crawl or "swarm" (see **Leviticus 11** and **Deuteronomy 14**).

Generally speaking, anything that lived off what was dead, anything that crawled or slithered along the ground was forbidden.

Any insect that had wings and went on legs without joints above their feet (like flies, for example) were forbidden.

The covenant laws concerning food always had a religious/theological dimension to them and food purity laws were no exception. But this didn't mean there weren't other considerations involved (humanitarian, health and social values). Sanitary laws, for example, had their "purity dimension" but there was an obvious health reason. So it was in regard to eating certain foods.

The so-called "Holiness Code" (**Leviticus 17-26**) stresses the religious dimension of the prohibitions. We hear talk of "defilement," "uncleanness" and the need for "purification" in connection with the handling and/or eating of certain foods.

Carcasses lying in the open would not have been bled as the law required, and flies with their detestable table manners would have been quickly on the scene (that is, those that weren't already on the live animal). For humans to share a table with flies and maggots—under normal circumstances—was to pollute themselves as well as subject themselves and the nation to the risk of disease. To choose to eat what the glutted flies had to leave or to chase off carrion-eaters so you could act like one of them was debasing.

But it was more than that. To live off things that dwelled with and lived off the dead was not for the children of the living God! Things that crawled on their bellies were a reminder of the curse and of Satan (**Genesis 3:14**). They were not to eat from the same table with such things or eat such things because they symbolized what was not *wholesome* (Knight) in either a health or purity sense. For a priestly nation, which was delivered that God might dwell in them and enable them to walk erect (**Leviticus 26:11-13**)—for that nation to eat these things was to defile itself.

To eat in a certain fashion, to eat only certain things and to avoid eating others *was part of telling the Story*. The whole of life; eating, drinking, dressing, farming, sexual behavior, family relationships, money, business, clothing, bereavement, marriage—all was geared to reflect the truth that their God was YAHWEH, and they were "different", holy. All was geared to draw lines between death and life, clean and unclean, blessing and curse devotion and drifting, gratitude and grabbing, good and evil.

Under normal circumstances, when an Israelite sat down to eat, *the Story* was being told, about him or her *and* about Yahweh.

But beyond the food, which had its own important place in life, is a world of the invisible. We can feed the body polluted food and we can feed the mind and heart corrupt and corrupting food. We have troubles enough as people without gorging ourselves on every rotting corpse laid before us in the name of entertainment. To join the drooling swarm, feeding in the stench and on the corruption is debasing to us and dishonoring to God. We're not to do it; we're holy people.

Every act of kindness to the alien, every kept promise, however costly it turned out to be, pointed back to Israel's God and Israel's rescue by that God

73

HOW IT FEELS TO BE ALIENS

Wouldn't you think that we who know our own history would be slow to develop a self-righteous and superior attitude?

"Do not oppress an alien; you yourselves know how it feels to be aliens, because you were aliens in Egypt" (**Exodus 23:9** and **22:21**).

An "alien" was one who lived as a guest in another's country and was expected to respect the host nation's ways (see the literature on this). Due to Joseph's being a blessing to Egypt, to his position of power, Israel was invited to live in Egypt as her guests. They went in good faith and experienced, by and by, oppression and insult.

He calls Israel not to act that way toward those they allowed to live with them. Israel was to be hospitable and keepers of their promises. This was expected of them since they had known Egypt's treachery. This was expected of them because their God, Yahweh, was opposed to all injustice and treachery. This was expected of them, also, because it kept their Story alive. Every act of kindness to the alien, every kept promise, however costly it turned out to be, pointed back to Israel's God and Israel's rescue by that God. "Why are these Israelites so hospitable and faithful to aliens?" would be answered by the telling of their Story. ("...that men may see your good works and glorify your Father who is in heaven," said Someone to his followers.)

Israel's treatment of the alien was to be a positive response, an outgoing kindness rather than simply a negative "not doing him an injury" attitude. **Leviticus 19:33-34** has this, "When an alien lives with you in your land, do not mistreat him. The alien living with you must be treated as one of your native-born. Love him as yourself, for you were aliens in Egypt. I am the Lord your God." And there is this awesome piece from **Deuteronomy 10:17-19**, "For the Lord your God is God of gods and Lord of lords, the great God, mighty and awesome, who shows no partiality and accepts no bribes. He defends the cause of the fatherless and the widow, and loves the alien, giving him food and clothing. And you are to love those who are aliens, for you yourselves were aliens in Egypt."

But here in **23:9** the stress is on Israel's personal experience. In light of that, they are to treat the alien kindly. It isn't only that it is like God to do so (which is the basis of all ethics) or that it is the practice of their own Story. In *this* passage the stress is on, "you know what if feels like so..." This principle applies to every phase of living. Paul calls Titus to urge the people to humility in the presence of all men, even the wicked, because "At one time we too were foolish, disobedient, deceived and enslaved by all kinds of passions and pleasures. We lived in malice and envy, being hated and hating one another. But when the kindness and love of God our Savior appeared, he saved us not because of righteous things we had done, but because of his mercy. He saved us through the washing of rebirth and renewal by the Holy Spirit" (**3:2-5**).

Wouldn't you think that we who know our own history would be slow to develop a self-righteous and superior attitude? Wouldn't you think we would extend help and kindness (in it various forms) without smugness since we know where we've been and who we are?

God will not tolerate he mistreatment of the vulnerable (**Exodus 22:21-24; 23:9**. As Wayne Meeks pointed out, *God went to a lot of trouble to free the vulnerable and the voiceless from slavery in Egypt and he isn't prepared to allow Israel to thrust them back into slavery!* If he will free the oppressed from Egypt at Egypt's expense, he will free the oppressed from Israel at Israel's expense. In Egypt the slaves became the head and Egypt the tail. If Israel takes to oppressing the aliens, the aliens will become the head and Israel the tail (**Deuteronomy 28:43-44**).

But we mustn't think any of us is anything more than a *ger* on earth. We are all only passing through. The Exalted king of Israel, even though he is preparing to stabilize the kingdom, acknowledges in **1Chron 29:15**, "We are aliens and strangers in your sight, as were all our forefathers. Our days on earth are like a shadow..." We're still vulnerable and dependent people even when living in the presence of God.

Yes, but we are God's aliens!

This was a gift God gave to them and on the basis of that grace of God they are to be gracious to others—animals included.

74

SO THAT YOUR DONKEY MAY REST

*Don't base your rest on their unending toil. Don't expand
your freedom and power through wealth by their enslavement. Don't
root your pleasure in their misery or your gladness on
their unending sadness.*

As we've noted, the Sabbath had power as a *sign* and as a
witness to an ethic based on God's prior Example but it also
has a humanitarian aspect. It remains true, of course, that this
humanitarian element is based on God's treatment of Israel, but it is
pleasing to hear God say they are to do and be to others (animals
included, as it applies) what he was to them. It isn't "do to others as
you would that they do to you," it's "do to others what has been
done already to you by God".

In **Deuteronomy 5:14** this is brought out with special clarity
with a phrase, "...so that your manservant and maidservant may rest,
as you do." *As you do!* This was a gift God gave to them and on the
basis of that grace of God they are to be gracious to others—animals
included.

Exodus 23:12 says this: "...on the seventh day you shall rest, so that your ox and your donkey may have relief..."

One doesn't need to follow "animals rights" activists everywhere they go in order to see that callousness to animals is objectionable. The heart that can be callous toward the voiceless and defenseless will show itself that way toward man as well as beast. A boy or girl who can be deliberately cruel to an animal shows a wicked spirit and an adult who works animals without rest until they die needs to take a long look into his heart as well as into the mirror.

The sweatshops around the world, in the west and elsewhere, are a witness against us in our capacity to force people to work without rest just to make enough to exist. I have no competence at all in the area of economics so how can I pretend to be able to know how to judge complex matters in this area but I can on occasion recognize greed (my own or that of another) and point my finger at places where the words "that's business" covers sub-Christian and sub-Judaic teachings and practice. Capitalism *can be* and *is* perverted by greedy men and women and defended on the basis of some economic philosophy. There *is* such a thing as predatory wealth just as surely as there are irresponsible and greedy employees.

However we slice it, in a world without sin and greed, exploitation wouldn't exist. Say that the issues are very complex; say that there are no easy answers, say that nearly all—perhaps all—the simple answers are nonsense. Say all that but let's not say there is nothing wrong! Nothing that needs righted! That there's no exploitation of people, animals or land.

To Israel, God said: "Those people and those animals who are under your power and who are the means by which God enables you to get wealth—give them a break! Don't base your rest on their unending toil. Don't expand your freedom and power through wealth by their enslavement. Don't root your pleasure in their misery or your gladness on their unending sadness."

75

THE HEART OF THE SABBATH

In the case of this woman, the ruler of the synagogue said, "There are six days for work. So come and be healed on those days, not on the Sabbath." Because her life wasn't threatened, she could wait. It was Christ's view that she had waited long enough.

When Christ came into conflict with some religious leaders of his day he claimed, "The Sabbath was made for humans, not humans for the Sabbath" (**Mark 2:27** and see **Matt 12:7**). In this he wasn't dismissing the Sabbath as irrelevant or to be ignored; the reverse is true. While Jesus would have opposed man-made rules that made the lives of people more difficult without bringing them nearer to God, he wasn't for a moment opposed to the Sabbath and what it stood for. He was a loving servant of Yahweh and his life was one of obedience to God's law (see **Matt 5:17ff**). In a real sense he wasn't delivering man from the Sabbath, he was delivering the Sabbath from man—they missed the point of it and the Sabbath in their hands had become a hindrance rather than help. Christ's teaching on the Sabbath kept its abusers from stealing the Sabbath and putting something else in its place. No, this day of joy, rest, refreshment was a gift from God to ensure the life and blessing of all who came under it. To take that away, to undermine that was to miss God's love of mercy that could be seen in all his teaching and ordinances, and nowhere clearer than in the Sabbath.

Jacob Neusner said this of Sabbath observance, "...those who compare the Sabbath of Judaism to the somber, supposedly joyless Sunday of the Calvinists know nothing of what the Sabbath has meant and continues to mean to Jews." In the tradition of the synagogue, the Jews were forbidden to fast and were called to rejoice. The liturgy for the Sabbath centered around the reading of the Torah with stress on creation, revelation and redemption. It was a day designed to allow Israel to bathe in the blessings of God and *live* in the life God had given them.

And this is what Jesus believed. It was a day to celebrate freedom, blessing and life to the full under Yahweh so when he healed on the Sabbath, bringing health and joy to people in the name of Yahweh (**John 10:25**), he believed he was acting in the very spirit of the Sabbath.

When in **Luke 13:10-17** he released a woman who was bound by Satan for eighteen years, "eighteen long years," he was acting out the spirit that the Sabbath proclaimed. If ever a day was designed to exult in deliverance, the Sabbath was it! The sages had agreed that doctoring or anything like doctoring (healing) would on occasions be the right thing to do on the Sabbath. They taught that Sabbath observance gave way to healing *when the situation was life threatening*. Their view was that anything that could be done on *the eve* of the Sabbath doesn't chase away the Sabbath.

In the case of this woman, the ruler of the synagogue said, "There are six days for work. So come and be healed on those days, not on the Sabbath." Because her life wasn't threatened, she could wait. It was Christ's view that she had waited long enough. These men pitted their interpretations against obvious need and exalted their interpretations over that need. To keep doctors from "making a killing" on the Sabbath they would forbid *God* to work, they would forbid God to rescue. It wasn't their desire to honor the Sabbath that enraged the Messiah, it was how they denied mercy to the needy while showing mercy to their own animals (the tools by which they did their work) *and* misrepresenting God!

It wasn't that meeting genuine human need was a "permissible violation" of the Sabbath—it was exemplifying the true nature of the Sabbath, it was the carrying out in practice what the Sabbath stood for. F.F. Bruce was absolutely right; "Any action which promoted the divine intention in instituting the Sabbath was an honoring of that day." The interpretations of these men took their point of departure from a flawed view of God. *I desire mercy and not sacrifice* he had said. Twice (on record) the Messiah said they were ignorant of God's character and therefore of how he prioritized things. [And it wasn't that they couldn't have known better. Their entire history with God was read to them every day in the synagogue. They missed the Story by exalting their wisdom over the Story.]

God would rather see acts of mercy from a merciful person than strict adherence to a set of *interpretations* that are produced with a view to honoring God. Interpretations that denied the exercise of much needed mercy are false and rise out of hearts that lack mercy! When those interpretations work in favor of the sages who have the power and influence and against the rank and file who are voiceless, lack of mercy is joined by hypocrisy.

Beyond the command to observe the Sabbath we find what Miller and others call the "sabbatical principle". The idea of "release" and "rest" and consequent joy are in God's teaching about the Sabbath, which, as we've seen, is based on God's creation rest and his release (deliverance) of Israel from Egypt.

In the Sabbatical Year the land is allowed to rest and the poor find food and refreshment. After six years, the Hebrew slave is freed on the seventh year and loaded up with good things to enable him and his family a fresh start. In the Sabbatical Year there is "release" of debts by the creditor. The Year of Jubilee follows, says the text, "seven Sabbaths of years" when release and the easing of burdens was a central element in Israelite social life. Jesus takes up the "sabbatical principle" of release or liberty and rest in his Messianic announcement in **Luke 4:16-20** when he promises the easing of burdens and the release from sin.

It seems very clear that all the laws of the covenant, in some way or another, have ramifications for the life of Israel at the human level and nurtured compassion, fairness and sensitivity.

76

BOILED IN MOTHER'S MILK

Deuteronomy 25:4 says the ox must not be muzzled while he treads out the corn. The law shows concern for the ox.

"Do not cook a young goat in its mother's milk". **Exodus 23:19**. It's been suggested that there were idolatrous practices that involved doing just this. Perhaps. But then there were idolatrous practices that involved roasting, butchering, bleeding and all kinds of things that were embodied in Mosaic ritual practice. A Ugaritic text has been offered as a parallel to **Exodus 23:19**. It's a text that needs reconstructed and the most likely reconstruction of it is debated. It might say, "Cook a kid in milk, a lamb in butter." In any case, this isn't a parallel to the biblical text which doesn't forbid cooking a kid in milk. This passage forbids cooking a kid in its *mother's* milk.

It's true the Mishnah forbids the cooking of any meat in milk (except fish and locusts—*Hullin 8:1*) but that was done to avoid the *possibility* of offending against this law. The rabbis even forbade the eating of cheese and meat together. But the covenant law three times forbids cooking a kid "in its mother's milk." Maybe there *is* a Canaanite fertility rite being opposed but there is no clear indication that this is so.

Maybe Chadwick is right, the simplest explanation is the correct one. In **23:5** the law urges Israel to assist the overburdened animal even if you have an emotional conflict with its owner. In **23:10** the law provides food for even the wild animals. In **23:12** the law provides rest for the domestic animals. The psalms assure us that God provides food and drink for the whole creation, animals and birds included (**Psalm 104:13-14; 145:15-16; 147:8-9** and elsewhere).

Exodus 23:19 may then be an expression of God's care for the animal world (which has theological and moral ramifications for us in terms of ecology and human relationships). In offering the first fruits sacrifice of animals, **22:30** tells us the animal is not to be separated from its mother for a full seven days (see **Leviticus 22:27; Deuteronomy 22:6-7**). While such laws have religious significance, there is no reason to choose the strictly *religious* significance and reject the *humane*. It seems very clear that all the laws of the covenant, in some way or another, have ramifications for the life of Israel at the human level and nurtured compassion, fairness and sensitivity.

Deuteronomy 25:4 says the ox must not be muzzled while he treads out the corn. The law shows concern for the ox. Paul's use of it in **1 Corinthians 9:9** does not deny that, it simply makes the point that if indeed God's care for oxen—which he does—he certainly cares for his human servants. To accuse Paul of denying not only what OT texts taught but also what every Jew of his day believed is nonsense! Just the same, we need to note what he did with a passage that legislated concerning a non-reasoning creature. He believed that the *principle* of the text went beyond oxen to people. Should that surprise us? His Master said, If God feeds the birds which are sold two for a farthing, he will feed his people who "are much more valuable" (**Matthew 6:25-26** and parallels).

In a fairly well controlled and self-sufficient community such as Israel things were simpler than they are today in a world of international commerce. It isn't always possible to assess fairly what is gratuitous violence, greed or cruelty. The killing of baby seals for food and clothing by those who live in that part of the world is not in the same league as killing them to make luxuries for bored people who have more money than they know what to do with. To abort a developing human to save the life of the mother, whatever else one might think of it, we shouldn't put in the same category as using aborted developing humans to manufacture cosmetics.

Whatever else is true about Exodus 23:19, people have always felt it shows a kind of callousness and perverseness, a perverting of nature, to take what was meant to sustain and nourish the offspring and make it the instrument of its death; to use what the baby delighted to cause its death.

To force a defenseless mother to choose or assist in the death of her child has that kind of spirit in it. The Nazi camp-commander, approached by the Jewish mother, begging him to spare her two little boys, cruelly said he'd allow one to live but she had to make the choice or both would die. He "cooked a kid in its mother's milk." To seduce a girl, by well-oiled speech to choose between her family and the baby growing within her is to "cook a kid in its mother's milk." For a young man (or woman) to use the deep emotion of one who loves them as the means of getting them to dishonor themselves is "to cook a kid in its mother's milk."

There are many ways to engage in this kind of perversity.

There are people who use their illness as a tool to hurt those who love them deeply and dearly. *Counting on* that love and devotion, in a fit of spite and with sly purpose, they sometimes feign pain or feign worse pain than they're really experiencing, or injure themselves to break the carer's heart. He (or she) has done something that has offended them, you see, so *they use their sickness as a weapon* but it can only work as a weapon when they can be sure of the love of the one they wish to hurt. Such people are ill in more ways than one. They "cook a kid in its mother's milk."

Children, in spite, to inflict pain, sometimes engage in things they *know* will grieve the hearts of the parents ["I'll make them sorry! If I end up on the streets or addicted they'll feel guilty!"]. They count on

315

the love of the parents and they use that love to bring about grief and profound pain. They "boil a kid in its mother's milk."

Astonishing! Yet, so common, so widespread, so perverse!

77

HAVING DINNER WITH GOD

But God did not raise his hands against these leaders of the Israelites; they saw God, and they ate and drank. **Exodus 24:11**

Chapter **24:1-11** tells us of the confirmation of the covenant God made with Israel. Moses returns from God with the concrete applications of the Decalogue and delivers this "Lesser Law" to the people who give their covenanted word that "Everything the Lord has said we will do" (**24:3**). They weren't professing they would be sinless, they were offering heartfelt covenant loyalty which while it would fall short of sinlessness, would always be a genuine effort to please and honor Yahweh. That's what they promised but they didn't give it. Moses committed the laws to writing, either personally or by the hand of someone else (**24:4**).

Next morning he built *an altar* that signified the presence of Yahweh and access to him through sacrifice. *He set up twelve stone pillars* that spoke of the tribes of Israel who covenanted themselves to Yahweh (**24:4**). Since the special priesthood had not yet been set up, young men were appointed to offer the sacrifices as peace offerings (**24:5**). Half of the blood he dashed against the altar which related the covenant toward God, who graciously receives it as atoning blood but also as a token that he is bringing himself under the vow of covenant loyalty (see **En 15:9-18** with **Jeremiah 34:18**). Moses reads all the words of the Law and formally declares the words of covenant enactment as he scatters the rest of the blood on the people (see **Heb 9:19-20**). To this covenant the people formally commit themselves.

In fulfillment of the instructions in **vv. 1-2** Moses, Aaron, his two sons and seventy elders of Israel climb the mountain.

It's hardly surprising that **24:11** tells us "But God did not raise his hand against these leaders of the Israelites" since he had invited them there to meet him. But this was the Lord who buried Egypt; this was the Lord who dwelled up a mountain in the midst of quaking, fire, smoke and deafening trumpet sounds. This was the God whose voice melted their spines and who threatened with death any man or animal that so much as touched the mountain (**19:16-24**). Would it surprise us if they had gone up with smiles on their faces? The only God they knew had delivered grace through judgment.

This time they were seeing a different face of God. They went up the mountain and into his presence and, wonder of wonders, he didn't kill them. Note how the text reads—They saw God and instead of keeling over dead. They ate and drank (**24:11**).

The meal may have been part of the covenant enactment or it may have been a meal that celebrated the fact that the nation was now in covenant relationship with Yahweh (see **Genesis 31:54; Exodus 18:12**). One thing is sure, they were up the mountain at God's invitation so they knew they were doing right and they saw another side of God. He isn't forever severe or judging or condemning. *God wishes us well!* If judgment falls, it must be a severe mercy and although he may not satisfy us with a long list of reasons for the severity of his judgment, his record assures us on our behalf that he doesn't afflict without cause.

Once when Ezekiel was aghast at what God was doing to the people he protested against the severity of the judgment. God tells him to hold his peace while he showed him what they were doing (**Ezekiel 8—11, esp. 11:13**). Later, he repeats that he will judge them severely but assures the tormented prophet (**14:22-23**), "They will come to you, and when you see their conduct and their actions, you will be consoled regarding the disaster I have brought upon Jerusalem—every disaster I have brought upon it. You will be consoled when you see their conduct and their actions, for you will know that I have done nothing in it without cause, declares the Sovereign Lord."

But here in **Exodus 24** they see another side of God. A God who seeks peace with the offenders, a God who seeks friendship and fellowship with sinners. The glory of what they did see was all they could take (and all God was willing to give) but it was enough to underscore the fact that not only did they not die, they feasted in the presence of the awesome Lord.

They had an opportunity not only of seeing God in a new and fresh way; *they had a chance to see each other in a new and fresh way*. A few days ago they were just seventy more men, all with ordinary names, having grown up together, learned their alphabet and sums together, played together, got married and lived in one another's daily sight; all that would tend to make them "good ole Jacob" to one another. But today, as they looked around at each other, they saw someone who had been invited by the sovereign Lord to eat with him. The White House? Ten Downing Street? The Kremlin? No, this was an invitation into the presence of Yahweh. Had they the eyes to see, their fellow-feasters would never be the same. A long look at each other in this setting of privilege and blessing and glory could make a profound and lifelong difference to how they would view each other.

And *they had an opportunity to see themselves in fresh light.* There's the need for balance in how we view *ourselves* as well as others. It's possible, of course, to think too highly of ourselves but on reflection, the sensitive people I know find it hard to think well of themselves. It wouldn't surprise me if the seventy men who climbed that mountain to meet Yahweh were thinking about their shortcomings. What they needed to think of also was the fact that he who knew them better than they knew themselves and who saw their shortcomings more clearly than they—that one was the one who had invited them in friendship into his awesome presence. Later, as the days became weeks and the weeks months and the months years they had the chance to think of that wonderful day when God's invitation came for *them* to eat in his presence. (And Christians can relate all that to the Christ of the cross and resurrection.)

For *sensitive* Christians who tend to dwell too much on their guilt there is a difficult but needed lesson to learn. If the one who needs the cup of cold water for thirst, the warm clothes for a naked body, the word of forgiveness for sins committed—if that one happens to be yourself, you must not withhold these things. You are no more your own Lord than you are mine. *Whoever* needs the kindness and the arm around the shoulder should be given it—even if it's yourself.

But there were *seventy* of them up that mountain at dinner with God (**24:9**) and that means they represented the entire people. What God was extending to this representative group, he was extending to the entire nation. What God extended to Israel he was extending to all the nations. What he has offered to disciples of Jesus the Messiah, he offers to all people everywhere. And *that's* good news.

Israel submits to the covenant and it is ratified. After that God calls Moses up the mountain to receive the two tables of stone and more covenant material concerned with the Tabernacle, priesthood and offerings (**24:12—31:18**). It is while he is gone for forty days that the golden calf rebellion breaks out.

WORSHIP IN THE
PRESENCE OF YAHWEH 25:1-40:38

They were to work with God to ease the burdens of the less fortunate and in this way, point to their sovereign and gracious Lord who dwelled in their midst.

78

GIVING AS WORSHIP

There is so much talk of "free will" offerings, there is tireless encouragement to generosity rather than a tight-fisted approach (Deuteronomy 15:7-8,10).

"Tell the Israelites to bring me an offering. You are to receive the offerings for me from each man whose heart prompts him to give." (**Exodus 25:2**)

"All who were willing, men and women alike, came and brought gold jewelry of all kinds...they all presented their gold as a wave offering to the Lord. Everyone who had...Those presenting an offering...every skilled woman spun...all the Israelite men and women who were willing brought..." (**35:22,23,24,25,29**).

I had always "known" Israel was to be a giving people and always knew that God wanted them to give from a heart that didn't grudge but I hadn't really known it until a recent closer look. J.G. McConville and Chris Wright drove it home for me in the course of discussing the nature of Israel's laws and their life as the People of God.

Think of the *cost* of obedience for Israel. There was the sacrificial system which required animals and crops (**Deuteronomy 12**), then tithes (**Exodus 23:19; 34:22,26; Deuteronomy 14**), the remitting of debts and slaves and generous gifts in association with that (**Deuteronomy 15:1-18**), the Feasts and the feeding of the needy (**Exodus 22:29-30; Deuteronomy 16:9-12,16-17**), the support of Levites (**Josh 21:41-42** as well as tithes and sacrifices), lending without interest (**Exodus 22:25-27**—but not just on money, see **Leviticus 25:35-37; Deuteronomy 23:19-20**), leaving crops and fruit unharvested (**Exodus 23:10-11; Deuteronomy 24:19-22**), paying servants wages (**Deuteronomy 24:14-15**).

McConville has helpfully stressed that the obedience called for in the Covenant Law is not the legal response to a legal demand kind— there is the recurring idea that people *forfeit rights* in their obedience to *this* law, if insisting on your rights is to the detriment of others. (So Paul's NT teaching about forfeiting rights in **1 Corinthians 8—10** and **Romans 14** is not unknown in the OT.) There is so much talk of "free will" offerings, there is tireless encouragement to *generosity* rather than a tight-fisted approach (**Deuteronomy 15:7-8,10**).

Behind all their *giving*, of course, is their *getting*—from Yahweh. The land is God's (**Leviticus 25:23**) and he causes it to be fruitful (**En 1; Deuteronomy 8:6-9,17-18;** see **Hosea 2:8-9; Jeremiah 14:22**). And when he calls them to give, give, give, he assures them that he will provide all that they need and more. See **Deuteronomy 14:28-29; 15:4-6,10,18; 16:16-17**. In **Deuteronomy 24:19** if they miss a sheaf in harvesting they are to leave it for the poor "so that your God may bless you" ensures a source for the future it is "so that it may go well with you and you may have a long life". *Of course* there's sense to covenant laws like this one and those that forbid the felling of fruit trees during war, but it isn't *just* a question of ecological sense. To honor father and mother (and all lawful authority) brings social reward but in the biblical setting, reward is more than "the natural outcome" of social cohesiveness, it is the promise of God to Israel.

Running throughout the entire covenant Law is the idea of self-denial, self-control and Genesis of spirit. The concept of *giving*! Behind that runs the truth that they have been *given*. They know what it is to be debtors, helpless and needy. God came to their rescue and continues to give to them. They are shaped and encouraged to give in response to the blessings they have been and continue to be given. They are to treat their neighbor, fellow-human, as God has treated them. See **Exodus 22:21; 23:9**.

But God is no slot machine. The mechanical use of scripture that says, "so much in, you get so much out" is bad. This "health and wealth gospel" is no gospel at all. It bruises the hearts of sufferers and innocent victims in the economic crashes. Israel was called to be a *caring* community because there would be those among them who needed cared for! It's tough enough that people go through the fires of pain and loss but it's worse still when over-dressed, over-fed, oily-mouthed, sun-tanned preaching dandies tell them their pain and loss is their own fault, the result of their faithlessness. The victims cannot live heroically for God under pain, when the pain, they're told, is their shame. A pox on that whole system of interpretation!

No, the Jewish nation was taught that they were to give sacrificially in a world where Sin has cheated and robbed people. They were to work with God to ease the burdens of the less fortunate and in this way, point to their sovereign and gracious Lord who dwelled in their midst.

All of this demonstrates that *worship* and *giving* for Israel were not divorced from each other. *Giving was worship*. It also disposes of the fallacy that "grace giving" (as *practiced* by Christian people) is neither more fruitful nor gracious than the OT teaching.

...the structure God had built was theologically significant. Everything about it taught the people who he was and therefore who they were.

79

A HOUSE FOR GOD TO LIVE IN

It's a good question when we're formatting programs or building a congregation. Is this for God's honor and glory and consequently for the benefit and ennobling of people?

You'd wonder, wouldn't you? The God the heavens can't contain wants a tent-house built for him. The God who speaks the world's vast wealth into being asks people to give him materials to built it with. The God who invests wisdom, skill and creativity in people requests them to use it on his behalf. When they were finished, what did they have? A grand tent-house for someone who didn't need it.

I have been angry in the past, and might be again in the future, when I looked at church buildings that cost millions. The end result was more comfort for the worshipers. More room, warmer in the winter and cooler in the summer, finer offices for the preachers, pastors and other staff, more comfortable library and an easier-access parking lot. A grander pulpit, more splendid classrooms, more entertainment spaces, a higher tech sound and recording system.

How can you criticize it? "Are we supposed to sit on wooden pews, freezing in the winter, roasting in the summer, elbow to elbow...?"

No, God forbid that we should have to suffer like that twice every week or that we should ask that of our guests.

I was just thinking that the structure God had built was theologically significant. Everything about it taught the people who he was and therefore who they were. I wonder how our structures fare if looked at from that angle? If we had asked, "What does this mean?" or, "Why is this so?" about the Tabernacle structure and furniture, we would have heard profound truths about God and about ourselves in relation to God. I'm afraid to think how we'd respond if someone asked us about our structure and furniture, "What does this mean?" I suspect we wouldn't understand the question or, if we understood it, would be afraid to say.

I don't think we consciously build to exalt ourselves but I would be afraid to think we do it *unconsciously*. That our concern for ourselves or for our preachers has gone beyond the conscious, gone deeper than the conscious— that would be sad indeed. That we could parade or please ourselves without even trying, might be worse, under some circumstances *would* be worse, than doing it consciously. This should lead us to prayerful self-examination (which isn't the same as morbid self-preoccupation). What exactly are we building?

That question has relevance even when we aren't talking about physical structures. It's a good question when we're formatting programs or building a congregation. Is this for God's honor and glory and *consequently* for the benefit and ennobling of people? What's being paraded here? What is seen as a priority? Our marvelous staff? Good taste? Preoccupation with entertainment? Our respectability? How modern we are? What?

One day—one day we're going to see things in a different light. If it's been the case, we'll see our emphasis was in the wrong place or that we were looking altogether in the wrong direction. We'll feel some guilt about it, realizing we didn't do enough and some of us may feel searing pain when our eyes are open because we'll conclude we were *completely* off the mark. *What are our priorities? What are we building? Who are we building for?*

A memorable scene in *Schindler's List* comes at the close when he's fleeing the allied advance. Surrounding by hundreds of people and saying his good-byes he is overcome with grief about the many people he didn't save. And between groans and sobs he says to Stern,

"I could have got more...I could have got more...If I could have made more money...I threw away so much money...(weeping)...you have no idea, If I'd just— I didn't do enough...(he moves toward his fine car)...what good bought this car?...why did I buy this car?...Why did I keep the car?......I could have got ten people, ten more people...(he takes the Nazi party pin from his lapel)..This pin...two people...this is gold...two more people, it would have given me two more, at least one. It would have given me one, one more person...that person's dead...for this...(weeping)...I could have got one more person and I didn't...I didn't."

"The Tabernacle meant God wanted to dignify those among whom he would dwell."

80

WHAT DOES THE TABERNACLE MEAN?

The phrase "so that I might dwell" acts as a purpose clause to say why God rescued Israel from Egypt. He wished to dwell, live among them.

The writer to the Hebrews has taught us that the Tabernacle is filled with teaching for Christians but he said he didn't have time to go into details. He did illustrate what he meant when he spoke of the veil representing the body of Christ through which we enter God's presence (**Hebrews 10**). **John 1:14** would carry its own Christological message and numerous other NT texts make a Christian use of the OT Tabernacle. What did it mean to the pre-Messianic Israelites?

The Tabernacle meant God wanted to dwell among humans. **Exodus 29:45-46** says this: "Then I will dwell among the Israelites and be their God. They will know that I am the Lord their God, who brought them out of Egypt so that I might dwell among them. I am the Lord their God."

The phrase "so that I might dwell" acts as a purpose clause to say *why* God rescued Israel from Egypt. He wished to dwell, live among them. I wonder if any generation ever recovered the feeling that must have filled a sensitive Israelite in those days when God said such things and finally made his entrance in glory into the Tabernacle (**Exodus 40:33-34**)? No doubt because of our sinfulness and consequent lack of appreciation of this condescension on God's part as well as his infinite glory, the truth that God wants to dwell with people is lost on us. Perhaps it will come to us one day and leave us forever breathless that this is indeed true.

J.B. Phillips, in one of his little books, speaks of a senior and a junior angel surveying the universe. His senior guide showed one galaxy after another to the junior. I suppose galaxy after galaxy after galaxy finally bored the junior and then the senior took him to one little galaxy, with a central star that wasn't very bright and then to look at a planet that had nothing much to say for itself by reason of its appearance. "And that," whispered the senior angel, "is *the visited* planet!" The junior was astonished. "He...himself...?" Yes, out of all the galaxies and all the heavenly bodies, this was the one visited by the Prince himself. There's something about that that forbids me to offer further comment.

The Tabernacle meant God wanted to dignify those among whom he would dwell. **Leviticus 26:11-13** has this to say: "I will put my dwelling place among you, and I will not abhor you. I will walk among you and be your God, and you will be my people. I am the Lord your God, who brought you up out of Egypt so that you would no longer be slaves to the Egyptians; I broke the bars of your yoke and enabled you to walk with heads held high."

"I will not despise (abhor) you". The verb is often used to mean to pollute. God assures Israel he will not regard them as vile or polluted, despicable. He redeemed them to dwell among them, redeemed them and enabled them to walk with their heads up. Mark Rutherford said he wanted to add a beatitude: "Blessed is the person who gives us back our self-respect". Every time a sensitive Israelite gazed at the Tabernacle he knew God dwelled among them to ennoble and dignify the nation.

The Tabernacle meant that worship was to be a central element in living. The Tent was placed at the center of the Israelites encampment. The Temple that replaced it was built high in the land, the people streamed *up* to it. The situation of God's dwelling place meant worship was to be central in their national/individual life. To live in the presence of the living Lord and with him dwelling at the center was to lead to worship.

Josipovichi has pointed out that the mass of details about the Tabernacle and the service related to it is not *just* laying down the rules of the Tabernacle. (There are hundreds of things that aren't dealt with in regard to that. This is one of the reasons we have the *Mishnah.*) No, chapter after chapter "lovingly lingers" over the building of the Tabernacle *so that* we understand that worship is of central importance to Yahweh.

The actual making of the golden calf is covered in three verses! It is an act of impulse, an act of passion that issues in more lust and passion. "I threw it in the fire and out came this calf," said pathetic Aaron. In the twinkling of an eye, there it was. It came in, in a rush of passion, remained for a while supported by passion and was crushed and swallowed. Not so the Tabernacle. Chapter after chapter [thirteen in Exodus alone] is taken up with the directions and the making. Worship really matters!

The Tabernacle meant that God was to be center of Israelite life. Worship was not an end in itself—a Person was. As in **Revelation 5** the throne that ruled the universe was at the center of everything and on that throne sat the Almighty, so it was that Yahweh was enthroned above the cherubim in the heart of the Tabernacle which sat at the heart of the Israelite nation (see **Numbers 1:53** and **chapter 2**). The physical position of the Tabernacle made a theological point. It wasn't simply worship Israel was to engage in; it was to be God-centered worship. He will not be sidelined or made peripheral by *anything* or *anybody*. Not prayers, special song-services, preaching excellence, revamped procedures. Nothing!

The Tabernacle meant that God must be invited to dwell if he is to make his home among people. **Exodus 25:1-9** spells out the circumstances under which the materials to build the sanctuary were gotten. The materials were an offering as each person was moved in their heart to give (**25:2**) and, then, having provided the materials, the people were to build it for him (**25:8**). If they did that, he would be willing to dwell in the midst of them.

35:5,21,29 asks for a gift from "everyone who is willing". But that wasn't enough. Then the skilled men and women were to take the contribution and shape it into a place for God to dwell in (**35:10,25,26**).

As it turns out, the people are so willing they have to be instructed to stop bringing offerings (**36:5-7**). God also gifted the people who were willing with skill to do the needed work on the Tabernacle (**35:25,26; 36:1-2**). The gifts they gave, of course, were things God got them from the Egyptians when they were leaving Egypt (see **Exodus 3:21-22; 11:2; 12:35-36**) which would act as payment, no doubt, for the years spent in service to the Egyptians.

Nevertheless, when all was said and done, the Tabernacle was reared on the free-will gifts and the willing work of the Israelites when God asked them for it. The only Tabernacle we know anything about in the OT is one built by the people for God when God asked for it.

The Tabernacle meant that God was willing to be a pilgrim with his people. The Tabernacle was a "mobile home" for God. That isn't just a preaching point, it was a point God made himself in **2 Samuel 7:6-7**.

The Tabernacle was constructed as a tent, a house always being built and dismantled again, a house for a God on the move. A house for a God on the move *because* his people were always on the move. **Exodus 25:15** tells us the poles of the Ark of the Covenant were never withdrawn from the rings through which they were placed. It remained in constant readiness to be carried.

This erecting and dismantling said Israel was a pilgrim people but it also said God who dwelled with them was willing to be a pilgrim with them. When compared with all the great shrines and temples of Egypt and the rest of the world, the Tent would have looked ridiculous. What kind of a God lives in a little skin tent? But this didn't bother God. He's even described by Moses in **Deuteronomy 33:16** as the one who "dwelled in the bush".

When David in **2 Samuel 7:1-2** plans to build God a permanent and more glorious place in which to dwell there were obviously mixed motives since God reacts both positively and negatively. David must have had some thought of glorifying God since God responds by saying he would build David a house (see **1 Kings 8:18**).

But there may have been a political agenda also in the purpose since God does repudiate the word of Nathan and says to David, "I have not dwelt in a house from the day I brought the Israelites up out of Egypt to this day. I have been moving from place to place with a tent as my dwelling. Wherever I have moved with all the Israelites, did I ever say to any of their rulers whom I commanded to shepherd my people Israel, "Why have you not built me a house of cedar?" There is reason to believe David wanted to centralize God for political reasons (to stabilize his kingship, to heal the breach between the northern and southern tribes which tore the nation apart under Solomon and Rehoboam). However that may be, this much is clear, God was more than willing to be a pilgrim with "all the Israelites" and bear whatever reproach that might bring from the outsiders. Compare **John 1:14; Mark 6:3** and the sneering of Celsus, an educated Platonist of the late 2nd century A.D.

The Tabernacle meant that God was sovereign and not easy to approach. There is always that purposed tension in the worship structure in the OT. God longs to dwell with humans but it isn't easy for him to dwell with humans. That is, both truths must be constantly maintained: God is infinitely "other" than humans; holy and majestic but *that* God longs to dwell with sinful people.

The laws concerning the Tabernacle stressed God great holiness. See, for example, **Exodus 30:20-21** where strict adherence to the laws was required on the pain of death. It's from his place above the cherubim (**25:22**) that God will meet with Moses ("you" is singular) and give his "commands" for Israel. **Leviticus 1:1** gives us the impression of Moses as a "message boy" for Yahweh and in **Exodus 40:35** even the great Moses is put in his place when we're told he couldn't enter the Tent of Meeting because the glory of God was manifested there. The Tabernacle was nothing less than a portable Sinai!

The Tabernacle meant that Yahweh was a God of redemption and joyous life. The Ark of the Covenant was the most important piece of furniture in the Tabernacle and it was there that we find the "mercy seat" (which acted also as the lid). At the center of the whole Israelite worship structure was *mercy*.

There was the great Day of Atonement (Yom Kippur) when sins were dealt with after all the harvests were complete and the nation was well provided for. The silver sockets in which the frame of the entire Tabernacle were set were made of redemption money (**Exodus 38:25-28, f. 30:11-16**). Joy is called for on numerous occasions (**Deuteronomy 12:4-7; 16:10-12**) and elsewhere. Whatever else the holiness of Yahweh meant to Israel, it wasn't meant to depress them to lifelessness.

81

SO WHAT'S WORSHIP FOR?

*Was worship meant to be something done as a substitute for
what they could not (did not) do or as a symbolical
expression of how they lived outside the Tabernacle?*

The instruction God gives about sacrifice, priesthood and tabernacle makes it clear that "worship", however "natural" it feels to worshipers is something that God crafted, shaped and even initiated. In that sense, "worship" is *God's* idea and while it may feel perfectly natural, almost instinctive, to us, it's nevertheless true that God is in it at the beginning and through to the end.

But what was it all about? How many purposes did it serve? Was it for God more than people or people more than God? Was worship something people did or did worship do something to people? Was it confession or promise? Were worshipers rehearsing what God had done or promising what they would do? Was worship meant to be something done as a substitute for what they could not (did not) do or as a symbolical expression of how they lived outside the Tabernacle? Was it meant to be one of the ways people *placated* God, kept him from angrily destroying them for not living right or was it one of the ways people were to *wheedle their way into his good graces* so he would give them things and protect them?

Did the people "go to church" so God wouldn't stay mad at their ugly lives? I'm sure they did. Did they "go to church" to bribe God on to their side in some dispute or some personal agenda? The prophets said they did. Did they "go to church" because it was "what we do"? Prophetic texts make it clear that happened. But whatever people did with the experience, it's clear that worship was *intended* to *be* and *do* certain things. "When your sons asks you, "What do these things mean?" you shall tell them…"

Worship was addressed exclusively to God. Behind and beyond, over and above, at the beginning and end of all the butchering, burning and bleeding of the animals, or the waving and heaving of the grain, the pouring and anointing, after all the soul-searching and motive-assessment of the worshiper—there was God! The programs and procedures, the method and ministering, the verbal recitations and the bodily prostrations all found their ultimate object in communion with *Yahweh*. No details, no rituals, no verbal rehearsals were to cloud this truth: we approach *Him* who is the center and heart of our life!

Worship was the divinely appointed rehearsal of foundational and gracious acts of God. The three great festivals, Yom Kippur, the Tabernacle service and priesthood were all to keep alive the memory of the events in which God redeemed Israel from the brickyards of Egypt in faithfulness to his promises to the fathers. These events (though not in isolation) created and defined Israel in the beginning and it was in the ongoing acknowledgment of this by each generation that Israel remained "Israel". Worship reminded Israel of and gave each generation an opportunity to bring itself under the meaning of those gracious, creative events.

Worship was the national/personal response of gratitude and commitment to Yahweh who was their Redeemer and Lord. When the worshiper brought his basket of first fruits (**Deuteronomy 26**) he came thanking God out of a heart that was aware and grateful. To no other god was thanks given for the blessedness of the worshiper's life and the first fruits given to God, as God's "share," was the confession that all was God's and that the worshiper was simply a guest at God's table. What was true of crops and herds was true of all that counted for *shalom* in the life of the worshiper.

Worship was the heartfelt offering of himself by the worshiper—by giving that which was representative of himself. In the end, what God wanted was the worshiper. In offering a sin-offering, for example, to cover his sins, the worshiper was giving to God in the sacrifice what he could not in fact give God—himself. A spotless sacrifice stood in his place as a confession that the self had not been spotlessly given to God. It was a confession that the whole person of the worshiper and nothing less than the worshiper was due to God. [I've developed this somewhat in my little book *The Dragon Slayer.*] In offering a part of *anything* (of time—the 7th day; of space—holy ground; of family—firstborn; of herds—firstborn, etc), the worshiper confessed that *all* belonged to God. What belonged to God couldn't be treated as "profane" and must be withdrawn from "public" or profane use (see **3:5**). If that were carried out, nothing could be used in "ordinary" life so God condescended to receive that which *represented* all.

Worship was the revelation of the character of Yahweh. The structure and laws of the Tabernacle, the separation and institutions of a special priesthood, the system of sacrifice, these all said things about the God Israel worshipped. Worship was not simply something Israel was to *do*, it was something they were to understand and to be taught by. Yahweh was awesome, "other" than the worshipers, removed from them, different ("holy").

Worship was the revelation of the worshiper's place before the Almighty. All the "obstacles" placed in the way of the worshiper, the "difficulties" which he had to overcome, the forbidden places, the substitutions which had to be made for the worshiper to approach God acceptably—all these were a constant reminder that God was not someone you just walked up to and said hello; they told of the difference between God and the worshiper, of the blinding holiness and majesty of Yahweh.

Worship was a way Yahweh assured Israel that he was present and available. For all his awful holiness—he was there! For all the curtains, washings, incense, special persons and rituals, Yahweh was there in their presence and was pleased to be so. Worship was a wonder of grace! At once it spoke of God's unapproachable person and of his gracious approachableness. It wasn't just *awe* that struck an enlightened Israelite in worship it was the *grace* that allowed him to approach that filled his eyes and heart with wonder.

82

WORSHIP THE OXYGEN OF THE SOUL

*The God who knew the difference between "mere" worship
and social usefulness still planted the Tabernacle in the
center of the nation.*

Harry E. Fosdick rightly reminded people, again and again, that worship was no substitute for a socially useful life. He said God was no vain being who insisted on our telling him how wonderful he is while refusing to carry out his desires in this life. Would Lincoln, he asks, have preferred that his socially redeeming policies be carried out or hear himself be praised as "America's most loved president"? We know the answer to that. Really great people would rather be forgotten if their grand and humanitarian schemes were remembered and acted on. Can we think less of God? Didn't the Christ himself say: "Why call me "Lord, Lord" when you won't do what I say?" It's too easy to substitute emotional hymns and fervent prayers for doing God-imitating justice. Worship, however fervent, sincere and correct is no substitute for "doing the truth".

Nevertheless, at the heart of the Israelite encampment was the "worship house". The God who knew the difference between "mere" worship and social usefulness still planted the Tabernacle in the center of the nation. When they were finally and fully freed from Egypt, they built the tabernacle and established the priesthood as God commanded. The Exodus culminates with the building of a place where the nation can meet and worship God. The instructions for the construction of the house for worship and what is related to it are not passed over in a few verses. Whole chapters are devoted to it. Precise instructions are given on a multitude of things necessary to the worship of Yahweh. If worship means little to us it simply shows how we differ from those ancients who were fresh from a great deliverance. If we dismiss it easily, we do something no enlightened Israelite would do. And when we remember that the Lord God himself laid down these instructions and this purpose to worship, in our better moments we can't make light of the worship experience or obligation.

Who and how we worship not only reveal our inner workings, they shape our inner world as well. Worshippers bear witness to the existence of a world beyond the senses or at least, to the truth that reality is more than what the senses can grasp. To worship is to act out our conviction that there is more to the rainbow than an optical phenomenon resulting from the refraction of light by water droplets. Yes, the rainbow's that but there's also **Genesis 9**. Drawing aside and entering, in a peculiar way, into "the house of God" allows us time to be in his presence, realize our relationship to him, recognize his sovereignty, praise his goodness, marvel at his "personalness" and honor his majesty. During these periods we not only do something, something is done to us.

Outside the Tabernacle, of course there was life and service (which is worship), but God still called for the Tabernacle. Something happened there that was peculiarly worship even though it was of one piece with their whole lives. To insist that the entire life is to be and can be worship is biblical and right. Not to recognize that there are times when "worship" takes on it a peculiar complexion is a serious blunder. In practice, to hold all days equally precious or holy doesn't result in every day being dignified and lifted. To hold that "all of life is worship" doesn't, in practice, make life more worshipful. The reverse is true, or so it seems to me. It appears that it takes special times of worship to remind us that all of life should be offered as a living sacrifice. It appears that special days like Thanksgiving, and anniversaries bring into focus our every day blessedness that we gratefully acknowledge. In the daily round of "getting" and "doing" and "giving" and "saying" and "seeing" and "planning" and "executing" and "learning" and "teaching" we can be seduced and lose contact with a world beyond the senses, a commonwealth in which we are citizens even while we're aliens here. It isn't our business to withdraw from human society (what does the Incarnation mean?) but it's important that we remember that humans (believers or unbelievers) do not *live* by bread alone.

All healthy worship has at its heart a sense of awe and reverence. An unalterable conviction that there is Someone infinitely greater than we. Healthy worship has a central feeling of dependence that insists that we aren't "self-made"; that we owe our blessings to Someone higher and beyond ourselves. Part of worship is that kind of confession. It humbles us and deepens our humility. Great worship leads us to acknowledge the majesty of the Lord God. However desirous God is to befriend and bless us, he is not our "Chum". It won't do to lose sight of the fact that God is God and we are his creatures. Kierkegaard was right, it's only infants who tug on the dress of a queen or pull the spectacles off a king. When they mature they lose some of their ignorance and acknowledge greatness. It is not to our credit that we cannot recognize majesty. One cartoonist shows us a man reading a sign that says: PREPARE TO MEET THY GOD. The next box shows us the man in front of a mirror straightening his tie. A graphic summary of a "worshipless" human. An aspect of healthy worship reminds us that "God is in heaven, thou art on earth, let your words be few".

All healthy worship strengthens our trust in him whom we can't see. The bowed head and bent knees in the presence of the unseen anchors us more firmly in the realities beyond this life of tangible and visible things. It underscores for us the existence of timeless relationships that are beyond our handling or control. In worship we acknowledge the existence of truths and mysteries beyond our power to explain. Martin Dalby has said: "Bad religion answers the unanswerable. Good religion cherishes the mystery." He's absolutely correct! Change "religion" to "worship" (says Robert Davidson) and the same truth emerges. All worship leads us into a realm of healthy mystery. A realm about which we have some answers but more mystery. A realm about which the answers we have give us sure grounds for hope and rejoicing but a realm of glorious mystery just the same. And puny little people are made punier by reducing everything to what they can explain. Healthy worship carries our hearts and minds into that glorious world which is bigger and finer and purer than the one we construct in our heads each day and having breathed that exhilarating and mysterious air we leave our places of worship invigorated and more socially useful in Jesus-imitating righteousness in the realm of the visible.

In light of the fact that Jesus took his apostles aside on the last night of his earthly ministry and engaged them in worship, among other things, prepared them for the tough road but redemptive work ahead—the rescue of a world—that must give us a hint that worship and "life in the real world" come into contact somewhere.

83

WORSHIP & THE SECOND GREAT COMMANDMENT

To refuse to involve ourselves in the righting of wrongs, the feeding of the hungry, clothing the naked and housing the homeless is a repudiation of the spirit of the incarnation of God in Jesus the Messiah!

At least since the rise of theological Liberalism, and especially as seen in people like Albert Ritschl, there has been a tireless call for Christians to spend more time dealing with the needy than "going to worship," the "natural" rather than the "supernatural," the "here and now" rather than the "by and by". The "social Gospel" note has been sounded with increasing insistence from the days of Walter Rauchenbauch in the dead-end quarters in New York to Liberation Theology in the "developing" countries. Too much talk of worship, too little involvement in the injustices of life; too much huddling around Scripture and too little "visiting the widows and the fatherless in their afflictions"; too much preaching and scant attention to the social injustices like unemployment, homelessness, physical and sexual abuse of women and children.

And how can we say, or why would we *want* to say that these issues aren't of great importance and must be addressed? **Matt 25:31-46** forbids us to dismiss them as of little consequence. The Incarnation itself forbids us to stand apart from the needs of people, forbids us to be uninvolved. To refuse to involve ourselves in the righting of wrongs, the feeding of the hungry, clothing the naked and housing the homeless is a repudiation of the spirit of the incarnation of God in Jesus the Messiah!

Did the Ten Commandments speak to these things? Is not the covenant Law filled with warnings against injustice, calls to just behavior and a tireless call to minister to the needy? Isn't it filled with compassion toward the widows, orphans and the impoverished? Riddled and permeated with it! And not just in independent laws—the entire covenant and Israelite existence as a nation grows up out of the soil of "social involvement" by God in the lives of the exploited, vulnerable and needy. It was the word of Jesus himself that the second greatest commandment of God was: *Love your neighbor as yourself!* And of him it was written that he went around doing good and healing all that were under the power of the Devil. Doing it, mark you, "because God was with him" (**Acts 10:38**).

If believers down the years had forgotten or ignored the needy it was *their* crime, they didn't learn it from their faith. When they sidelined the needy they were sidelining a central element of their faith. It was right for Liberal theologians to call men away from cold rationalism, mere theological correctness and "pie-in-the-sky-so-don't-rock-the-boat-in this-life" teaching! But in doing this they were only calling believers to what the Scriptures had been calling them to all along.

Nobody knew better than God that *mere* worship was vain, "The multitude of your sacrifices—what are they to me? says the Lord...I have no pleasure in the blood of bulls and goats...Your incense is detestable to me...I cannot bear your evil assemblies...your appointed feasts my soul hates... (**Isaiah 1:10-14**). He scalds the worshipers in **Isaiah 58**, who worship and fast so he will come down on their side in a court case. "Is this not the kind of fasting I have chosen: to loose the chains of injustice and untie the cords of the yoke, to set the oppressed free...to share your food with the hungry and to provide the poor wanderer with shelter—when you see the naked to clothe him...." (**58:6-7**). How could those who profess allegiance to him ignore this or explain it away; how could they *want* to?

What has a God like this to learn from preachers and theologians about a "social aspect of the Gospel"? If they know anything about it, *he* showed it to them!

Just the same, at the center of the camp God built a house of worship. It is there that people learn who they are and who their neighbor is. Worship must set the tone for social involvement. We're not to give the impression that organized worship and social involvement are competitors but the visible and social must not be allowed to dictate to the invisible and spiritual. The second great commandment must not be given first place (**Matthew 22:37-39**).

It is wrong to give the impression that those who teach us about God and ourselves are not socially involved! The very act of calling people to turn to Christ is an active piece of social involvement. It calls for change, change in *us* if not change in our conditions.

It's important for us to keep our priorities right. Israel must be involved in social justice, must be concerned about how men stand in relation to each other; but their first concern had to be, "how did they all stand in relation to God?" The Church must not involve itself in social concerns *in such a way* as to generate less concern about sin and salvation than about social issues of great importance. The Church must not remain silent about flagrant injustice but it mustn't generate consuming discontent and banners demanding, "Give us our Rights," "More Jobs Now," "Shorter Hours & More Money," at the expense of *God's* rights! If God is not given "his rights" the human family won't enjoy his blessings. [But see Philippians 2:5-8.]

Easy to say when I'm not suffering? Easier, I'm sure. I would talk differently if I lived in the countries where civil rights are non-existent? Almost certainly! But even those sad people who languish in stinking prisons have a greater need than political and physical freedom. Even those sad, starving people have a deeper need than much-needed food for their bodies.

Social involvement that didn't take its cue from worship didn't exist for Israel. There was no basis for ethics apart from the covenant and worship. Worship had its indispensable place in shaping, promoting, sustaining and inspiring social justice on the basis of the God who liberated them that they might be his instruments to bless the world. I wish Christian ministers would stop treating worship like a barely tolerated stepchild. I wish they'd help us see its foundational role in social activism. I wish they'd stop publicly contrasting it unfavorably with "real Christian service".

Worship helps us to keep the first great commandment first without neglecting the second great commandment.

84

HOLY FURNISHINGS

God lays special claim on these furnishings and their being removed from common use recognizes that claim.

Exodus speaks of two "tents of meeting". One was obviously a temporary arrangement until the "main" Tabernacle was constructed. It was placed outside the camp and people went out to it to Moses when they needed to commune with God (**Exodus 33:7-11**). Then the Tabernacle proper was raised and was placed at the center of the camp. The holy furnishings and altars related to that Tabernacle rather than the former tent of meeting. See the dictionaries for a discussion of the theological significance of the sacred furnishings.

How can furniture or furnishings be sacred?

They are separated from other furnishings by the will of God. God lays special claim on them and their being removed from common use recognizes that claim. They are no longer common (profane) and by the will of God had become sacred (holy).

Beginning with and based on God's peculiar claim on these things, they are used, handled, carried and stored by uncommon people and in uncommon ways. This further marks the things out as peculiar.

They are known to belong to "the house of God". Each Jewish family had its own dwelling place with things peculiar to it. The furnishings of the Tabernacle were not like their own tents. Since God was holy, what belonged immediately to him and what was always in his house was holy in ways that no other furnishings were.

They are invested with deep spiritual significance by the will of God. Each of the furnishings carried a message from God to the people. They reminded them of truths by which they existed, were shaped, nourished and challenged.

The most sacred piece of furniture was "the ark of the covenant" (**25:10-22**). It's the first piece mentioned, it's the piece that rests in that awful place where the Glory of God dwells, it's the piece that contains the covenant which was written by the finger of God, it's the piece above which the sovereign Lord sits enthroned between the awful cherubim.

In building a shrine unto God, Israel is to understand that the first thing to be enshrined is God's will—the covenant is placed at the heart of the Tabernacle. In that ark is the will of God for the nation—the Decalogue.

The ark had attached rings through which poles were placed for carrying. The poles were never removed from the ark. Portability and sacredness are underscored in this way. The Tabernacle was always on the move and God was a fellow-pilgrim, living in a tent with his people. Nor must hands touch the ark, not even the hands of the priests. The poles made this clear and enabled them to honor God in the transporting of it. (This was chillingly stressed in the death of Uzzah when David tried to manipulate God so as to secure his throne—see **2 Samuel 6:6-10**.)

On the top of the ark, not just as its lid (**37:1 & 6**), but also as a distinct though not independent entity was the "mercy seat" (that is, the covering). The fierce cherubim who are the executors of God's wrath, the avengers of his honor and the protectors of his holiness

350

(**1Chronicles 28:18; Ezekiel 1& 10; Genesis 3:24**) are gazing downward, as though into the ark where the covenant Law was (**25:20**). That covenant Law which was being broken day after day would (as it were) call the cherubim into fierce judgment were it not for "the cover" which hid it from their gaze.

In all this the Lord of the covenant gives his commandments from above the covenant (**25:22**), administering the covenant with judgment and mercy. For Israel to really enthrone God is to enthrone *that* God by having the covenant in their hearts also. Nevertheless, they must understand that the very existence of such a covenant, the very existence of Israel as God's nation is a matter of divine mercy, pure and simple. Again and again we are reminded that God is enthroned above "the mercy seat" (**Leviticus 16:2; Numbers 7:89**). The very holy of holies in Solomon's temple is called "the room for the mercy seat" (**1Chronicles 28:11**, NRSV).

And there was the Table on which "the bread of his Presence" was placed each Sabbath (**25:23-30**). Like the Ark of the Covenant, it was made of acacia wood and overlaid with gold. Had they been of pure gold (like the "mercy seat") they would have been extremely heavy. It would appear that the bread and the wine made the confession in the presence of God, in his house, that he was their sustainer and provider and that they devoted to him all he had supplied them with. The priestly representatives of the nation ate the "showbread" of the previous week and confessed on behalf of the nation their dependence on God by placing a new batch of twelve hot loaves for the incoming week. See **Leviticus 24:5-9**. (It is because the priests *do* represent the nation and it's because God *did* provide for the whole nation that David and his followers, when in need, could eat the showbread without violating the spirit of the ordinance.)

And there was the seven-branched lamp stand (**25:31-40**) on which little saucers of olive oil were set (**Leviticus 24:1-4**) so that there would be light burning in the holy place all the time, night and day. The priestly representatives on the nation kept this light alive (using the oil supplied by the people). This was Israel's light answering to God's glorious light, which hovered over the

Tabernacle—*the Shekinah*. The almond buds that were worked into the structure of the candlestick seems to speak of God's and Israel's wakefulness; he to their needs and they to his desires. The almond tree was the first tree to bud in the spring. See **Jeremiah 1:11-12**. The NT makes use of "lamps" and candlesticks of Christians and churches (see **Revelation 1:12,20** and **Matt 5:14-16**).

There was the "altar of incense" (**30:1-10**), also overlaid with gold and also, with rings connected so it could be carried on poles. Incense is a universal symbol of prayer. The psalmist will say (**141:2**), "May my prayer be set before you like incense..." and it is at the time of incense offering when the people are gathered outside the temple praying in **Luke 1:10**. In the pictures of **Revelation 5** the incense is said to be the prayers of the saints. This altar reminded the people that behind the visible was the invisible, behind the formal was the intangible, behind the rock hard physical realities were the mysterious and wondrous realities, hiding behind, as it were, the shimmering cloud of incense which itself soon became part of an invisible world.

Here in a peculiar, but not exclusive way, the hearts of the people went up to God in their prayers. Although it sat in the holy place, it belonged, said the Hebrew writer to the holy of holies (**Hebrews 9:4**). It's been suggested that the veil had a vent in it and the incense from the altar of incense poured from the altar into the holy of holies. In **Leviticus 16:13** when the high priest entered the holiest he had to bring with him incense which was meant to overshadow "the cover" where he would sprinkle the blood.

There was "the laver" (**30:17-21**) at which the priestly representatives of the nation were to purify their hands and feet before entering to minister to the Lord of the covenant. This is used as a figure of NT baptism in **Titus 3:5** and in the temple of Solomon it becomes the "bronze sea" (**1Kings 7:23-26**) and perhaps in **Revelation 4:6** the sea of glass. In any case, between the worshiper and the Lord of the covenant lay the bath of purification.

It's too easy for Christians to dismiss all this with impatience. It's too easy to dismiss all that is physical as of no consequence. It's too easy to say "the real house of God is people" and not buildings. Don't we think that enlightened Israelites knew that? Haven't we heard even Solomon insist that God can't be contained by the heavens, so he couldn't be contained by a physical structure; that God doesn't dwell in temples made with hands? Are we so enlightened and they so ignorant?

We know "the church isn't the building, it's the people"! Of course! Israel knew that too. They were God's "church" (congregation, assembly) in the wilderness ("qahal" or "ekklesia"). Structures aren't holy! Hmmm. We moderns are so wise. Because some things are true about physical structures, we dismiss physical structures as utterly irrelevant. As if they can't mean and be made to mean things that are noble; as if they can't teach and be made to teach profound truths.

A holy mountain, a holy city, a holy temple, a holy people, holy dishes, pots and pans, holy furniture—all proclaiming a message to the world. Church buildings with spires (fingers pointing Godward, proclaiming for whose honor the building was built). We "spiritualize" everything to the point that we lose our balance and perspective. *Nothing* is left holy. The possible theological content of physical structures is sneered at or argued against. Just as long as the preacher can be heard and can be front and center, just so long as the worshipers and their guests can be comfortable, just so long as the children can be put somewhere—nothing else matters.

Centuries ago when people couldn't read, windows in buildings told the Story in pictures, or at least, told central and crucial events in the Story. (Since we all can read now (!) we don't need such things. Maybe we can read but are we biblically literate?) These buildings had their special places (taking their cue from the OT) that weren't like other places; they had degrees of sacredness, places set aside for special purposes. "Rubbish, the building isn't holy even if devoted to special purposes!" And, in practice, so it seems to me, instead of making everything more spiritual, we profane everything (making it all equally common) and have our entertainment rooms right next door to our "sanctuary" (see **Ezekiel 43:8** where God condemns kings for separating his house from theirs only by a wall).

So what is all this? It's less about physical architecture than it is about our loss of the sense of the holy. It's less about buildings than it is about our missing *the point* of OT holy places and holy spaces. It's less about the physical than it is about our uninformed high-mindedness about the use of the physical for sacred purposes and ends. We're too wise, too spiritual, too up-to-date, too modern, too Christianized.

So must our buildings be used only for prayer, praise, Bible reading and Holy Communion? I'd hardly think so. But must all of it be used like an entertainment center where well-fed, well-clothed, well-entertained, well-catered-to people can find even more comfort? Has the Torah *nothing* to teach us?

There is something in Daniel 5:1-9 that we need to pay heed to. Belshazzar's doom was announced when he used God's temple furnishings in support of something other than God. They were only pieces of metal—but they were *God's* pieces of metal!

85

HOLY CLOTHING

Maybe we can't wear special clothes while ministering
before God but perhaps we can think our way through the point
behind the holy clothing of God's ancient people.

"They are to make these sacred garments for your brother Aaron" (**Exodus 28:4**). How strange this sounds in the ears of many modern and western people. "Sacred garments"? Were they made of some special "holy" material? Did they have a different molecular structure? No, spaces and places, garments and gadgets were holy because God claimed them and purposed them for a peculiar use. People invested offerings with holiness when they purposed them to and for the Lord in keeping with his will. (Note **Leviticus 27** for the laws about things devoted to God in a vow.)

But when those of us who aren't raised in a setting where sacred garments are part of the landscape, look at religious figures in the world today, tripping over robes, covered in rings and regalia we find it hard to be patient. We also find it hard to believe that the person in that regalia *isn't* exalting himself. For myself, I think the first question is not, "Are the clothes he's wearing objectionable?" but, "Is the position he claims objectionable?"

An enlightened Jew would never have had our problem. He might have thought the high priest was arrogant or "full of himself" but it wouldn't have been on the basis of the clothing he wore when he was ministering! The clothes spoke of his function, don't you see. He was the representative of both God to the people and the representative of the people to God. If his spirit and life outside his regalia was pride-filled and hypocritical, he would have been judged severely by good-willed people—his clothes on formal occasions wouldn't have entered into it. The truth is, his clothes would have witnessed against him; his clothes would call him hypocrite!

We're fond of saying clothes don't matter and we have a healthy fear of creating a crass "clergy/laity" arrangement and we can't always keep these two things in their place. Clothes *did* matter once. "Ah, but those days are gone, special clothing is now dispensationally objectionable." There's truth in that, but it isn't all the truth. What we don't want to do is this: we don't want to dismiss the special clothing and miss *the point* of the special clothing. *What's behind God's choice of sacred clothing for his ministers in the OT arrangement?*

Something wondrous was happening when the priest ministered and he was not permitted to minister in those ways without the special clothes. *The very sight of his garments bore witness to the fact that he was approaching God on behalf of the people.* The clothes spoke their own message. In addition to the man, his family background, his marital status, his physical condition, his known orthodoxy, his devotion to God and the people—in addition to all this, his special clothes spoke of a special time, a special function; an approach to a holy God on behalf of his People is signaled by his appearance in these special clothes. The clothes didn't *make* the man; they *identified* him. The clothes didn't *create* the moment; they *marked* it out. They said, "This moment is not like all other moments. Something special is happening at this time between God and his People."

Yes, yes, but what does all that mean to us? Maybe that's not the correct question. Maybe the question is, "What *should* that all mean to us?" We say, "Clothes aren't important!" only when we aren't thinking well. We know better when some special occasions come around. We don't expect women to wear lingerie to the supermarket or men to wear swimsuits to a downtown worship assembly. We even smile at top executives who are dressed in business suits and running shoes. We would wonder (under normal circumstances) at someone coming to a grief-stricken home to offer condolences while wearing a jazzy shirt and Bermuda shorts.

And we know the significance of clothing when a loving husband or wife dies and we see their dresses or shirts hanging in the closet or when some time after a tragic death we come across a pair of baby shoes or a teenager's sweatshirt.

Maybe we can't wear special clothes while ministering before God but perhaps we can think our way through *the point behind* the holy clothing of God's ancient people.

It's worthwhile noting that the garments of the priest are discussed before the priesthood itself. This surely adds emphasis to the point that the garments are filled with significance for Israel's worship and life before God.

There are white linen undergarments (**28:42-43**) that assured modesty and a tunic (**39**) that was common to all priests. The other four pieces relate peculiarly to the high priest. See the dictionaries for discussion and description of these articles.

So the high priest would wear undergarments, a tight-fitting shirt or tunic over which he wore a splendid blue robe ("the robe of the ephod") that went down to his feet. The robe had bells on the bottom so that when the high priest was in the holy of holies ministering on behalf of the nation, those outside could follow his movements. In addition he must announce his coming into and his leaving the presence of the Lord by the sound of the bells; he wasn't allowed to "barge into" God's presence. **28:31-35**.

Over the robe he wore a beautiful jacket (the ephod itself) that was made of two pieces. It went on over his head, was joined at the shoulders and tied with a sash at the waist. On the shoulders there were two stones placed which represented the twelve tribes. He was their representative and carried the burden of them before the Lord (**28:9-12**).

On the ephod/jacket the High Priest wore a breastplate (**28:15-30**). It was attached to the ephod with rings and sashes and on it were two rows of six stones, worn over his heart for Israel's sake (**29**). There were also two stones, the Urim and Thummim (**30**) which were the stones of judgment. Apparently in some critical times the Lord gave his "yes" or "no" judgment to something put to him by the nation's representative.

The High Priest ministered before God with his head covered (see **1Cor 11:4ff**) with a turban on which a "plate" of some kind was placed. On the "plate" the words "HOLY TO JEHOVAH" were to be engraved. The man who wore this was "Israel" and not just an individual.

*In **Exodus 28:40** we hear this, "Make tunics, sashes and headbands for Aaron's sons, to give them dignity and honor."*

Clothing considerations aside (but not quite), is there not a tendency for those who minister representatively to play down the dignity of the position to which they've been called? Are we not so anxious to be "one of the boys" and "no different than anybody else" that the people have begun to see us in just that light? In our mad dash to "equality" in every conceivable area, have we not lost something not only precious, but also something important? I hear ministers who are now treated like "one of the boys", a "good ole Joe"—I hear them lament the fact that their position is no longer respected. Maybe the people lose respect for the "office" when the "officers" themselves have lost it; maybe the people have simply taken the minister at his word.

Something similar happens to politicians. They forever top the list (or stay near the top) of those least trusted by the general public. They're amazed at this despite the fact that they tirelessly and publicly roast one another as liars and prevaricators. Socrates is quoted as saying, "You can always tell when a politician's lying, you can see his lips moving." Adlai Stevenson is alleged to have said, "A lie is an abomination unto the Lord, a very present help in time of need." When asked if politicians told lies, especially foreign ministers, former presidential hopeful, general Haig, said, "Of course!" As a profession, politicians have undermined their own credibility in many ways.

I think the same is true with those of us who minister the Word. It isn't *just* the failure of many of us to live consistent lives of integrity that I'm talking about. Those of us who have failed in important areas to bring our behavior into line with our Story have a lot to answer for. At this point, however, I'm talking about those among us who minister the Word but who have no word to minister. Willimon is right. In response to someone who said, "The troubles in the Church begin when the pastor forgets he's a person" he insisted, "No, the trouble in the Church begins when the pastor forgets he's a pastor". We are so anxious to be part of the "helping professions" that we have no "word from God" for the people because we now don't *know* any "word from God". Part of the reason we don't know any word from God is because we've come to see ourselves as just another one of the "helping professions" and begrudge any time spent in prayerfully reading, studying and teaching that Word.

I'm not suggesting that counselors, administrators, benevolence officers and such are unimportant, God forbid! *I'm saying they aren't in the same area of service as those who are called to minister the Word* (see **Acts 6:2-4**). Levites worked with the Tabernacle and service but they weren't priests! Ministers of the Word ought to acknowledge their calling and get on with it. If we ourselves play down "ministry of the Word" why should we expect people to view it as something special? Yes, yes, we all know about those ministers who are virtual recluses who do nothing but study and are cut off from people. They need to have their heads and hearts examined. But for every one of those I know or have heard of, I know or have heard of a hundred of the other kind.

Arthur Gossip told of an assembly that was looking for a preacher. The deputation listened to the speaker and later gathered to discuss their response to him. A serious, shy man finally spoke with deep intensity and yet hesitantly, as if very afraid that he would be misunderstood. He said, "The fact is, I for one am set down

359

among earthy and material and sometimes squalid things; these make my life; and the church services are my one chance. Unless I see God there, I shall forget about him altogether, shall lose sight of him, amid the din and dust and press of life. And while this preacher taught me, interested me, even fascinated me, while he was preaching I was given none of that needed sense of God."

A cartoon I saw sums it up well (almost). A depressed-looking preacher is sitting at his desk, head in hands, trying to understand, and behind him is a chart that plots the downward spiral of church attendance. A friend leans over his shoulder, offering sympathy and wisdom, "Maybe," he says, "it would help if you didn't end every sermon with, "But then, what do I know?"."

What has any of this to do with holy clothing?

*Read **Exodus 28:40** and think about it!*

86

THE BLESSING OF REPRESENTATION

Any healthy sense of representation carries with it the notion of on behalf of and where that does not exist there is no true representation.

A community cannot live without representation in some form. Democracy carried to a pure extreme would be anarchy and people fear anarchy more than tyranny. The only form of democracy that can survive and function is *representative* democracy, that is, where some are chosen to represent all. Without some being empowered to act *for* all, the weak would become prey for the strong who used their strength for evil purposes. Richard Niebuhr's often-quoted remark is true: *Man's capacity for justice makes democracy possible; but man's inclination to injustice makes democracy necessary.*

Any healthy sense of *representation* carries with it the notion of *on behalf of* and where that does not exist there is no true representation.

That was one of the reasons for the choice of a special priesthood that we find initiated in Exodus 28:1-4.

361

It was a part of the nation which stood as representative of the nation. There was a practical aspect to all this—the whole nation, every individual, could not offer his/her own sacrifices and offerings nor would they be acceptable in any old fashion. It wouldn't have worked if the Tabernacle were the center of a "free-for-all" with masses of individuals bumping into one another, no order or organization. There had to be people who knew what constituted a blemish or uncleanness or the proper way to offer the offering. *It was through this special group that the whole nation was able to offer its worship to God.*

But it was more than a matter of practicality. Everything without exception belonged to God. When he chose Israel to be his peculiar treasure (Exodus 19:5) he reminded them that all the nations of the earth belonged to him. Israel is peculiarly marked out *not* to suggest that they alone are his—the reverse is true. The existence of Israel, among other things, was a claim by Yahweh that all the nations belonged to him. We see this truth throughout Exodus and the rest of the Bible.

OT worship had *sacred places,* which were the indicators that every place belonged to Yahweh. There were *holy days* that proclaimed the truth that all days really belonged to Yahweh. The *holy feasts*, like the Feast of First fruits, for example, said that all the crops belonged to God. The firstborn of the flocks and herds were devoted to God as a confession that all the flocks and herds were his (see **Psalm 50:7-12**). The firstborn male children were redeemed from God and that was a confession that all the children were God's.

But if God did not sanctify *a portion* of the land, the time, the food, the herds and the families and the nation then it *all* would have to be withdrawn from profane use, none of it could be used for "non sacral" living. God then is willing to receive a part of all and allow the rest to be used commonly; not that the rest is not his, not that it isn't sacred or that it can be used in a way that would offend his honor. The reverse was God's point. The portion proclaimed that *all* belonged to him even though he allowed most of it to be used "profanely," that is, for common use.

The Lord was making the same point in claiming the family of Aaron as peculiarly his ministers. He was claiming the whole nation in terms of *the part represents the whole*. Since the whole nation could not withdraw itself from daily "pollution" as a result of contact with the dead and numerous other everyday experiences, God withdrew some members of the nation. This pollution of the nation on a daily basis must not lead them to think that holiness was an *option* or a casual matter. The choice of a special priesthood proclaimed that holiness was *indispensable* if they were to live with a holy God.

The high visibility of the holy priesthood was a constant reminder of the nation's responsibility before God and the nations around them. As a single nation they were to be a separated (holy) nation and the special (holy) priesthood in their own midst not only reminded them of that but was also an expression of it.

But since they could not give God his due and live their lives as humans in society one with another, they endorsed, approved of and gladly received the Aaronic priesthood as representing them. The nation endorsed the priesthood and the truths the priesthood stood for by acting under its ministration and in submitting to the priesthood that represented them they were offering their worship and service to the Lord.

The worship they offered was not personal worship, that is, worship that was to be offered by each individual—it was national. These individuals did not live with God as a crowd of disconnected and free-standing units. They were a single community and their personal relationship with God was experienced within and not outside the community.

This modern religious individualism that is destructive of community and unity is a pox! This lust: "Never mind the "body", what's in it for me?" is a curse.

In electing a special priesthood God was not creating an elite group but an elect group; not a "lording it over" group but a servant group

87

ELECT OR ELITE?

*While the priests had to understand and act on that truth, Israel
needed to understand that the choice of Aaron and his family was
God's choice and as such, when they opposed Aaron,
they were opposing God.*

One of the dangers in choosing a special group to act on behalf of a larger group is that misunderstanding and envy may arise. In choosing a special priesthood out of a nation that was, at least, priestly in calling, God was willing to risk the misunderstanding and envy of some of the people. There are numerous texts that show that envy and bitterness were indeed a problem connected with this.

The book of **Numbers** has this as one of its recurring themes. Chapters **12**, **16** and **17** deal with the problem. In chapter twelve Moses' authority chafes Aaron and Miriam and in chapter sixteen Korah and his companions are maddened by the peculiar claims of Aaron and his family.

In electing a special priesthood God was not creating an elite group but an elect group; not a "lording it over" group but a servant group; not a "self-chosen" class but "an obedient to a call" class of men.

It's clear from a reading of the biblical text that God didn't make these priests paragons of virtue, he didn't work a moral miracle and make them into sinless beings. The behavior of Aaron, Nadab and Abihu, Eli's sons, Hopni and Phineas— this and the frequent denunciation of the priesthood by the prophets leave us in no doubt that priests had their character flaws.

This being the case, there was no ground for priests to act as though butter wouldn't melt in their mouths. They were chosen not because they were uniformly of wonderful character. In this they were like the nation that God reminded again and again—"I didn't choose you because of your righteousness". Israel had no more reason to look down on their neighbors than the priests had to scorn their fellow-worshipers, the Israelite nation.

But while the priests had to understand and act on that truth, Israel needed to understand that the choice of Aaron and his family was *God's* choice and as such, when they opposed Aaron, they were opposing God. And when God called Aaron and his family, Israel needed to understand that for Aaron to say no would have been to rebel against YAHWEH.

Finally, both priests and the nation need to understand that the special priesthood was *on Israel's behalf*. They were called to serve Israel. Envy against the priestly representatives is out of order for many reasons but it misses the point because it is leveled against those whose every existence was to serve them.

And the priests needed to understand that they were called to *serve* not to enslave. Authority in the form of representation is *for* others rather than *over* others. And this remains true even though the priests are given decision-making power. The people in many things must submit to the instructions of the priests and are required to regard them as *God's* representatives to the nation as well as the nation's representatives to God.

Democracy and egalitarianism can foster dangerous tendencies.

88

SERVICE OR POWER?

*The gift of service [and it was a gift of "service"!] was given
only to the family of Aaron.*

Hebrews 5:1 says priests are appointed by God "on behalf
of" people and **Numbers 18:7** says priesthood is given to
Aaron and his sons as a "gift" which is service. How easy it is for us
to see that and how difficult it is for us to understand the envy and
chagrin of those who were not given such a status.

"Why would some Israelites object to being given servants?" we
ask. "If they only understood that the priests were God's gift to *them*,
to do them service they would not be envious but grateful." Indeed!

Yes, but the gift of service [and it was a gift of "service"!] was
given only to the family of Aaron. If others decided to take on them
the service that was committed to the Aaronic family, they would be
destroyed by God (**Numbers 18:7**). At least that's what Moses and
Aaron claimed.

"But what difference does that make, that only the Aaron family
could serve in that way? It was still *service* and it was still for the

367

benefit of the nation. All right, so everyone else was excluded from the priestly function; that shouldn't disturb people or make them envious. It was *still* a matter of serving the nation." Indeed!

This is the correct response. Korah and company (**Numbers 16**) were angry with Aaron and wanted the right to act as priests. That need not have happened. But it did! Yes, but it shouldn't have! Yes, but it did!

It seems that no matter how clearly God makes his intentions known, there is always another way to view them. God meant the priesthood as *service* but Korah and others saw it as *exercising power* or being the boss. That the priests represented Korah and his followers (as well as the whole nation) was true, "But why do they alone get the right to be the only representatives? We're all holy," was the Korah response. Korah said these priests had taken too much on themselves. We've heard complaints like that before but have we ever heard a serious complaint against someone that he or she *served too much or too well*?

No, it was a controversy over *power*, over who has the right to *call the shots* in this area. The notion of *service* was lost in the will to power. It was a question of "everybody's right" to exercise authority. It was construed as a matter of discrimination—"We've been discriminated against." *We even hear about some people being "enslaved" because they are not allowed to be "servants".*

No one would have *said* YAHWEH was discriminating against them—he's too big to take on directly. No, the easier route to go is to say Moses and Aaron aren't truly representing YAHWEH. "We're all holy" and God wouldn't discriminate between his holy ones. The family of Aaron was no better than the other families. They weren't any smarter; not more charismatic; not more holy; not more anything!

And so? What Korah and his company were fighting for was to be allowed to be servants to the nation! Really? *Is that how the Numbers text reads?* And in **Numbers 12:2** when Miriam and Aaron whine about God speaking to them as well as Moses was it because they wanted to *serve* more? All these gripes were from people who wanted to *serve* more? *Or was it not that they sought the power that* *came with the service?* Was it not that they were offended at having been passed over for the job? Was it not that they felt they had been demeaned? Others were made to look better than them?

Perhaps if Korah and his henchmen could have been *absolutely certain* that God had chosen only the family of Aaron they would have been content. Maybe if **Numbers 17** had preceded **16** they wouldn't have rebelled as they did. Why didn't God give the undoubted proof of Aaron's call prior to the death of Korah? If he had done that surely everything would have been all right and division and tragedy would have been avoided.

Yes, God should have known better. It was nothing but a misunderstanding and God viewed it as envy and malcontentment. It was simple fairness Korah wanted, it was clearer testimony and the right for "all God's servants" to serve. It wasn't a heart problem, it was an information problem and God blew it all out of proportion and distorted the facts as well.

On the other hand, maybe God knows more about motives than we do. Maybe God made things sufficiently clear and it wasn't a clearer understanding they needed or wanted. Maybe they just resented the will of God and maybe that resentment made it hard to accept the witness brought to them by Moses and Aaron. Maybe a search for "proof" is less a search for "proof" than it a search for justification for what we want to do.

Part of our problem is that we take too seriously the distinction between service and power. If all those who exercised power were serving as they did it and all those who wanted to exercise power saw it as service we would be competing to see not how many we could get under us, but how many we could get under.

Maybe then there'd be less clamoring for "our rights".

Money, which is a symbol of power, can accomplish a lot but it has its limits.

89

MONEY THAT MAKES A CONFESSION

The rich weren't to give more—there was no need to overstate with a monetary flourish how humble they were in confessing how dependent on God they were. The poor were to give no less—there was no reason to underestimate their need.
The same amount from all of them leveled all of them.

C ross this line and join the number of the congregation that is listed as the people of Yahweh!" Surely only the people of God in their most listless moments could find that truth to be ho-hum. Stepping across the line each man was numbered with the holy nation, the kingdom of priests (**Exodus 30:13-14**) and this was a greater honor that these people could appreciate. But they *needed* to appreciate it and they needed to know their unworthiness in respect to this incredible honor.

It would appear that this "atonement money" was paid each time there was a census taken for whatever reason and however often (**verse 12**). Censuses are made for numerous practical purposes but such an occasion could offer profound temptation.

The nation could be tempted to see its own strength, admire it, attribute it to its own power (see this alluded to in **Deuteronomy 8:10-18**) and find God's blessing withdrawn and curse brought on them (**Exodus 30:12**). It's possible that when David took a census of the fighting men he was motivated by pride and self-congratulation. It would only serve to inflate the national ego. At least, that's how Joab saw it, believed it would be an occasion for national guilt (**1 Chronicles 21:3**) and it resulted in plague (**2 Samuel 24 & 1 Chronicles 21**).

The book of **Numbers** (**1 & 26**) has two censuses, which caused no problem so it seems best to see censuses simply as an *occasion* when temptation would be especially strong. This being the case, "atonement money" (in the form of ransoming silver) stressed their danger but in stressing the danger, it stressed their true status before Yahweh. Others might excuse themselves the self-worship of a census taken in smugness but Israel, in the midst of whom dwelled their redeeming Lord—they dare not. In effect the ransom money was the extension of the principle taught in the redemption of the firstborn (**Exodus 13:12-13**). *This ransom money made a confession at a particularly tempting moment!*

Money, which is a symbol of power, can accomplish a lot but it has its limits. Simon (**Acts 8**) found it couldn't buy the Holy Spirit. It can buy medicine but not health, books but not wisdom or learning, satellites but not friends, a house but not a home. It can assure us a place in many of the world's leading clubs but it can't buy us acceptance with God.

In **Exodus 30**, rich or poor, they all had to pay the half shekel as ransom money (**30:15**). The rich weren't to give more—there was no need to overstate with a monetary flourish how humble they were in confessing how dependent on God they were. The poor were to give no less—there was no reason to underestimate their need. The same amount from all of them leveled all of them. God determined the amount and it was laid on all of them, equally. The poor were accountable and responsible; their circumstances did not excuse them or lessen that accountability. The rich wore the same brand: *Needy.* Their social or financial status couldn't cover their nakedness before God and their consequent need of him for all they had and were.

The money gathered was to be used in the service of the Tabernacle (**30:15**). It was wise of God, and fitting for Israel, to pay close attention to times when the nation might flex its muscles or count its national blessings and turn it into an occasion to stress *their utter dependence on God.*

Now they had a god they could see. Now they had a god they could manipulate and control. Now they had a god that they themselves created.

90

GOLDEN CALVES AND ELECTRON MICROSCOPES

How many men and movements since we outgrew God, have promised us utopia?

"Absence makes the heart grow fonder". Maybe! This saying has proved true often enough for it to become a proverb; but it isn't always true. It depends on the heart and who it is that's absent. Moses had been up the awful mountain for nearly six weeks and their hearts grew restless. Here they were, stuck in the desert and "this man" Moses may well have been dead (Exodus 32:1). What they needed was "a god" to go before them to Canaan. So they chose the bull-calf which was known everywhere as the symbol of power, liberating power, life-giving power, sexual power. It was well known in Egypt, of course, but it was especially at home in Canaan where Baal, the powerful giver of life was supreme.

They took their golden ear rings, made the god and worshipped it while decked out in all the fine ornaments that God had gotten for them as their wages from Egypt (Exodus 12:35-36). There was worship and reveling; the kind of degenerate behavior characteristic

375

of Canaanite Baal worship where the worshipers by their erotic service excited the gods into sexual activity. That resulted in the fruitfulness of the earth and the people. *This, they said, was the god who brought them freedom!*

Now they had a god they could see. Now they had a god they could manipulate and control. Now they had a god that they themselves created. What more could they want? Well, yes, now they had a god whose worship made them feel good! This was so much better than a god who hid himself from them. A god who when he was asked for his name refused to give it or, at best, cryptically called himself: I AM WHO I AM. What sort of god is it who will not be controlled or manipulated and who is utterly independent of his worshipers?

The sudden return of Moses, the shattering of the tablets of the covenant, the fierce Levites and a later plague (Exodus 32:15-35) made them think again. Yahweh told them that their survival depended on his drawing back from them. He said he'd kill them if he went with them and he commanded this thoroughly frightened and chastened people to remove their ornaments (33:2-6). They removed them—permanently. But when Moses asked for precious things and finery to help build the Tabernacle, God's "home" among the people (35:4-9), they went to their homes and came back with such a flood of gifts that Moses had to call a halt to the generosity (36:2-7).

But what's all that to us? We in our sophisticated, enlightened, modern West? We don't worship golden calves or bow down to tree stumps. We worship little or nothing and have no need of any god. We definitely need no story from an ancient and discredited book. For pity's sake, it's the 21st century! We've outgrown all that. But is that true? Are we really so wise? Really so self-assured? Haven't we created a god in the image of MAN?

Think about it. How many men and movements since we outgrew God, have promised us utopia? A revolution of the working class would bring us heaven on earth said one political "golden calf". If only nations could be freed from Communism and allowed to direct their own destinies, that would solve the world's problems.

376

We said that in pre-Gorbachev days when Yugoslavia was still Yugoslavia. You think it's better today? Education would atone for all our sins and bring us out of the dark, others said. Medical advances and scientific discoveries will heal our cosmic loneliness as well as our diseases, we told ourselves. No, no, said our latest Western savior, understanding ourselves and treating ourselves with respect and tender loving care—*that's* what we need and that's the way to heaven on earth. Well now, here are gods we can understand and explain in terms of Math, sociology and behavioral patterns; gods we can control and use, gods who are predictable, whose names we know, gods we ourselves have created with our brilliance, gods who are dependent on us. Gods whose worship puts us at the center and makes us feel good! The question used to be: "Is it true?" Now it's, "Does it make me feel good?" We moderns have gods that can *really* "go before us" and bring us safely into an earthly heaven. We're not like those poor ancient ignoramuses in biblical legends.

But if all these gods are so adequate, how come we feel so bad? So lonely? So empty? If our philosophy is so wonderful why was poor Nietzsche so troubled and Hume so cynical? Why did the agnostic Julian Huxley, when he was a full-grown man, desert the Humanist Manifesto and turn to drugs in search for meaning? If science and medical advances are so uplifting and life-bringing, how come we're killing 36 million developing humans every year? If psychotherapy is so satisfying how does it happen that the dean of Humanistic Psychology, Carl Rogers, has seances and claims to have made contact with the dead? How come Elizabeth Kubler-Ross, famous for a no-nonsense approach to preparation for death—how come she's been pursuing the dead and claiming they've contacted her? And, tell me this, why did Richard Alpert, the Harvard psychologist, disappear and then surface as Baba Ram Dass? How come an approved segment of the American Psychological Association has seminar offerings on "Kundalini Awakening and Spiritual Emergence"? How come it sells mantra meditation beads and has the appearance of Swami Muktunanda as a highlight ?

If our secular gods are so great, how come the West has been flooded with eastern gurus? You think it's only the young drifters who listen to these? How come Tarot cards, astrology and mediums never had it so good? Why is the New Age phenomenon spreading all over the West and why are more and more psychologists buying into the eastern doctrines of karma and the transmigration of souls? If we're so wise and sophisticated, how come shrewd business men in the autumn of 1989 paid $625,965 for 27 Robert Mapplethorpe photographs? How come our acclaimed art critics oohed and aahed over the brilliance of the technique and were blind to the utter muck of the sadomasochism which Mapplethorpe himself, in a farewell interview just before he died of AIDS, described as "sex and magic"? In dismissing the true God, said Chesterton, we don't come to believe in nothing, we believe in anything!

The truth is, we're never going to be free from the need of God! Down inside us, beyond the reach of transactional analysis and electron microscopes, there's a deathless hunger for meaning. An undying longing for purpose and for the assurance that human love, joy, dreams, bravery, courage, compassion and hope (yes, hope) are not just chance products in an eternal mausoleum called the universe. And it isn't only that we feel this hunger; it makes sense and stubbornly refuses to be obliterated by the arguments of "experts". Because when life is ending, the things we praise, the things we want to talk about are the good things. Not the scientific, medical, psychological or political things (fine as these may be in the service of an over-arching purpose)—I mean the morally lovely things. Like love and justice and compassion. The things that make men and women what we call, "great". A large Numbers of scholars think Karl Barth was the greatest theologian of this century and some would go even further. When they asked him what the most profound truth he had encountered in all his studies was, it's said he quoted the child's hymn, "Jesus loves me this I know for the Bible tells me so." Jamesy, my Ethel's uncle died. He was unemployed, had a serious heart condition that killed him, but he was well known and loved in the district. At his funeral the things they talked about over and over (besides God and the blessed Savior Jesus Christ) were the

378

lovely and simple deeds of his transformed life. For both the utterly brilliant Barth and the simple, uneducated Jamesy, the final realities were God, relationships and the grandeur of simply loving in the light of God's self-revelation.

But there's a price to be paid for all this purpose and blessing; for all this assurance and life. Our ornaments and our finery, intellectual and otherwise, which we've used in the service of lesser gods, must be used when they're called for, to construct a home for the God we gladly welcome as a guest and friend; a God that, incredible as it sounds, is willing to pitch his tent among us.

making of the golden calf and
the making of the Tabernacle
are set over against each other

91

THE ART OF BUILDING

All the while they build to the destruction not only of themselves but many around them who will join in the marvel of this "golden calf".

When Israel called to Aaron to make them gods (a god), **Exodus 32:2** says, "Take off the gold earrings that your wives, your sons and your daughters are wearing, and bring them to me". So all the people took off their earrings and brought them to Aaron. He took what they handed him and made it into an idol cast in the shape of a calf, fashioning it with a tool. Then they said, "These are your gods, O Israel, who brought you up out of Egypt."

3:22 tells us the jewels of silver and gold given to them by the Egyptians were to be put on their sons and daughters and it seems probable enough that the gold earrings these former slaves were wearing were part of that booty. See the use made of it here in contrast to the use God made of it in **35:4ff**.

It's clear to me that Josipovichi is right when he says the record is deliberately structured so that the making of the golden calf and

381

the making of the Tabernacle are set over against each other. The speed, the passion and impetuosity involved in the making of the calf is in contrast to the "loving lingering" over the Tabernacle as it is constructed. There's no hurry, we are *made* to slow up, *even in the reading of the text,* while skilled men and women of willing hearts build for God and the nation (and the world).

But isn't it common enough to see people, carried away by passion which isn't honorable, gather materials that could and should be used to build something to glorify God and construct something fit only for destruction? And it isn't unusual to see people gather information and piece it together into something vile but something they stand back to look at, praising themselves, and it, as something wonderful, when in truth it's an offense to God. "How well written," they say, "how well documented, how well argued" as they congratulate one another on their artistic ability. All the while they build to the destruction not only of themselves but many around them who will join in the marvel of this "golden calf".

Then there are those, equally intelligent and biblically rigorous, just as genuine and no less in love with God, who see it as part of living to gather that they might build unto God. People who seek out whatever will come to hand, as wise master-builders (see **1 Corinthians 3**) to make a place where God can dwell, a building to his honor and glory where his Spirit finds himself at home. A place, where those who don't know God in a personal relationship, would look to in their felt time of need, when God comes nibbling at the edges of their minds.

I'm not suggesting that disciples of God must always be sweetness and light but when people make a career out of gathering to build what takes men and women down, when that is what's characteristic of them, you find yourself stopping to wonder. In any case, I know the Lord would urge us to "take heed how you build" and "unless the Lord builds...they labor in vain that build it".

92

A GRASS-EATING BULL

"At Horeb they made a calf and worshipped an idol cast from metal. They exchanged their Glory for an image of a bull, which eats grass." Psalm 106:19

Psalm 106 is a hymn to God's loving patience with an Israel that refused to maintain covenant integrity with him. **Verse 19** says, "At Horeb they made a calf and worshipped an idol cast from metal. They exchanged their Glory for an image of a bull, which eats grass." That Aaron in **Exodus 32:5** covered the act by declaring it was the worship of Yahweh made no difference to the psalmist— he saw it as a straight swap.

It was rank stupidity. In doing what they did, they traded the glorious Lord for a shiny fake. Not even a real bull, mind you! A dead thing, a copy of life, a brainless production from their brainless heads and a heartless image from their heartless souls. The reason it had to be an image of a bull is because the real thing would die before their very eyes, it would rot away. This makes the point that the image was an image of a dumb, dying, brute. It was Billy Sunday, I think, who used to say, "Sin is forgivable, stupid is forever!"

383

The good news is we moderns are delivered from all that kind of nonsense. Knowing better we wouldn't bow down to anything that rots away and dies, that fades or loses its power and/or loveliness. We'd never make men or women into gods, we'd never worship and adore education, health, wealth, acclaim or any other passing, limited, reality.

She needed someone to clean house for her and met the down-to-earth lady who applied for the job. Satisfied she would suit, the owner showed the lady around the house. In the master bedroom, on a dressing table sat the picture of a newly married girl. The new employee took a long look at it, then asked, "Is that you?" The new employer smilingly granted that it was. The newcomer took another look and with awe in her voice said, "My, my, ain't time a killer". Indeed!

It was crass defiance. Whatever they *meant* to do in worship, they knowingly violated the second word from Sinai: "You shall not make for yourself an idol...You shall not bow down to them or worship them; for I the Lord your God am a jealous God..."

When asked for a name that would sum him up, God refused to give one. He wouldn't be boxed in, sewn up, known completely. The very covenant name *YAHWEH* forbade them to do what they did. Aaron couldn't speak his name without convicting himself and them of the evil they were committing.

You would have thought Israel knew better. Intellectually they did but their problem wasn't intellectual. Of idolaters, Paul (**Romans 1:22-25**) said, "Although they claimed to be wise they became fools and exchanged the glory of the immortal God for images made to look like mortal man and birds and animals and reptiles...They exchanged the truth of God for a lie, and worshipped and served created things rather than the Creator—who is forever praised. Amen."

It was self-defeating. This is another mark of the stupidity of it all. They gained nothing by shrinking the Almighty. They wanted *more* and got *less*. They wanted *life* and got *death*, they had a dead god on their hands.

The Corinthians did the same thing in choosing one preacher over against another. "Why would you choose Paul over against Peter? Or Apollos over against Paul or any of them over against Christ?" we hear Paul saying in **1 Corinthians 3:21-23**. *All* things belonged to them, including the Messiah to whom they belonged. To pick and choose was to lose!

To worship our *views of God* would be an awful mistake, wouldn't it? To worship our understanding of God would be tragic. "All there is to know of God is marked on the margins of my Bible". How does that sound? Or if not on the margins of my Bible then in my filing cabinet or computer. A pox on all that! What are all these things but grass-eating bulls? If we aren't careful we have shrunk the living God into a man-made image on the basis of some passing theological fad or sectarian impulse. Historical theology is littered with gods created in light of some marvelous insight that came to wonderful Man, brilliant Man. Gods that grew old and rotted away even before their creators.

To be delivered from this was

a severe mercy, a ruthless

kindness; the surgical removal

of a cancerous growth on the

body of the nation.

93

A HARD PILL TO SWALLOW

All that he distanced himself from, all that he forced down their silly throats. He said, "That isn't me, that isn't anything like me!"

Exodus 32:20 has this to say: "And he took the calf they had made and burned it in the fire; then he ground it to powder, scattered it on the water and made the Israelites drink it". So much for the new god!

This was done out of anger. Yes! And no wonder. If ever anger was justified this was it. But surely such anger was out of place, surely a man that angry didn't understand the people, didn't care to understand them, didn't care for them. All untrue! It was because he *did* understand them that his action was anger-filled and fierce. And it was because he *did* care for them (as **32:31-32** shows) that he acted as he acted. And bear this in mind, he was acting as God's regent so the anger was fully justified.

But he was also acting as Israel's protector. Had he not acted on their behalf grinding their god to powder, savagely demonstrating the stupidity of their apostasy the sovereign Lord might well have ground *them* to powder and made the earth to drink *them*.

All that that calf stood for, a god of human creation, a god that could be controlled, a god that would be predictable, a god that would be visible and dependent on its worshipers—all that God damned and destroyed. All that he distanced himself from, all that he forced down their silly throats. He said, "That isn't me, that isn't anything *like* me!"

We think that was their loss? We think because he so judged them that this was their loss? It was their *gain*, for pity's sake! To be delivered from this was a severe mercy, a ruthless kindness; the surgical removal of a cancerous growth on the body of the nation.

And if the day arrives, however painful it is, that God pulverizes our cherished god, the lovely thing we worship, and forces us to see the stupidity of our thinking and our behavior—if that day arrives and he enables us to survive it, we need to fall down on our knees and pour out our gratitude for his commitment to us.

A god is someone or something which is a guiding and motivating principle in my life; that to which I turn as a "given" which must not be tampered with; that which I defend whatever the evidence against it and for which I will sacrifice friendship with God or man. An idol I take out on a regular basis and find consolation in, though in my heart of hearts I'm aware that such affection or devotion compromises my prior commitment to God and others.

Did the Israelites gag on it as the raging Moses stood over, perhaps the leaders of the rebellion, commanding them to drink it down? There aren't many people who can graciously "eat their words". And how many of us do you know who easily retract something we've cherished and taught for years? We're shown a narrow and mean view of God that creates pseudo-scandals and in horror we see it as our own. Easy to swallow? *Essential* to swallow, easy or not!

94

GOD IS IN EARNEST

He's no heavenly hit-man who enjoys his work but when he must, he will bring down severe judgment.

What happened in **Exodus 32:25-28,35** should end forever our tendency to believe God is a "heavenly sweetheart" about whom those of us who croon romantic ballads. The God of this section is in deadly earnest. He isn't hair-triggered and irritable, watching with eagerness for our every mistake so that with a blow from his huge fist he can dispense with us. He's no heavenly hit-man who enjoys his work but when he must, he will bring down severe judgment. He describes himself in **34:6-7** as one who slow to anger because he is compassionate and gracious, nevertheless, he says he does not "leave the guilty unpunished."

What Moses ordered in the name of God is not a measure either of Moses' or God's vindictiveness, it is a measure of the sin committed and the earnestness of God in the pursuit of his purpose to bring life and blessing to the world through Israel.

Moses commends the fierce Levites for doing what they did. They slew brothers, sons, friends and whoever chose to engage in the apostasy which had happened that day and in doing this, gave

389

the promise that they would be the defenders of the truth of God no matter what it cost.

But isn't that awfully harsh? Not only were the idolaters and betrayers of Yahweh killed, children would be robbed of a parent or maybe completely orphaned. How can it be right to inflict suffering on the innocent for what the parents did? "He is the Lord; let him do what is good in his eyes," said Eli when he heard that the Lord would reject his house and kill his wicked sons. This old priest recognized that whoever else was in error, Yahweh did what was right. Others may have their private agendas and special interests but God had the saving of a world in mind.

It's important that we get our minds clear about this. We need to have a clear conception of the kind of God we're dealing with [the God, rather, who is dealing with us] because our view of our God will affect our view of our world—inner and outer. And if we think that an earnest God who works with sweet ruthlessness and who carries out severe mercies, if we think that kind of God is confined to the OT, we need to think again. It was Jesus the Messiah who passionately urged, "If your eye offends you, pluck it out; better to end life with one eye than have both and end in Gehenna. If your hand offends you, cut it off...". He's the one who called his followers with assurances of trouble and pain to come his way and he was the one who turned to a multitude and told them to count the cost before they enlisted with him

The complexity of human society is like a nervous system. A judge sends a criminal away—the family suffers. A father drinks—a family suffers. A mother loves the night-life—a family suffers. Artists turn to indecency—a society suffers. Movie-makers turn to moral ambiguity and downright perversion—a generation suffers. Ministers practice deceit and wickedness—churches and movements suffer. Governors and generals lust for power—countries suffer. Nations go to war—future generations pay the price. Men and women with influence say nothing—a nation suffers.

Since God is bent on blessing the whole world through Israel he will not allow Israel to get in his way. To make her/his instrument of blessing he will chastise her or completely reject her (**Exodus 32**).

And to bless her (because he loves her) he will not allow her just to walk away from him, will not allow her to kill freedom and choose slavery, to murder life and choose death.

To have listened to Joseph's tears and deliver him back to his father would have pleased Joseph and Jacob but what then of the nation and the nations around? (**Genesis 42:21; Psalm 105:18**) To allow Israel to choose or reject him at their will would have been a choice against the nations of the world as well as Israel herself.

It just isn't enough to say we must be kind to hardened criminals. Of course we must! But what of the victims? Rehabilitate criminals we *will if we can* but punish them we must. And it's not a matter of vindictiveness and it's not even simple raw retribution! We mustn't by our treatment of hardened criminals encourage vindictiveness or cruelty in the victims of crime; but the victim is the victim and the tension raised about "punishment" has been created not by the law-abiding victim but by the criminal.

If to "over-punish" the criminal nurtures the threat of his future offending, the absence of punishment (that fits the crime) nurtures the widespread scorn of laws that in turn produces more and more criminals. If ill-conceived systems of punishment produce more hardened criminals, benevolent bungling and lack of justice produces more.

It makes no sense to say that because we are to be kind we will not discipline or dismiss an employee who endlessly abuses the clients. Be kind to whom? The employee? What of the customer? Do we owe the customer anything? It's weakness on our part that we give in to the persistent demands of one child when we know it will go ill with another because of our "yes". We can claim we are too caring to exercise discipline or lovingly confront but somebody suffers because of such decisions. Our refusal to act when the circumstances are crying out for us to act is not to our credit. Instead of bragging on such weakness as though it were something wonderful, we should keep it quiet.

We need to learn from this God who has chosen to rescue the world. This *God is in earnest!*

Truth and honor and loyalty
are the fruits of good sowing
and good nurturing.

95

I'LL TAKE MY CHANCES

An offer he couldn't refuse—and he refused it!

God said to Moses (**Exodus 32:9-10**), "I have seen these people and they are a stiff-necked people. Now leave me alone so that my anger may burn against them and that I may destroy them. Then I make will make you into a great nation." Sounds like God was speaking to Abraham: "I will make you a great nation". What an offer. One he couldn't refuse?

Moses refused it! This wasn't the first time. He had refused to be known as Pharaoh's son and turned his back on all the riches of Egypt and chose rather to suffer affliction with the people of God than the pleasures of sin for a season. That was back there in Egypt. He had already suffered affliction not only *with* but also *from* the people of God. How did he feel about them now? I mean about those who tirelessly called his integrity and leadership into question, who endlessly muttered and complained against him.

Israel is not now an unknown quantity. The immediate thrill of (under God) rescuing them, if it had ever existed, had passed. When he chose them in this text he knew what he was choosing. And it wasn't *riches in Egypt* he was turning down—it was *his* life with God! And his immediate emotion was fear, fear for his people, fear that they might lose what they dared not lose, what he could not bear to see them lose. How do you explain that kind of response?

I'm not fool enough to think that Moses always *felt* that way or that he was always so gallant. I know better than that. I recognize that this was a high point, a response so noble that it takes our breath away but such a high point isn't possible for one who is utterly without finer feelings, without deeper purposes than to serve himself. This kind of response is prepared for, is nourished in the lives of those who experience them, by the nurture of a great heritage, by the practice of honor and loyalty.

It's true that we sometimes see amazing responses from those we'd least expect it from, but that's only because we haven't seen, don't know, what has gone before in the lives of such individuals. You don't get figs from thistles or grapes from thorn bushes. Such beauty grows out of good seed sown, however long ago doesn't matter. Truth and honor and loyalty are the fruits of good sowing and good nurturing.

So Moses' response, while it is breathtaking is, in some sense, not really surprising since he was who he was. (I say that with little conviction even when I know there's truth in it. The wonder of this behavior is spellbinding.) Paul felt that drive too as we can tell from **Romans 9:3** where he speaks of his continuing anguish for the pain and loss of his own nation. "I could wish that I myself were cursed and cut off from Christ for the sake of my brothers, those of my own race." Just *precisely* what Paul was saying isn't clear but the grand direction he was moving is clear enough. If it were to their benefit, he would wish his loss. But Christians expect that from Paul, don't they?

Grenfell told of an incident that further illustrates this spirit. An old British chieftain of centuries ago was stepping down into the baptistery to be baptized into Christ when he posed his question.

"And what has happened to all my forefathers who died unbaptized?" The minister quickly assured him that they were burning in hell. For a long time the old man stood there in the water, silent. Then he turned and walked back up the steps as he wrapped his wolf-skin around him. Gently but decisively he said, "I believe I will take my chances with them." Spellbinding.

...it can hardly be difficult to see that change at a more demanding level could be traumatic.

96

LEAVE THIS PLACE

Now they have a covenant relationship with God, a sacrificial system and priesthood set in order. Is that not enough? No! They are told to move on (Deuteronomy 1:6).

It was time for Israel to move on to better things. In this case it was to move from the wilderness to Canaan. It wasn't only better because it would be more comfortable, it was better because it was the fuller outworking of the purposes of God for Israel and for the world.

It's too easy to become too comfortable and satisfied with the status quo, isn't it? Peter sees something wonderful up the mount of Transfiguration and wants to build booths there but Christ urges him back down the mountain to where the people are (**Matthew 17**). Sometimes we grow weary with the pursuit of growth, progress or (even in the healthy sense) success. Our emotional, mental and physical surroundings become familiar and comfortable. Our "furniture" is well worn and we fit snugly into it. Our creed has now wrapped itself around us; we've worked out the kinks (or most of them) in our stated beliefs and contentedly flow with our worship patterns. It's hardly surprising we wish to remain where we are. If changing from old and comfortable shoes to a new an unfamiliar pair can be traumatic, it can hardly be difficult to see that change at a more demanding level could be traumatic.

Israel has been around the mountain for about a year. They have their food and water supply, they are prospering and healthy. Now they have a covenant relationship with God, a sacrificial system and priesthood set in order. Is that not enough? No! They are told to move on (see **Deuteronomy 1:6**).

But people will only move on if they are convinced that the change is for the better. (Even then there are those who don't think *the better* is worth the trouble.) But convince people that the change will really benefit them and half the battle is won (only half). Aladdin's lamp was traded in for a piece of shiny junk because the shiny junk was thought to be better and a world was traded in for a piece of metal. The people of River City in the movie: *The Music Man,* traded in their pool-hall for a school band because they became convinced the band would save their kids from a fate worse than death. In the parables told by Christ (**Matthew 13**) the merchant of pearls traded all he had for a very special pearl. The laborer sold all he had to buy the field and its treasure. Neither one would have gone to that much trouble if they hadn't thought they were gaining. Once they passionately believed they were gaining, their *sacrifice* was no sacrifice. *Not* selling all they had to get the other would have been sacrifice to them.

So one of the safeguards against stagnation is the conviction that better things are ahead and "you ain't seen nothing yet". This is one of the reasons hope looms so large in the Bible. This is why there is optimism even in the midst of much pain. Boredom is only possible because we think we've seen or heard it all. It is only a real possibility for a people who have *arrived*. Observe a Bible student in class; lethargic and listless. Then the teacher introduces something new, exciting, profound, full of promise, unlocking a mystery and broadening horizons. Now see the student's jaw go slack, the eyes widen and off he or she goes with new zest into the Scriptures.

This is why we need people with a prophetic spirit, with zest for living. This is why we must never make God or the Bible appear to be dull. This is why we mustn't encourage people to be satisfied to drone out the stock answers, borrowed and inherited creedal statements or to be content with stale ritual. A child's creed is good for a child, adults need to move on. We don't need to jettison enduring truths to leave the mountain in search of further experience with God. In our bones we all know we "ain't seen nothing yet".

He doesn't want the land if

God's presence does not go

with them

97

GO WITH US OR DON'T SEND US

It's no difficult thing for many of us blessed ones to think of people who interceded for us in a costly, powerful and fully effective way.

The golden calf. All that that calf stood for: A god of human creation, a god that could be controlled, a predictable god, a visible god, a time and space-bound god, a god that depended on humans for his existence and whether he stayed put or moved on— all that YAHWEH damned and destroyed, all that he forced down the throats of the worshipers, all that he distanced himself from. He said: "That isn't me! That isn't anything *like* me."

Moses, lover of his people that he was and frustrated with them though he was, pleaded with God to forgive them. If God would blot them out of the book he had entered their names in, Moses wanted to be blotted out with them. And God was gracious, forgave them and chastened them—but he forgave them. Chastening and forgiveness have never been enemies so they don't need to be reconciled.

And having forgiven them he renews the promise that he will give them the land he had promised their fathers (**33:1-3**) so he sends them forth. But because of their stubborn and evil hearts a less exalted being will go with them to guide and secure for them the land (**33:2-3**). One divine being is the angel of God's presence (**33:14**), the angel promised in **verse 2** is aptly called by someone, "the angel of God's absence". Even though that angel would go before them and win the land for them, the fact that it was he rather than "my Presence" was God distancing himself from Israel.

There is a clear distinction drawn between the angel of verse two and the "I" who would not go up among them for fear of having to destroy them *but*, despite the "I" who wouldn't go up there was the assurance that God would send his angel so they would secure the land he had promised on oath he would give their forefathers, Abraham, Isaac and Jacob. (**33:1** is more than a command to leave the Sinai area. It is a full-blown assurance that they were to go to the land that God would give them even as he had sworn.)

But to Moses' everlasting credit, he asks for more than the assurance that they would receive the land. He doesn't want the land if God's presence does not go with them (**33:14**). Without God dwelling in the midst of them, they are no more than another nation among other nations; they are nothing more than the descendants of another ancient pilgrim who has vanished off the earth (**33:16**).

What is the gift of God without God? What is a piece of land without the presence and fellowship of the gracious Giver? How could they make it a home if the "Father" of the nation wasn't there and pleased to dwell with them?

That God would send an angel before them (**33:2**) doesn't say enough. What precisely is the function of the angel? Yes, the angel would help them drive out the nations before them but does that exhaust the description of his work and nature? This angel is the angel of God's absence, what does that mean (**33:12**)? And so Moses pleads for more than such an angel, pleads for God's own Presence. After all, these people aren't Moses' people (**33:13** and see **Ezekiel 20:4-12** where this whole period is alluded to). And God had said Moses was singled out and known by him (**33:12**). If indeed that is

402

true, Moses asks for grace, that the Presence of God might continue with Israel and him so that Moses can get to know YAHWEH even more intimately. Before this really selfless kind of intercession (do see **32:31-32**) God "repents" and assures Moses the threat has been averted. The glory, covenant and Presence of God would remain with the nation and they would remain his peculiar treasure and kingdom of priests (**14**). Blessed intercession! Israel didn't know what it had in having such a one as Moses.

And it's no difficult thing for many of us blessed ones to think of people who interceded for us in a costly, powerful and fully effective way.

To be someone like that—is that not heavenly?

Isn't this a lovely thing to learn--that God can feel warm about humans?

98

AS A FRIEND TO HIS FRIEND

I didn't merely break a law, I broke a heart! The sooner we see our sins as crimes against our Friend and our friends the better.

"The Lord would speak face to face with Moses," we're told in **33:11.** "Face to face" is explained for us, "as a man speaks with his friend". Here's another of the many texts that function to confirm Moses' leadership under God. Others were leaders also but this was a unique person in Israel's history. But there's more than a formal confirmation of the man's call to a place of leadership—isn't there? It's warm as well as formal—there's affection there and all the more it stresses God's serious to complete his overarching purpose that he will not allow Moses to enter the promised land.

Isn't this a lovely thing to learn that God can feel warm about humans? It's true that this isn't said of all men and women and it's true that only one is expressly called God's friend (**2 Chronicles 20:7; Isaiah 41:8; James 2:23**) but if it happened to one human or a few humans, it is a possibility for all humans. To be God's friend! To be *called* God's friend *by God*! See **John 15:13-15.**

What a difference it makes to religion to know that it can be viewed as friendship with God. It makes a difference to "sin". Sin is more than the breaking of a law of God, it is more than a falling short, a missing of the mark and a transgression and the like. It is the violation of a friendship. It is disloyalty and treachery against a loved one, one who holds me dear, who cherishes me and always wishes me well.

It is right to speak of sin as the violation of law! But it's wrong to view it only from that angle. God is more than a lawgiver, more than a judge, more than a moral governor.

I'm caught speeding, I have broken a "law", a wise rule of society so I pay my fine for transgressing this faceless rule; this wise faceless rule—but this *faceless rule* for all that. There is no anguish here, maybe personal embarrassment, but no pain. No one was hurt, no person was crippled and local government got a little more income. There is nothing in all that to encourage remorse or repentance. The personal is absent.

But I sin against my wife/husband/children/parents/—friends! Why is it that tears well up? Why do I have guilt-filled eyes and a remorse-filled heart? I didn't merely break a law, I broke a heart! The sooner we see our sins as crimes against our Friend and our friends the better. Maybe then, by God's grace, we will be able to harness the power of friendship against sin rather than simply depending on moral legalities and our awareness of them.

Being God's friend and being befriended by him will mean we will cherish what he cherishes and give him our support in what is noble and honorable. Christ believed if we were his friends we would keep his commandments. We can hardly offer friendship to God while making a covenant with organized evil (**James 4:4**), which is his mortal enemy. How could we cherish that which sought Christ's destruction and the destruction of the world he so loves? Friendship makes its demands just as laws do even though the demand comes from a different direction.

99

MY FACE SHALL NOT BE SEEN

It would seem that God comes to their room every morning for a private briefing on what he will be up to in the world that day.

God spoke with Moses as with a friend and the thought of it might well fill us with two distinct feelings. One of joy that such a God exists and would make a friend of a human and in so doing, allow us to think of the infinite possibilities in such a relationship. And one of jealousy; the right kind, we would hope, when we too would want in on the blessedness of such a relationship.

Nevertheless, there is **33:22-23** which says, "When my glory passes by, I will put you in a cleft in the rock and cover you with my hand until I have passed by. Then I will remove my hand and you will see my back; but my face must not be seen."

Not in this life will we see God's face. Not in this life will be behold all his glory. Not in this life will be given the opportunity to absorb all that "his face" means. Even for a friend as close as Moses there must be an opening in the rock, a place to be hidden by God as an act of protection (**20**).

And it was that—an act of protection. But it also says to us that the person of God must always remain too big for us, unfathomable, beyond our grasp, "his ways are past finding out."

There must surely be this element in all healthy relationships between humans and God. I confess to some irritation with those for whom God is so familiar. No word of his has mystery and no plan of his is unknown to them. They know why "God allowed" this or that to happen. They have the answer to why "a door was shut" when some fine person with noble intentions tried to go through it. They understand what God wants to teach people when they have suffered bereavement or some great loss. They recognize God's hand in everything and are never at a loss for words. It would seem that God comes to their room every morning for a private briefing on what he will be up to in the world that day.

Colin Morris scathingly says, "There are preachers who chat about God with a folksy familiarity that is breathtaking. They would be modest enough to confess they haven't the foggiest idea what is going on in the head of their family pet but lay claim to sure knowledge of what their **Pal Up There** is thinking about the National Economy, the Middle East conflict or even the future of Mankind."

There is no mark of humility in such people. They are never stunned into silence! Their steps were guided by God. He opened up this or that or closed this or that or promised them to say this or that. They never open a Bible but God opens it for them at just the right text for that very moment and gives them a revelation about its meaning and application. If one protests that their use of the text doesn't seem admissible we're as likely as not to hear, "Well, you aren't arguing with me, you're arguing with the word of God!" as though there is no possibility that "a word of man" might issue from them and that they could be mistaken in their interpretation.

But the text allows us to muse over this: while God's ways are beyond searching out because he is too majestic and grand for us, he sometimes *chooses* to work incognito. Wondrous things are done for us and we know not how they were done or who did them but we have a sneaking suspicion that if we listened hard we might, so to speak, hear the dying whisper of **33:23**. Fervent prayers are answered, much-needed help arrived without our asking, the well-timed letter, the desperately needed success—these arrive much to our joy-filled wonder and total surprise. It could all be explained by others as coincidence but we, too filled with joy to believe such reasoning, look eagerly around to see who we can thank and only manage, as it were, to catch a glimpse of Someone's back. We scramble to see more but he's gone and on a moment's reflection we gladly respect his wish for hiddenness.

And having seen him graciously act in a hidden way, now and then we're moved to that kind of action ourselves and no one knows who did the lovely thing—they get only a glimpse of our back parts as we hurry away. I love the thought of that. I have so much experience in being helped by those who wouldn't show their faces.

We aren't to suppose that God punishes the innocent children of transgressors although his punishment of the transgressors often means suffering for their children

100

THE DARK LINE

If there is anything the voiceless and marginal people of the world need to hear us teach and live out it is this: All wrongs will be righted!

They rebelled against God even while Moses is up the mountain receiving covenant instruction (**32**). The tables of the covenant are smashed and the Lord in fury is prepared to destroy them (**32:9-10**) but Moses pleads their case (**32:31; 33:1-6,12-15**) so that mercy prevails. Now in **Exodus 34:1-10** God is renewing the covenant with Israel (**34:10**) through their intercessor who has again pleaded for them (**34:8-9**). In the course of the renewal God manifests himself to Moses, not showing him what he *looks* like but what he *is* like and he does that by declaring his own name, "Yahweh, Yahweh" (**34:6**). The name is given content, the sound was meant to bring to the minds of Israel what God here says about himself. If we ask what the name "Yahweh" means, we are to go beyond etymology and linguistic arguments and note what he says of himself and how he shows himself in his doings (**34:10**).

411

In response to Moses" pleas and Israel's awful need in connection with the golden calf, God describes himself as one who is compassionate and forgiving, gracious and slow to anger, faithful and maintaining his covenant love toward those who will have him as the covenant Lord (**34:6-7**). But he doesn't stop there! Gracious, forgiving, compassionate and loyal—yes, but "Yet he does not leave the guilty unpunished; he punishes the children and their children for the sins of the fathers to the third and fourth generation" (**v.7**). See **20:5-6** where similar words are used in connection with the breaking of the second commandment and note how the second commandment is phrased here in **34:17**.

W.M.Clow call this "the dark line in the face of God". His willingness to punish the transgressor. (We aren't to suppose that God *punishes* the innocent children of transgressors although his *punishment* of the transgressors often means *suffering* for their children.)

We're tempted to call **verses 5-6** "gospel" and **verse 7** something else but we need to think this through. Whether we like it or not, the God who revealed himself here (and more fully in Jesus Christ) is a God who is compassionate and gracious and *yet* he punishes the impenitent transgressor.

If there is anything the voiceless and marginal people of the world need to hear us teach and live out it is this: *All wrongs will be righted!* We *want* a God who will take sin seriously. Because injustice, the porn industry, the vice and drug barons, the war-mongers, the sadistic, brutal and cruel matter to us, we don't want a God who yawns at it all, who murmurs at all these and this, "There, there, it's all right, you didn't mean it". We *want* him to take it all seriously; we *want* him to have a "dark line" down his face. We *want* to be able to say to the people who turn to us in despair and shock, with a plea in their eyes, *"Believe me, all wrongs will be righted."*

The witness of Scripture tells us that Yahweh is a God to whom justice matters. The garden, the flood, Sodom and Gomorrah, the Korah, Dathan and Abiram rebellion, the Assyrian and Babylonian exiles—all bear witness to that dark line. The cross of Jesus Christ—whatever one we choose among the theories of the atonement—

makes it clear that God takes sin seriously. And nowhere more seriously than among his own people!

We *want* a God who can become judicially angry but whether we want it or not, he himself has said that's how he is! It's a lovely thing to sing of the grace and compassion of the Father of our Lord Jesus Christ (and praise God that it's true) but we need to remember that it is of *that* Father that we read, "He that spared not his own Son but delivered him up for us all..."

But even this is not bad news for the fierceness of God's fury against evil is the assurance that he will bring us to holiness. It is *his* holiness that is the guarantee of ours! He will not allow us to live like pigs! If there had been no "dark line" on the face of God there would have been no cross on that hill and if there had been no cross on that hill it would have meant that God had left us to our own devices. We can bear the thought of **Exodus 34:7** more easily than we can bear the thought of his washing his hands of us all and eternally walking away!

I lay prostrate before the Lord those forty days and forty nights because the Lord said he would destroy you. I prayed to the Lord and said, "O Sovereign Lord, do not destroy your people "

101

HE WAS NOT AWARE

Why didn't his face shine earlier? Was it because that on this stay in the mountain he was overwhelmed by selfless love for the people?

So where are we at this juncture? Israel had arrived at Sinai, prepared themselves for the self-manifestation of God, were frightened by the spectacles and the sounds, especially the Decalogue spoken by the awesome voice (**19:1—20:18**). Moses received the "book of the covenant" material when he entered into private communication with God (**20:19—24:11**). Later, God called Moses to join him on the mountain to receive the two tables of the Decalogue and additional material connected with the Tabernacle, priesthood and offerings (**24:12—31:18**). It's while he's gone on this occasion that the rebellion focused in the golden calf incident occurred.

This section (**Exodus 34:29-35**) is especially interesting for numerous reasons, not the least of which is that Paul makes extended use of it in **2 Corinthians 3**. We're told that Moses spent another forty days in God's presence (**34:28**, see **Deuteronomy**

415

9:18) after the golden calf incident. That time was spent, not only receiving the renewed covenant and other covenant instruction; it was spent in intercession, begging God not to destroy the treacherous nation.

"I lay prostrate before the Lord those forty days and forty nights because the Lord said he would destroy you. I prayed to the Lord and said, "O Sovereign Lord, do not destroy your people...Overlook the stubbornness of this people, their wickedness and their sin" (**Deuteronomy 9:25-26**).

No wonder the psalmist makes Moses one of the three paramount interceders for Israel (**Psalm 99:6-7**); no wonder the Jewish nation exalted Moses almost to the point of worship; no wonder all non-Jews who take seriously the record of this man, shake their head at the wonder of his life.

He'd been in the presence of God before for forty days, when he first received the Tables and "the book of the covenant", why didn't his face shine then? Is there anything to Chadwick's thought that what brought him closer to the glory of God was a deepening desire to know God (**33:18**) and the fact that on this stay in the mountain he was overwhelmed by selfless love for the people? I want to believe that, and think there is as much ground for it as for any other educated guess.

And a striking mark of his unselfconscious devotion is the fact that he is unaware that his face is glorious (**29**). He was so long in the presence of God's glory and so united in heart with God's purpose that he reflected it. Here was another proof indeed that this Moses, the one they had so recently despised (**32:1**), not once, but on many occasions—this same Moses was in the very presence of his Friend (**33:11**)—his commission was real.

Surely the loveliest brand of goodness is the kind that is so much a part of the character of a person that they are unaware of it. They *do* it because they *are* it. They serve the Lord as naturally as they eat a meal, without affectation or flourishing. If you were to say to them, "Your face is shining!" they might say, "Oh, dear, is it really?" and rise to look in a mirror, sure that you're mistaken.

416

Wilbur Rees put it like this, "Saints never know they're saints. That's why they are saints. They are too busy talking to God to look in the mirror. The same moles and wrinkles are there, but contact with the divine has given them a borrowed glory. Divine conversation has left a residual luster. The saints are not conscious that they are different, but the dark world is quite aware of the light that has invaded it. The world does not need to ask, "Have you been talking to God?" but only, "What did he say?"."

...this Tabernacle, this they built gladly and with pride.

102

A HOME BUILT OUT OF SUFFERING

Israel had built treasure cities for Pharaoh but it was under the whip, they built nothing that had their heart in it. Now, this Tabernacle, that was something else!

The Tabernacle was a glorious place with the blues and reds and yellows, the blacks and whites, the sparkle and shine, the brilliance of silver and the warm glow of gold. The woven threads, the flashing jewels, the multi-colored curtains, the leaping flames and the clouds of sweet-smelling incense. For all the truth there is to tell about the awful "throne room" where the Glory dwelled, for all the truth about the need for sacrifice in approaching Yahweh—this was a house of glory, color, joy, life, forgiveness, prayers, praise and unity. Here in **35—40** there must have been singing and laughter and a new sense of hope—"God wants a house! He must be intending to dwell with us, despite the golden calf affair!" There must have been something in **chapter 40**, when the Tabernacle was erected, as there was at the dedication of Solomon's temple and, later, under Ezra. What a day! What days!

419

Israel had built treasure cities for Pharaoh but it was under the whip, they built nothing that had their heart in it. Now, this Tabernacle, that was something else!

They had even built a golden calf. Built it in a moment. Built it out of passion, treachery and self-assertion. Not this Tabernacle. Over this they lovingly lingered; this they did to please God rather than themselves; this they built as a token of loving obedience.

Looking back at the treasure cities of Egypt they would curl their lip and deny the worth of the cities, they would stress their unwillingness and feel no joy. Looking back on the golden calf they would, at least for now, be filled with genuine remorse at their betrayal and feel ashamed. But this Tabernacle, this they built gladly and with pride.

All the lovely things they used in the building were brought with them from Egypt. The gems, the garments, the curtains, the precious metals they would have brought with them—the fruit of their sufferings. And with the fruit of their pain, the "wages" of their slavery they joyfully created a place for God in their midst and in their hearts (**Jeremiah 2:2**). Not only had the slavery and injustice of Egypt not killed their heart, they had used what came at the end of their pain to initiate a new phase of life with God!

If that story came to us only from ancient days and from an ancient book, we could have more patience with those who dismiss it as nonsense. But every day, in some home or street, in some village or town, in some city or metropolis we see or hear of it happening again. People, by the grace of God, taking their pain and forcing it to serve noble ends; taking their suffering and forcing it to yield joy and greater service to God and man. What happened in a wilderness thousands of years ago has been happening again and again and again ever since. You yourself can bear witness to that, can't you! Of course you can, praise God!

And I suppose, in the end, that's what points out the difference between the *real* men and women and the rest. Nearly anyone can make a splash with a full paint-box but what kind of picture can we paint with only red (as in blood) and dull gray (as in a life without perks)?

103

BEZALEL AND THE MESSIAH

The Lord has chosen Bezalel...and he has filled him with the Spirit of God, with skill, ability and knowledge in all kinds of crafts...
Exodus 35:30-31

It isn't necessary to deny the inexpressible glory of Moses' place before and under God in order to say there was glory in the life of Bezalel under God. One was filled with the Spirit of God to lead a nation and the other was filled with the Spirit of God to be a gifted craftsman unto God. We hear from **35:30-31** that, "The Lord has chosen Bezalel...and he has filled him with the Spirit of God, with skill, ability and knowledge in all kinds of crafts—"

Bezalel and the Messiah had one thing in common, they were working men and they worked by the Spirit of God unto God's glory! J.C. Carlile told of a speaker who addressed a roomful of young educational experts on creative ability. Referring to the cups, tablecloths and other things, he gently reminded them that there wasn't one in the room who could make them. The more he talked, the more they listened until he stepped back and asked leave to introduce them to someone. He moved as though he drew back a curtain and introduced a young Galilean carpenter. They had been interested, said Carlile, now they were spellbound. The speaker asked this "guest" if there was anything here he could make and he walked toward the table, pulled back the tablecloth, looked at the corner and carved legs of the great table and said, "Yes. I could make the table—I am a carpenter." Spellbinding. An old tradition says that above the door of Christ's carpentry shop there was a sign that said: MY YOKE IS EASY.

It's surely a mistake to ooh and aah over everything we see, it's surely a mistake to exaggerate the glory of deeds that, while they're honorable, are commonplace. This is hard to say well, but we *expect* mothers and fathers to be good to their children (when they aren't we're shocked and, sometimes, astonished). We can't go around making heroes out of people for doing what common decency would lead anyone to do *and yet...* We need to learn balance here. We must not exalt the speakers or writers who have influenced half a world and begrudge praise to the people whose names aren't known beyond their own walls but have lived lives of moral grandeur. Workers of the world, men, women, boys and girls have followed in the steps of the God who made yokes—Jesus Christ. And while we won't roll out the red carpet for them, and they would never dream they earned it, we will acknowledge the Spirit of God at work in their work just as surely as in the famous and prominent.

What George Eliot said in *Middlemarch* is well worth repeating, "The growing good of the world is partly dependent on unhistoric acts; and that things are not so ill with you and me as they might have been, is half owing to the Numbers who lived faithfully a hidden life and rest in unvisited tombs".

104

THE KING IS IN RESIDENCE

Then Moses set up the courtyard around the tabernacle and altar and put up the curtain at the entrance to the courtyard. And so Moses finished the work. Exodus 40:33

In Bangkok once, Larry Henderson, as we drove by the royal palace, pointed out the flag that was flying in the grounds and told me, as I'm sure he would all his visitors, "that means the king is in residence right now." That was nice to know. The likeness and difference between that and the Tabernacle are striking.

The building of the Tabernacle was delayed by the monstrous apostasy of Israel in the "golden calf affair" (**Exodus 32**) but the covenant was renewed and work on the Tent of Meeting began. **40:33** offers us this, "Then Moses set up the courtyard around the tabernacle and altar and put up the curtain at the entrance to the courtyard. And so Moses finished the work." There's a nice sound to that last phrase; as if it were written with a sigh of contentment and relief. "Done! All we're waiting for now is for the King to take up residence!" we can imagine someone saying to Moses. The next thing we hear is (**34-35**),

Then the cloud covered the Tent of Meeting, and the glory of the Lord filled the tabernacle. Moses could not enter the Tent of Meeting because the cloud had settled upon it, and the glory of the Lord filled the tabernacle.

The text seems to suggest that Moses tried to enter but failed. But what a glorious failure. His failure gives us some impression of the splendor of God's glory at that time and it's likely that that is precisely why we're told Moses could not enter—we're supposed to reflect on how glorious the glory must have been.

I'm reminded how hard one of the Marys tried to find her beloved Lord whom they had murdered. Her poor mind was distressed, she was beside herself, they had laid him reverently in his grave, she must find him. And she couldn't! And wasn't she glad, later! And aren't we glad beyond words. Had she been able to find him, wouldn't we all have been eternally the losers? Blessed failure!

From some distance the glory must have been visible and should one passing by the Israelite camp ask what the pillar of fire or cloud meant, they could have been told, "It means the King is in residence". What a "flag". But then, what a King!

And wherever they wandered (**36-38**) he didn't leave them alone. NT people hear echoes of this in **Matthew 28:20**, "And lo, I am with you always...." Night and day he was there, says **verse 38**. When they slept he watched over them, for he who is Israel's King neither slumbers nor sleeps, said a psalmist, with obvious pleasure. He was there, not only to give them protection but also to give them guidance (**verses 36-37**). And his presence with them was "in the sight of all the house of Israel". Open, obvious, easy to see.

SELECTED BIBLIOGRAPH

To offer a bibliography might be a mistake. It might suggest I'm making a claim to scholarship that I'm not competent to make. I'll risk it. I can only tell you that I consulted the works I've listed here [and many more] and they might have helped me to avoid some glaring blunders I might have otherwise made. The benefit I gained doesn't always show in this book. There are no devotional books included in the list.

R.K.Harrison's *Introduction to the Old Testament* and Gleason Archer's *Survey of Old Testament Introduction* will give the interested reader a robust conservative response to the liberal "documentary hypothesis," especially as it relates to the Pentateuch. For a brief and modestly stated liberal proposal you might want to see Edward Greenstein's piece on "Sources of the Pentateuch" in *Harpers Bible Dictionary*. For a readable, less modest but much more detailed treatment you might look at B.W.Anderson's *The Living World of the Old Testament* and his *Contours of OT Theology*.

Good Bible dictionaries are such a help. There are a number from conservative and liberal slants. *The Interpreter's Dictionary of the Bible*, *The International Standard Bible Encyclopedia* (the more recent revised issue, edited by Bromiley), *Harper's Bible Dictionary* and *The Illustrated Bible Dictionary* (Tyndale. This 3 volume set is the revised text of the 1962 *New Bible Dictionary* put out by Inter-Varsity Fellowship but with a wealth of added illustrative material, maps, diagrams and photographs).

Alter R. and Kermode, F. (eds), *The Literary Guide to the Bible*, Fontana/HarperCollins, 1989

Birch, B.C., *Let Justice Roll Down*, Westminster/John Knox Press, 1991

Breuggemann, W., *Hope Within History,* John Knox Press, 1987
The Land, Fortress Press, 1977
Bruce, F.F., *Tradition: Old and New*, Zondervan, 1974
Chadwick, G.A., *Exodus*, Eerdmans, 1956

Childs, B.S., *The Book of Exodus*, Westminster, 1974

Danby, H., *The Mishnah*, OUP, 16th impression, 1987

Daube, D., *The Exodus Pattern in the Bible*, Greenwood Press, Connecticut, 1963

Davies, W.D., *The Gospel and the Land*, UCP, Los Angeles, 1974

Durant, W., *Our Oriental Heritage*, Volume 1 of 11, Simon & Schuster, 1963

Durham, J.I., *Exodus*, Word BC, 1987

Ellison, H.L., *Exodus*, Westminster, 1982

Fairbairn, P., *The Revelation of Law in Scripture*, Zondervan, 1957

Finegan, J., *Myth & Mystery*, Baker, 1989

Fretheim, T.E. *Exodus*, John Knox Press, 1991

Ginzberg, L., *The Legends of the Jews*, Vol. 2 of 7 volumes, Jewish Publication Society of America, 1980

Goldberg, M., *Jews and Christians, Getting Our Stories Straight*, Abingdon, 1985

Harris, Archer,Waltke (eds.), *Theological Wordbook of the Old Testament*, 2 Volumes, Moody Press, 1981

Jordan, J.B., *The Law of the Covenant*, Institute for Christian Economics, Tyler, Exodus, 1984

Josipovici, G., *The Book of God, A Response to the Bible*, Yale University Press, 1988

Kaiser, W.C., *Toward Old Testament Ethics*, Zondervan, 1983

Kilpatrick, W.K., *The Emperor's New Clothes*, Crossway Books, Illinois, 1985

Knight, G.A.F., *Theology as Narration*, Handsel Press, Edinburgh, 1976

Martens, E.A., *Plot and Purpose in the Old Testament*, IVP, 1981

McConville, J.G., *Law And Theology in Deuteronomy*, JSOT, Supplement Series 33, 1986

Neusner, J., An *Introduction to Judaism*, Westminster/John Knox Press, 1991

Rad, G.Von, *Old Testament Theology*, Vol. I of 2 volumes, Harper & Row, 1962

Rosen, C & R., *Christ in the Passover*, Moody Press, 1978

Sanders, E.P., *Jewish Law From Jesus to the Mishnah*, SCM, 1990

Wenham, G.J., *Story as Torah,* T&T Clark, 2000
Wenham, J.W., *The Goodness of God*, Tyndale, 1975
Wright, C.J.H., *God's People in God's Land*, Eerdmans, 1990
Living as the People of God, IVP, 1983
The Mission of God, IVP, 2006
Zimmerli, W., *I Am Yahweh*, John Knox Press, 1982
Old Testament Theology in Outline, T&T Clark, 1984

www.ingramcontent.com/pod-product-compliance
Lightning Source LLC
Chambersburg PA
CBHW071204090426
42736CB00014B/2707